Contents

iii

Introduction –
Excel 2007 edition

Aims

The book is aimed at a number of Advanced courses of study within the National Qualifications Framework currently available in schools and colleges.

The book covers all the key software skills required in the practical components of ICT and computing specifications that require a study of spreadsheets using Microsoft Excel .

The materials and approach used in the book are also applicable to students on many computing and ICT-related courses in further and higher education where a study of Microsoft Excel spreadsheets is necessary.

As well as covering many features of Microsoft Excel 2007, the book offers advice and support materials for Excel projects including:

- designing the spreadsheet solution
- implementing the solution using Excel
- testing the implemented solution
- evaluating the solution
- user documentation
- choice of project.

Features of Microsoft Excel 2007 covered in this book

At this level, students are expected to make use of features beyond the simple arithmetic of +, -, *, / and straightforward formulas. The features of Microsoft Excel 2007 covered in this book are likely to be useful to many students.

Some of the features introduced are:

- linked worksheets
- named sheets, cells and cell ranges
- functions such as IF, COUNTIF, RAND and LOOKUP
- absolute references
- conditional formatting
- combo boxes, option buttons, spinners, scroll bars and check boxes
- macros to automate commonly used tasks
- spinners
- message boxes
- UserForms for aiding and automating input
- pivot tables
- multiple scenarios.

At the start of each unit, there is a list of the new features in that unit.

Students should be reminded that use of these features alone does not guarantee high marks – many marks will be for how well they document the solution.

The book is intended for guidance only. Teachers and students should use the book in conjunction with the course specification and examiners' reports.

How to use this book

The book assumes that students have a working knowledge of Microsoft Windows and Windows-based software.

The book can be used as a formal teaching aid by lecturers, or students can work independently through the self-study units in class or away from the classroom.

Part 1 – Spreadsheet starters takes the student through a series of short units. These don't take long to complete and are designed to remind the student of the features of Excel that they may have seen before and to look at some other important features of the software. We have found this part useful in:

- reinforcing student knowledge
- switching from previous versions of Excel to Excel 2007
- helping to get to know your students' abilities at the start of the course
- setting as homework
- giving practice in setting up a complete solution
- allowing students to work at their own pace.

Part 2 – The *Denton Gazette* takes the student through a series of 22 self-study units which demonstrate further useful features of Excel 2007. This is done through the scenario of calculating the cost of an advertisement in a weekly newspaper, the *Denton Gazette*.

The scenario is fictitious and has been designed to incorporate as many features as is possible for demonstration purposes only.

These units should be worked through in sequence as they set up a spreadsheet solution. If there are any problems, the files that should have been created by the end of each unit can be downloaded from the Internet.

There are also some exercises for students to practise the skills learned – these are printed in red.

Part 3 – Further Excel features looks at some more Excel features that students may wish to use in their projects through stand-alone self study units (Units 23 to 26).

Part 4 – UserForm exercises looks at two Excel solutions that are UserForm-driven. These can be used as extension material and as a source of ideas for projects.

In Part 5 there are two practice assignments. Each student should tackle at least one of these to put the skills they have learned into practice. This is followed by 12 ideas for projects – students could adapt a problem or undertake a similar problem to meet the demands of a real user.

Further ideas for projects can be downloaded from the internet.

Part 6 – Documenting your project gives advice on how to document an Excel project. It covers the design, the implementation report, the testing, the user guide and the evaluation. It includes pointers, hints and examples of good practice.

Part 7 – Practice exercises offers a range of exercises for students to practise their Excel skills.

Part 8 – Tips and tricks offers a range of useful tips that support the units and should provide interesting reading. These could be used as further activities for students – it is hoped that they can be the starting point for finding out even more about Excel.

Programming in Visual Basic

Generally, specifications at this level do not require the use of programming. However, some features in Excel – such as UserForms and Message Boxes – can only be implemented by using a line or two of Visual Basic for Applications (VBA).

Students can enhance their solution in such cases by inserting a few lines of code or by tinkering with existing code. Details of how to insert a little VBA code are included in Part 2 and Part 4.

Compatibility issues

All software manufacturers bring out new versions every few years, changing the features and adding new ones. Microsoft Excel is no exception.

The screen layout for Excel 2007 is different from previous versions. However, many features are similar or identical.

Excel 2007 stores files in *.xlsx format. It is also backwards compatible so that it can load files set up in previous versions of Excel. However, to load *.xlsx files in earlier versions of Excel you will need to download the Microsoft Office Compatibility Pack from www.microsoft.com – or Google 'Microsoft Office Compatibility Pack'. This pack enables you to load Microsoft Word, Excel and PowerPoint 2007 file formats in older versions of Microsoft Office. This is very useful if a student has a different version of the software at home from the version in school or college.

If you want to use macros in your spreadsheet, you will need to store your work as a macro-enabled worksheet. These files are in *.xlsm format.

A note to students and lecturers

It is important to note that solutions used in the text are not being put forward for particular grades at any level. Solutions are fictitious and are aimed at showing the student the potential of Microsoft Excel and how software features can be incorporated to produce a working ICT solution.

All awarding bodies provide exemplar materials, support and training. It is vital that students and tutors follow the specification they have chosen to follow.

The documentation of ICT solutions at this level follows the systems life-cycle approach of design, implementation, testing and evaluation. Again, though, different specifications and different solutions will have a different emphasis.

A word of real caution – on no account must students copy materials from text books and submit them for examination. Moderators, examiners and the examination boards are very aware of published exemplar materials. You will be penalised severely.

Julian Mott and Ian Rendell have written two coursework books:

- Spreadsheet Projects in Excel for Advanced Level
- Database Projects in Access for Advanced Level.

What's different in Excel 2007?

At first sight, Excel 2007 looks very different from previous versions of the software. This is due to the new wide toolbar called 'the ribbon' across the top of the screen – see Figure 1.

Figure 1 ▶

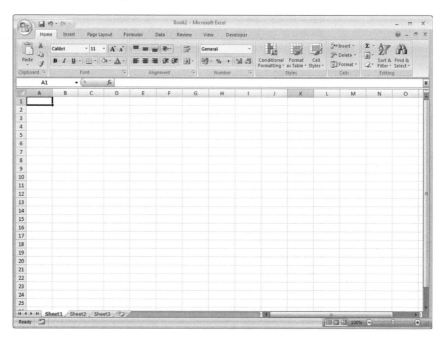

The ribbon contains buttons, many of which users of previous Excel versions will recognise. There are new buttons as well and it is a good idea to spend a few minutes investigating the ribbon and the menu structure.

Figure 2 ▼

As can be seen in Figure 2, there are tabs across the top of the ribbon labelled Home, Insert, Page Layout, Formulas etc. Clicking different tabs will bring up different underlying sections of the ribbon.

On each tab, buttons are arranged in groups – these are labelled at the bottom of the ribbon. In Figure 2, there is a Clipboard group, a Font group, an Alignment group, a Number group and so on. Figure 3 shows the Styles group in close up.

Figure 3 ▶

The File menu now appears on the Office Button at the top left of the screen, shown in Figure 4. Click this button if you want to open a new file, save a file, print etc.

Figure 4 ▶

Whichever tab you select on the ribbon, you can always see the Quick Access toolbar at the top left of the screen, shown in Figure 5. This toolbar contains important buttons and is customisable – you can add your own buttons or remove ones you don't use very often.

Figure 5 ▶

Hiding the ribbon

Sometimes you need to hide the ribbon to devote more space to the spreadsheet. There are several ways to do this:

- press CTRL and F1
- right click on the ribbon and choose **Minimize the Ribbon**.
- double click on the selected tab – for example, if the Home tab is selected then double click on the word 'Home'.

Showing the ribbon

You can:

- press CTRL and F1 again to show the ribbon
- right click on the ribbon and choose **Minimize the Ribbon** as before
- double click again on the selected tab.

Page Layout view

The Page Layout view shows the header and footer, as well as displaying a ruler along the top and down the left-hand side of the spreadsheet as shown in Figure 6. To enter Page Layout view, click the **View** tab and click **Page Layout** in the **Workbook Views** group.

Figure 6 ▶

To return to Normal View, on the **View** tab click **Normal** in the **Workbook Views** group.

Excel 2007 has a security feature called the Trust Center – this lets you set up trusted file locations. When you open an Excel file containing a macro, the Trust Center will disable the macro unless it comes from a trusted source. Click **Office Button** > **Excel Options** > **Trust Center** to edit the Trust Center settings.

1 Spreadsheet starters

Spreadsheet starter 1: Comparing mobile phone costs

Features used:
- column widths
- copy and paste
- formulas
- fill
- AutoSum
- absolute and relative references
- colours, backgrounds and fonts
- merge and center
- borders
- removing gridlines.

Selina is about to buy a 'pay as you go' mobile phone from B-Mobile, but they have three different tariffs to choose from. You are going to set up a spreadsheet model which will work out the cheapest tariff for her.

You will then use the same spreadsheet to work out the best tariff for her friend Bryony.

Typical rates for calls and texts are shown below – call charges are per minute.

	Everyone	Mates Rates	Text Appeal
Cross network calls	£0.12	£0.40	£0.40
Same network calls	£0.12	£0.05	£0.20
Landline calls	£0.12	£0.20	£0.20
Cross network texts	£0.10	£0.10	£0.03
Same network texts	£0.10	£0.05	£0.03

Entering the data

1 Open a new worksheet.
2 Click cell A2. On the **Home** tab in the **Cells** group, click **Format > Column Width** (Figure 1.1) and set the width to **18**.

Figure 1.1 ▶

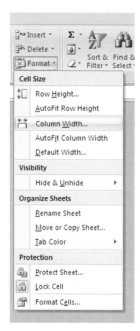

Figure 1.2 ▶

3 Highlight columns B to D and set their width to **12** in the same way.
4 Highlight cells B2 to D6. On the **Home** tab in the **Number** group, choose **Currency** from the drop-down list (Figure 1.2).
5 Enter the data as shown in Figure 1.3. (You do not need to enter the £ signs.)

Figure 1.3 ▶

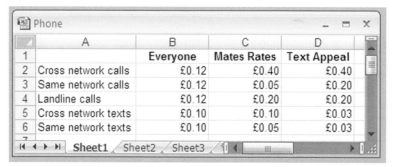

	A	B	C	D
1		**Everyone**	**Mates Rates**	**Text Appeal**
2	Cross network calls	£0.12	£0.40	£0.40
3	Same network calls	£0.12	£0.05	£0.20
4	Landline calls	£0.12	£0.20	£0.20
5	Cross network texts	£0.10	£0.10	£0.03
6	Same network texts	£0.10	£0.05	£0.03

Sheet1 / Sheet2 / Sheet3

6 Set the column headings in cells B1 to D1 to bold by clicking the **Bold** button.
7 Centre these column headings with the **Center** button.
8 Save your file as **phone.xlsx**.

Selina thinks that in a month her use might be:

10 minutes – Cross network calls

80 minutes – Same network calls

60 minutes – Landline calls

30 Cross network texts

80 Same network texts.

Bryony thinks that in a month her use might be:

100 minutes – Cross network calls

20 minutes – Same network calls

100 minutes – Landline calls

100 Cross network texts

100 Same network texts.

9 Put the name **Selina** in cell A8.

10 Enter the tariff names in cells A9 to A13. The best way to do this is to highlight cells A2 to A6. Then on the **Home** tab in the **Clipboard** group, click the **Copy** button as shown in Figure 1.4. Click cell A9 and click the **Paste** button.

11 Enter the data for Selina in cells B9 to B13 as in Figure 1.5.

Figure 1.4 ▼

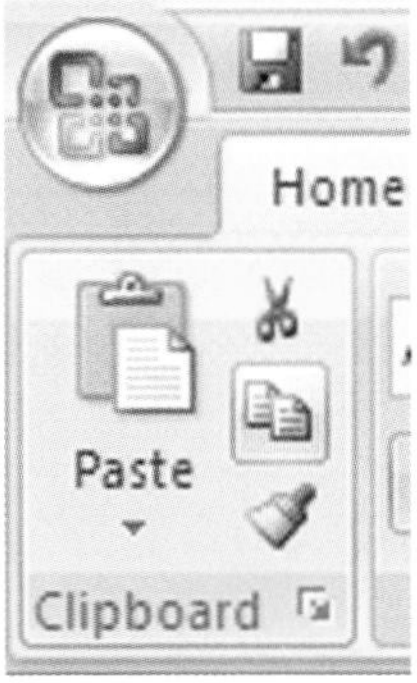

Figure 1.5 ▶

Phone

	A	B	C	D
1		Everyone	Mates Rates	Text Appeal
2	Cross network calls	£0.12	£0.40	£0.40
3	Same network calls	£0.12	£0.05	£0.20
4	Landline calls	£0.12	£0.20	£0.20
5	Cross network texts	£0.10	£0.10	£0.03
6	Same network texts	£0.10	£0.05	£0.03
7				
8	Selina			
9	Cross network calls	10		
10	Same network calls	80		
11	Landline calls	60		
12	Cross network texts	30		
13	Same network texts	80		
14				

Sheet1 Sheet2 Sheet3

12 Enter (or copy) the tariff names again in cells A16 to A20 and the column headings in cells B15 to D15 as shown in Figure 1.6.

Figure 1.6 ▶

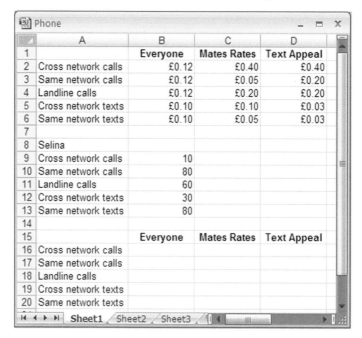

You now need to enter the formulas that will calculate the cost for each tariff. To work out the cost of the cross network calls in the Everyone tariff, you will need to multiply B2 by B9 and store the answer in B16.

13 Click cell B16 and enter **=B2*B9**. Don't forget the equals sign at the start of the formula.

You should get the answer £1.20 as shown in Figure 1.7.

Figure 1.7 ▶

	A	B	C	D
1		Everyone	Mates Rates	Text Appeal
2	Cross network calls	£0.12	£0.40	£0.40
3	Same network calls	£0.12	£0.05	£0.20
4	Landline calls	£0.12	£0.20	£0.20
5	Cross network texts	£0.10	£0.10	£0.03
6	Same network texts	£0.10	£0.05	£0.03
7				
8	Selina			
9	Cross network calls	10		
10	Same network calls	80		
11	Landline calls	60		
12	Cross network texts	30		
13	Same network texts	80		
14				
15		Everyone	Mates Rates	Text Appeal
16	Cross network calls	£1.20		
17	Same network calls			
18	Landline calls			
19	Cross network texts			
20	Same network texts			

Sheet1 / Sheet2 / Sheet3

14 Click cell B17 and enter **=B3*B10**.

15 Enter formulas in cells B18, B19 and B20.

Because the formulas are similar, there is an easier way. You can replicate (copy) the formula in cell B16 as follows.

16 First delete the contents of B17 to B20 – select the range and press **Delete**.

17 Highlight cells B16 to B20. On the **Home** tab in the **Editing** group, click **Fill > Down** as shown in Figure 1.8.

Figure 1.8 ▶

18 Click in cell B21. On the **Home** tab in the **Editing** group, click the **AutoSum** button shown in Figure 1.9. Press **Enter**. It will add the contents of cells B16 to B20.

Figure 1.9 ▶

19 On the **Home** tab in the **Font** group, click the **Borders** drop-down button and choose **Top and Bottom Border** as in Figure 1.10.

Figure 1.10 ▶

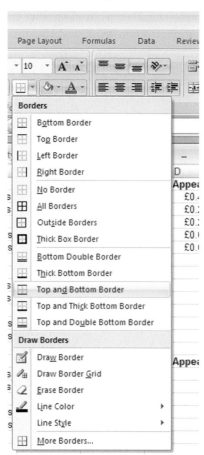

20 Your spreadsheet should look like the one in Figure 1.11.

Figure 1.11 ▶

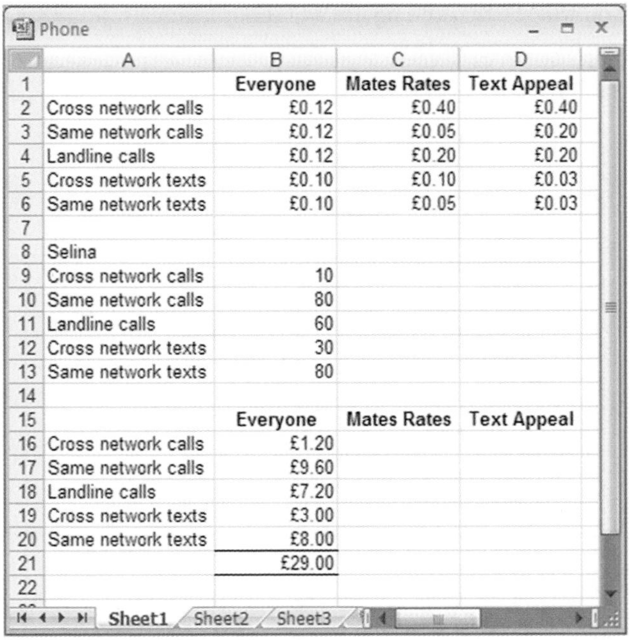

	A	B	C	D
1		Everyone	Mates Rates	Text Appeal
2	Cross network calls	£0.12	£0.40	£0.40
3	Same network calls	£0.12	£0.05	£0.20
4	Landline calls	£0.12	£0.20	£0.20
5	Cross network texts	£0.10	£0.10	£0.03
6	Same network texts	£0.10	£0.05	£0.03
7				
8	Selina			
9	Cross network calls	10		
10	Same network calls	80		
11	Landline calls	60		
12	Cross network texts	30		
13	Same network texts	80		
14				
15		Everyone	Mates Rates	Text Appeal
16	Cross network calls	£1.20		
17	Same network calls	£9.60		
18	Landline calls	£7.20		
19	Cross network texts	£3.00		
20	Same network texts	£8.00		
21		£29.00		
22				

Sheet1 / Sheet2 / Sheet3

21 Enter a formula into C16 to work out the cost of Mates Rates cross network calls. Use the **Fill** button and **AutoSum** again to fill in the rest of the column.

22 Repeat this for column D.

Your spreadsheet should look like the one in Figure 1.12. From this you can see that the Mates Rates tariff would be the cheapest for Selina.

Figure 1.12 ▶

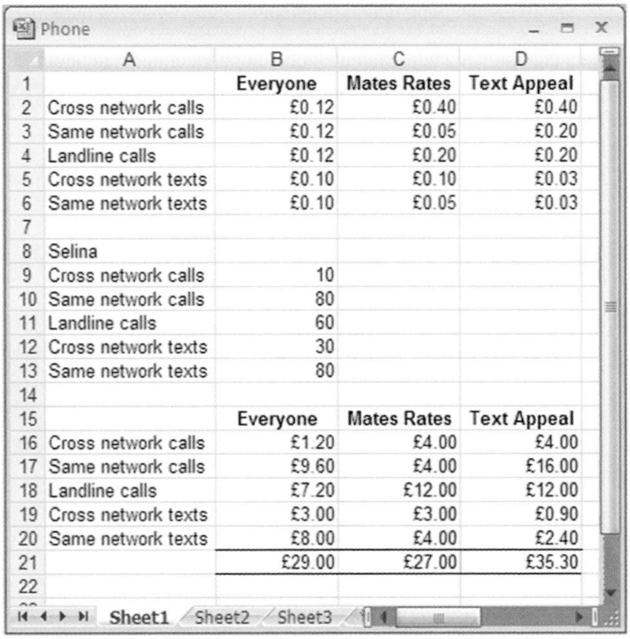

	A	B	C	D
1		Everyone	Mates Rates	Text Appeal
2	Cross network calls	£0.12	£0.40	£0.40
3	Same network calls	£0.12	£0.05	£0.20
4	Landline calls	£0.12	£0.20	£0.20
5	Cross network texts	£0.10	£0.10	£0.03
6	Same network texts	£0.10	£0.05	£0.03
7				
8	Selina			
9	Cross network calls	10		
10	Same network calls	80		
11	Landline calls	60		
12	Cross network texts	30		
13	Same network texts	80		
14				
15		Everyone	Mates Rates	Text Appeal
16	Cross network calls	£1.20	£4.00	£4.00
17	Same network calls	£9.60	£4.00	£16.00
18	Landline calls	£7.20	£12.00	£12.00
19	Cross network texts	£3.00	£3.00	£0.90
20	Same network texts	£8.00	£4.00	£2.40
21		£29.00	£27.00	£35.30
22				

Sheet1 / Sheet2 / Sheet3

23 Edit the data in cells A8 and B9 to B13 for Bryony.

You will see that the figures adjust automatically and that the Everyone tariff is much cheaper for Bryony (Figure 1.13).

24 Save your file.

Figure 1.13 ▶

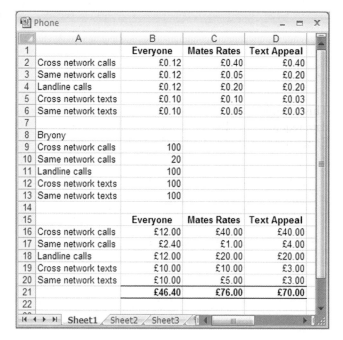

	A	B	C	D
1		Everyone	Mates Rates	Text Appeal
2	Cross network calls	£0.12	£0.40	£0.40
3	Same network calls	£0.12	£0.05	£0.20
4	Landline calls	£0.12	£0.20	£0.20
5	Cross network texts	£0.10	£0.10	£0.03
6	Same network texts	£0.10	£0.05	£0.03
7				
8	Bryony			
9	Cross network calls	100		
10	Same network calls	20		
11	Landline calls	100		
12	Cross network texts	100		
13	Same network texts	100		
14				
15		Everyone	Mates Rates	Text Appeal
16	Cross network calls	£12.00	£40.00	£40.00
17	Same network calls	£2.40	£1.00	£4.00
18	Landline calls	£12.00	£20.00	£20.00
19	Cross network texts	£10.00	£10.00	£3.00
20	Same network texts	£10.00	£5.00	£3.00
21		£46.40	£76.00	£70.00
22				

Sheet1 / Sheet2 / Sheet3

25 Adjust the figures in cells B9 to B13 again – choose your own figures. Which tariff is cheapest now?

You can also adjust the prices in cells B2 to D6.

Absolute referencing – copying the formula from B16 to C16 and D16

The formulas in columns C and D are similar to the formulas in column B. Couldn't we just copy them across? Let's try it.

1 Delete the data in cells C16 to D21 and then highlight the cells. On the **Home** tab in the **Cells** group, click the **Delete** button.
2 Highlight cells B16 to D16.
3 On the **Home** tab in the **Editing** group, click **Fill > Right**.

This gives £0.00 in cells C16 and D16 (Figure 1.14). Clearly this is wrong.

Figure 1.14 ▶

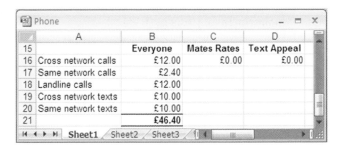

This is because the formula in cell C16 is = C2*C9. But cell C9 is blank – the data required is in B9. This should not change as you replicate along the row. So we need an **absolute cell reference** – one that stays the same when copied. You indicate an absolute reference with dollar signs – i.e. $B$9

4 Click cell B16 and change the formula to **=B2*$B$9**. It should still read £12.00.
5 Highlight cells B16 to D16 and click **Fill > Right**.
6 Click cell B17 and change the formula to **=B3*$B$10**
7 Highlight cells B17 to D17 and click **Fill > Right**.
8 Do the same for the other three rows.

The spreadsheet should now be working correctly again.

The formulas should be as shown in Figure 1.15.

Figure 1.15 ▼

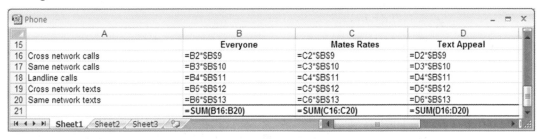

Hint **Switching to formula view**
If you want to see the formulas, hold down the CTRL key on the keyboard and press the back tick key (left of 1 on the keyboard). Press the same two keys again to switch back to normal view.

An alternative method using cell naming

Another way of setting up this table is to give a name to cells B9 to B13. Follow the instructions 1 to 8 as above.

1 Clear the data in cells **B16** to **D20**.
2 Select cell **B9**.
3 Click in the **Name** box at the left end of the formula bar.

Figure 1.16 ▶

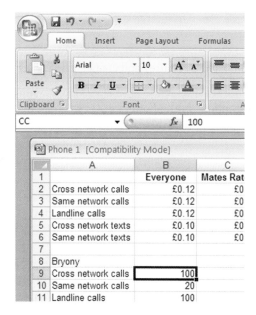

4 Enter the name **CC** (short for Cross network Calls) as shown in Figure 1.16.
5 Press ENTER.
6 Repeat this procedure to give names to cells B10 to B13.
7 In cell B16 enter the formula **=B2*CC**.
8 Enter similar formulas into cells B17 to B20.
9 Use **AutoSum** in cell B21 to add these figures.
10 Highlight cells B16 to D21 and click **Fill > Right**.

The formulas are shown in Figure 1.17.

Figure 1.17 ▼

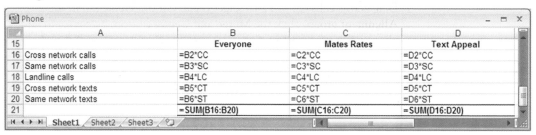

	A	B	C	D
15		Everyone	Mates Rates	Text Appeal
16	Cross network calls	=B2*CC	=C2*CC	=D2*CC
17	Same network calls	=B3*SC	=C3*SC	=D3*SC
18	Landline calls	=B4*LC	=C4*LC	=D4*LC
19	Cross network texts	=B5*CT	=C5*CT	=D5*CT
20	Same network texts	=B6*ST	=C6*ST	=D6*ST
21		=SUM(B16:B20)	=SUM(C16:C20)	=SUM(D16:D20)

Improving the look of your spreadsheet

It is important to present your spreadsheet professionally, paying full attention to its appearance and general layout.

In Excel you can:

- change fonts
- change text size
- change colour
- change backgrounds
- add borders
- align data (left, right or centre) and change many other appearance and layout aspects.

You will use the options in the **Font** group to improve the look of your spreadsheet.

1 Load the file **phone.xlsx**.

Start by positioning the sheet centrally on the screen by inserting rows and columns.

2 Drag across row headers 1 to 4 to highlight the first four rows.
3 On the **Home** tab in the **Cells** group, select **Insert > Insert Sheet Rows**. This will insert four rows.
4 Drag across column headers A and B and select **Insert > Insert Sheet Columns** to insert two columns.

In the same way, rows and columns can be deleted by highlighting the rows/columns that you wish to delete and clicking **Delete** on the **Home** tab in the **Cells** group. A number of formatting options are also available by highlighting the cell or cell ranges and right clicking the mouse button.

5 Highlight cell ranges C5 to F5 and C19 to F19 (hold down the **Ctrl** key while selecting the second range).
6 On the **Home** tab in the **Font** group, click the **Fill Color** drop-down > **Aqua, Accent 5**.
7 With the cells still selected, select **White** from the **Font Color** drop-down list.
8 In cell C2 enter the text **Mobile Phone Cost Comparison Table**. Don't worry about column widths.
9 Drag across cells C2 to F2 to select them. On the **Home** tab in the **Alignment** group, click the **Merge and Center** button. Select again and alter the font size to 14 point. Again set the Background to **Aqua, Accent 5** and the text colour to **White**.
10 The next step is to highlight key areas with colour. Select cells C6 to F10 and C20 to F24. Set the Fill Color to **Aqua, Accent 5, Lighter 60%**.
11 Highlight cells C25 to F25 and change the Fill Color to **White, Background 1, Darker 15%**.

12 Drag across cells C12 to D17 and click the **Borders** drop-down button and choose **All Borders** (Figure 1.18).

13 Set cells C12 and D12 to **bold**.

Figure 1.18 ▶

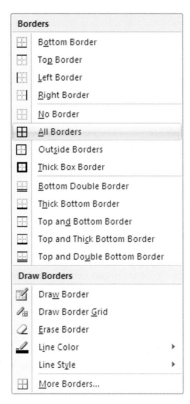

14 On the **View** tab in the **Show/Hide** group, click to uncheck the **Gridlines** check box (Figure 1.19) to remove the gridlines from your spreadsheet.

Figure 1.19 ▶

15 Add the heading to cell D12 and align the data as shown in Figure 1.20.
16 Save your file.

Figure 1.20 ▶

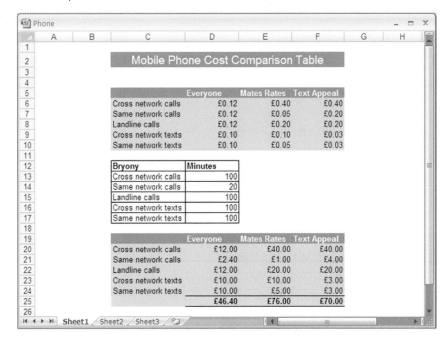

Printing your spreadsheet is covered later (Spreadsheet starter 5). When printing it is important to consider how your work will fit on the page, the paper orientation (portrait or landscape) and the addition of headers and footers.

You may wish to refer to the printing section now (page 48). Print your work with the page set to Landscape.

Spreadsheet starter 2: An invoice

Features used:
- column widths
- formatting borders
- formulas
- =TODAY()
- merging cells
- print area
- protecting and unprotecting sheets
- data validation.

Excel is ideal for creating invoices (bills). It is important that your invoice looks professional. It is a good idea to find an invoice such as a gas bill at home and use this as the basis of your design. Alternatively you could use a credit card bill, an electricity bill, a phone bill or a council tax bill.

Setting up the worksheet

1 Click the **Office Button** and choose **New** to start a blank spreadsheet.
2 Click cell C1.
3 On the **Home** tab in the **Cells** group, click **Format** and set the **Column Width** of this column to **40**.
4 Format the width of columns B and D to **15** in the same way.

Your spreadsheet will look like the one in Figure 1.21.

Figure 1.21 ▶

5 Now copy the headings from the screenshot in Figure 1.22 into your worksheet. Make sure that you format **Invoice**, **Quantity**, **Description**, **Unit Price** and **Total** to **Bold**.

Figure 1.22 ▶

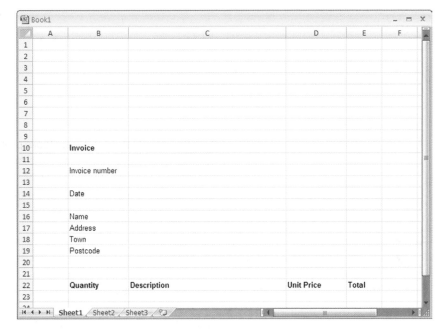

Formatting borders

1 Highlight cells B23 to B36. Click the **Borders** button and select **Outside Borders**.

2 Repeat this for:
- cells C23 to C36
- cells D23 to D36
- cells E23 to E36
- cells C16 to C19
- cell C14
- cell C12.

3 Highlight cells B22 to E22. Click the **Borders** button and select **All Borders**.

Your spreadsheet will look like the one in Figure 1.23.

Figure 1.23 ▶

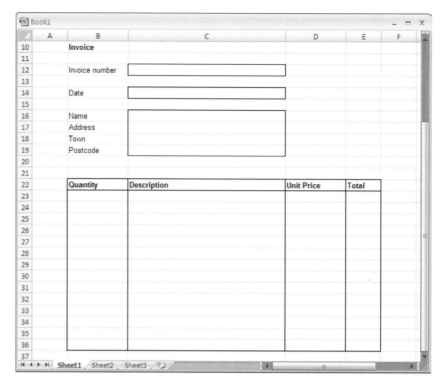

4 Save your file as **Invoice**.

5 Enter **4** into cell B23, **Dining Chairs** into cell C23 and **79** into cell D23.

6 We need to work out the price of four dining chairs. The number of chairs is in cell B23. The price of each chair is in cell D23. So in cell E23 enter **=B23*D23**.

7 You should see **316** in this cell.

Note: It is better to select the cells with your mouse rather than typing in the reference because you are less likely to make a mistake.

8 Highlight cells D23 and E23. On the **Home** tab in the **Number** group, select **Currency** from the drop-down list.

9 In the line below, enter **1 Dining table** costing **255**.

10 In the line below that, enter **2 Easy chairs** at **143**.

11 Enter the formula into E24 and E25. You can copy and paste from E23 or replicate using **Fill > Down** or the Fill Handles. (See *Tips and tricks 5*.)

12 Format cells D24 to E25 to currency.

13 Click in cell E37 and click the **AutoSum** button and press ENTER.

Check that the amount in cell E37 is £857.00 (Figure 1.24). The formula should be **=SUM(E23:E36)**

Figure 1.24 ▶

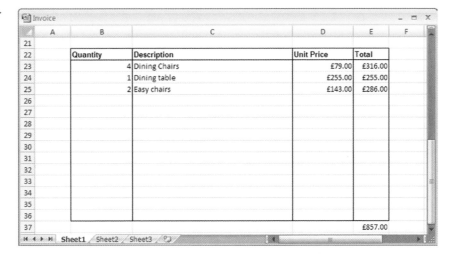

14 In D37 enter **Subtotal**.
15 In D38 enter **VAT**.
16 In D40 enter **Total**.
17 The VAT rate is 17.5%. In cell E38 enter the formula **=17.5%*E37**.
18 In cell E40 enter the formula **=E37+E38**. The total in cell E40 should be £1006.98.
19 Highlight cells D37 to E40 and select **All Borders** from the **Borders** drop-down list.

Entering the date

1 Click in cell C14. Enter the formula **=TODAY()**. When you press **Enter**, you should see today's date in cell C14.

Remember: You must start with the equals sign and finish with the two brackets, but it does not matter if the word 'today' is in upper or lower case.

2 This is the first invoice, so enter **1** into cell C12 (Figure 1.25).
3 Select C12 and C14 and click the **Align Left** button.
4 Highlight cells B1 to D5.
5 Click the **Merge and Center** button.
6 Put the company name in the merged cells. Format the size of the font to a suitable size, say 36 or 48 point. Add a logo near cells D1 to D5.
7 Merge the cells B6 to D6 in the same way and enter the company's address. Similarly enter the phone/fax numbers and the email address.

Figure 1.25 ▼

8 Click **Office Button > Print > Print Preview** to see what the invoice will look like when it is printed.
9 We don't need to print column A, so click **Close Print Preview**. Highlight cells B1 to F42.
10 On the **Page Layout** tab in the **Page Setup** group, click **Print Area > Set Print Area**. Now only these cells will be printed.
11 You can change the font, font colour and background colours now if you wish.

Protecting the worksheet

How can we prevent the accidental deletion of data? We don't want to lose the logo, the company name, the column headings or the formulas in cells E37, E38 and E40, for example.

You do this by protecting the worksheet. Firstly you have to decide which cells you want to be able to change. They are:

- B23 to E36
- C16 to C19
- C12.

1 Highlight cells B23 to E36. On the **Home** tab in the **Cells** group, click **Format > Format Cells** (Figure 1.26).

Figure 1.26 ▶

2 Click the **Protection** tab and uncheck the **Locked** check box (Figure 1.27), then click **OK**.

Figure 1.27 ▶

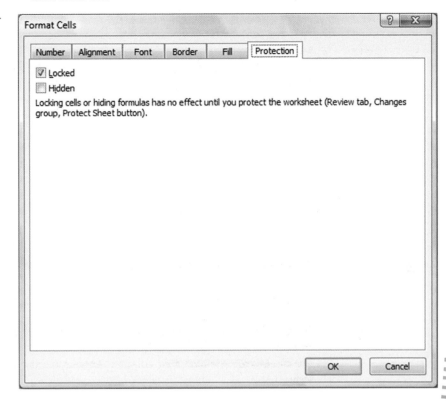

3 Do the same for cells C16 to C19 and then cell C12.
4 On the **Review** tab in the **Changes** group, click **Protect Sheet**. Click **OK**.
5 Test that you can change the invoice number or the furniture purchased, but not edit the company address or the date.

Data validation

We've all made clumsy typing errors, such as typing 44 instead of 4. It could be a disaster if you sent an invoice to a customer for 44 chairs when you meant 4. How can you prevent such mistakes in Excel?

We can use the Data Validation feature.

1 Load the file **Invoice**. You will need to turn off Sheet Protection while you set this up so click **Review > Unprotect Sheet**.
2 Select cell B23.

Normally customers do not buy more than 8 chairs.

3 On the **Data** tab in the **Data Tools** group, click **Data Validation**. A dialogue box appears (Figure 1.28).

Figure 1.28 ▶

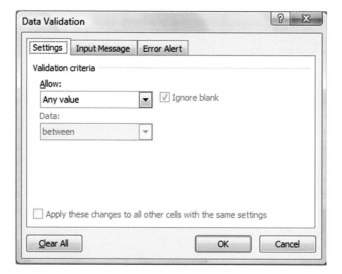

4 Click the **Allow** drop-down list and select **Whole number**.
5 Enter a Minimum of **1** and a Maximum of **8** as shown in Figure 1.29.

Figure 1.29 ▶

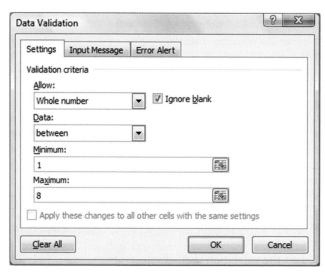

6 Click the **Input Message** tab and enter the details as shown in Figure 1.30.

Figure 1.30 ▶

7 Click the **Error Alert** tab and enter the details as shown in Figure 1.31.

Figure 1.31 ▶

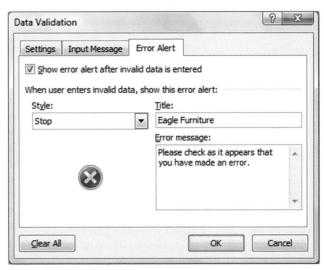

8 Test the validation check by entering the test data below in cell B23.

Test data

Data	Expected result
0	rejected
I	accepted
3.4	rejected
8	accepted
9	rejected

Figure 1.32 ▼

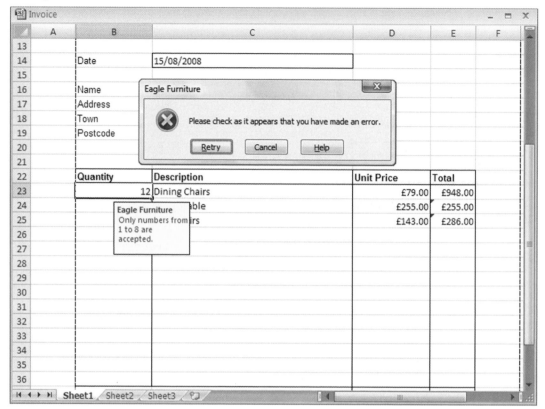

The Data Validation feature allows you to:

- set up maximum and minimum values for whole numbers (as seen)
- set up maximum and minimum values for decimals
- restrict the length of data in a cell
- let the user pick from a list
- select a date between a start date and an end date
- select a time between a start time and an end time
- allow the user to customise their own validation.

Spreadsheet starter 3: The school play

Features used:
- formulas
- AutoSum
- merge and centre
- column widths
- borders
- colours, backgrounds and fonts
- conditional formatting
- multiple sheets.

The school drama society wants to use a spreadsheet to store details of seat bookings and income from the sale of tickets and programmes.

The school hall has seats for 144 people. The seats are arranged in 4 blocks of 6 rows, with 6 seats in each row.

The layout is shown in Figure 1.33.

Figure 1.33 ▶

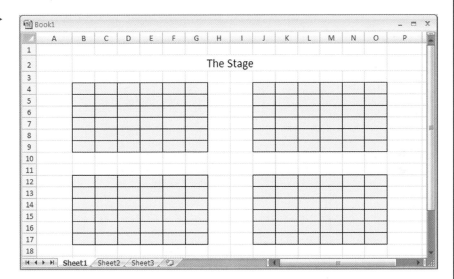

The cells of the spreadsheet are used for the rows of seats – each cell will represent one seat.

When a seat is booked a number **1** is entered in the cell. Seats that are vacant are left blank.

The seats in the front two blocks are priced at £5.00 and the seats in the rear blocks at £3.00.

Start by setting up the spreadsheet as shown in Figure 1.33.

1 You will need to work in Landscape mode – on the **Page Layout** tab in the **Page Setup** group, click **Orientation > Landscape** as shown in Figure 1.34.

Figure 1.34 ▶

2 Highlight columns B to O. On the **Home** tab in the **Cells** group, click **Format > Column Width** and set the column width to **5**.
3 Enter **The Stage** into cell B2. Highlight cells B2 to O2 and click the **Merge and Center** button to merge the cells for the stage.
4 Change the font size of the title to **16** point.
5 Highlight each of the four blocks of seats in turn and click the **Borders** button. Click **All Borders** to format the borders of each cell.
6 Similarly for each block, click the **Fill Color** button and select a suitable fill colour.
7 Enter **1** in some of the seats to show that they are sold (Figure 1.35).

Figure 1.35 ▶

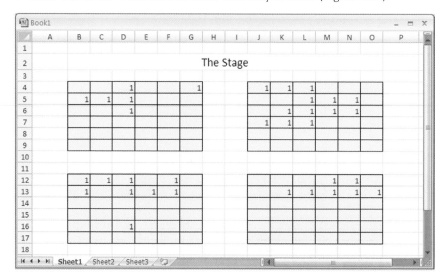

You are going to design a spreadsheet model to store the number of seats sold in each row, the total number of seats sold and the total income from the sale of seats.

1 You may need to adjust the width of columns A, H, I and P to make your spreadsheet fit the screen.

In Q3 and R3 enter the headings **Seats Sold** and **Income**.

2 In Q4 you will need to put a formula that adds up cells B4 to O4. Replicate this formula down to Q9 using **Copy > Paste, Fill > Down** or the **Fill handle**.

3 In R4 you will need to put a formula that multiplies the contents of Q4 by 5. Replicate this formula down to R9 in the same way. This formula multiplies the number of seats sold by £5.00, which is the cost of each seat in these rows.

4 You will need to repeat steps 2 and 3 for cells Q12 to R17 – but remember that the price in these rows is **£3.00**.

5 Format column R to **currency**.

6 In cell R19 set up a formula to add the contents of cells R4 to R17. In cell Q19 set up a formula to add the contents of cells Q4 to Q17.

7 Extend your spreadsheet to store details of income from programmes sold. Programmes sell at £1.00. Assume that you sell one programme for every two people in the audience.

8 In cell R23 set up a formula to add the contents of cells R19 to R21.

9 Test your model so that as a seat is sold, the total number of seats sold increases by 1 and the income increases accordingly. Use your formatting skills to try to present your spreadsheet professionally (see Figure 1.36).

10 Save your file as **play.xlsx**.

Figure 1.36 ▼

	A	B	C	D	E	F	G	H	I	J	K	L	M	N	O	P	Q	R	S
1																			
2								The Stage											
3																	Seats sold	Income	
4				1			1			1	1	1					5	£25.00	
5		1	1	1							1	1	1				6	£30.00	
6				1							1	1	1	1			5	£25.00	
7										1	1	1					3	£15.00	
8																	0	£0.00	
9																	0	£0.00	
10																			
11																			
12		1	1	1		1						1	1				6	£18.00	
13		1		1	1	1					1	1	1	1	1		9	£27.00	
14																	0	£0.00	
15																	0	£0.00	
16				1							1						2	£6.00	
17																	0	£0.00	
18																			
19																Tickets	36	£146.00	
20																			
21																Programmes		£18.00	
22																			
23																Total		£164.00	

Sheet1 / Sheet2 / Sheet3

Conditional formatting

You can use conditional formatting to make cells stand out if they meet certain criteria. For example, we can colour seats that are sold with a red background.

1 Highlight all the seats.

Hint To do this, highlight one block of seats in the normal way. Then hold the CTRL key down and highlight another block. Repeat this until all four blocks are highlighted.

2 On the **Home** tab in the **Styles** group, click **Conditional Formatting > Highlight Cells Rules > Equal To...** as shown in Figure 1.37.

Figure 1.37 ▶

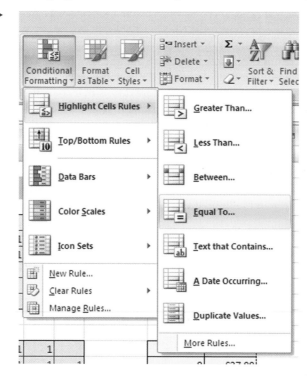

3 Set the value to **1** and **Custom Format**.

4 Click the **Fill** tab and choose a red fill (Figure 1.38). Click **OK**.

Figure 1.38 ▶

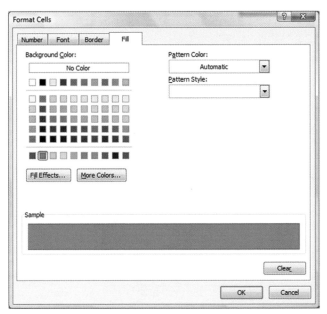

5 Click **OK** again. You can quickly see which seats have been sold as shown in Figure 1.39.

Figure 1.39 ▼

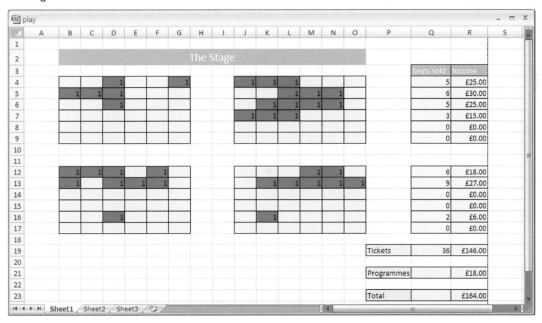

Note: Sometimes it is hard to tell where you have applied conditional formatting. Press **F5**, click **Special** and check **Conditional formats** (Figure 1.40).

Figure 1.40 ▶

- Click OK.
- The cells with conditional formatting will be highlighted.

Multiple worksheets

The school play is running on three nights – Thursday, Friday and Saturday. We will use a different worksheet for each performance to store details of ticket sales and a fourth sheet to store the total sales.

1 Double click the sheet tab for Sheet1 and rename the sheet **Thursday**.
2 Rename Sheet2 as **Friday** and Sheet3 as **Saturday**.
3 On the **Home** tab in the **Cells** group, click **Insert > Insert Sheet** to add another sheet – name it **Total** (see Figure 1.41).

Figure 1.41 ▶

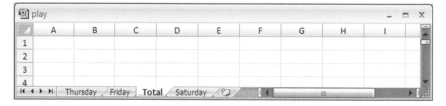

4 You will need to move the new sheet to a new position by holding the mouse down button and dragging as shown in Figure 1.42.

Figure 1.42 ▶

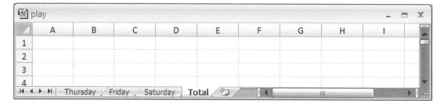

The next step is to copy all the detail on the Thursday worksheet, including the formulas, to the Friday and Saturday worksheets.

5 Go to the **Thursday** worksheet by clicking the Sheet tab.
6 Press CTRL and **A** on the keyboard to select all or click the **Select All** button (Figure 1.43) to select every cell.

Figure 1.43 ▶

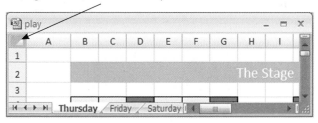

7 Click the **Copy** button.
8 Switch to the Friday sheet. Select cell A1 and click the **Paste** button.
9 Go to the Saturday sheet. Select cell A1 and click the **Paste** button again.

The formulas, borders, background colours and conditional formatting will all be copied. You now have a sales system for each performance.

Setting up the Total spreadsheet

1 Go to the Thursday sheet, **Select All** and click the **Copy** button.
2 Switch to the Total sheet, select cell A1 and click the **Paste** button.

Now you need to add formulas to the Total worksheet that will sum across the worksheets Thursday, Friday and Saturday.

3 In cell B4, type in **=Thursday!B4+Friday!B4+Saturday!B4**
4 This adds the values of cell B4 on the Thursday sheet, B4 on the Friday sheet and B4 on the Saturday sheet. If it has been sold on all three nights it should say 3.

Alternatively, in cell B4 of the **Total** worksheet:

- enter **=**
- switch to the Thursday worksheet and click B4.
- enter **+**
- switch to the Friday worksheet and click B4.
- enter **+** again
- switch to the Saturday worksheet, click B4 and press **Enter**. The formula builds as you go. (See Figure 1.44.)

Figure 1.44 ▼

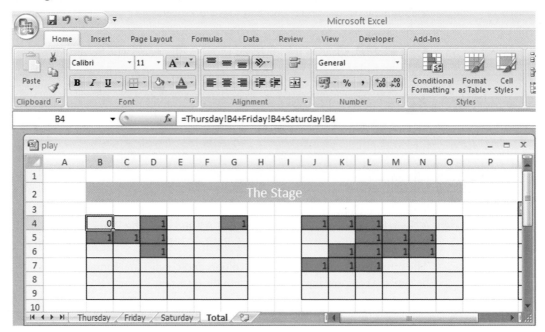

5 Remove the conditional formatting from cell B4 by clicking **Conditional Formatting** in the **Styles** group. Click **Clear Rules > Clear Rules from Selected cells.**

6 On the Total worksheet, select cell B4 and click the **Copy** button. Select cells B4 to G9 and click **Paste.**

You should see the totals for the first block of seats (Figure 1.45).

Figure 1.45 ▶

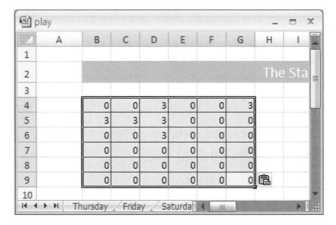

Now copy across to the other three blocks.

7 Highlight cells B4 to G9 and click **Copy.**

8 Select in turn B12, J12 and J4 and click **Paste.**

9 The spreadsheet will now show you how many times each seat has been sold (Figure 1.46).

Figure 1.46 ▼

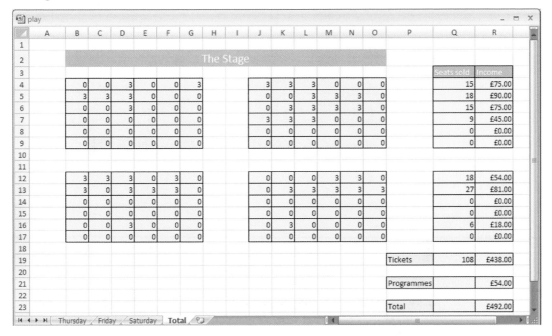

10 Save your file.

Viewing multiple sheets

To view more than one sheet in the same workbook at a time, open a new window for each sheet that you wish to view.

1 On the **View** tab in the **Window** group, click **New Window**. Nothing appears to happen, but it has created another window with your file in.
2 Click the **Friday** tab.
3 Click **New Window** again and click the **Saturday** tab.
4 Click **New Window** again and click the **Total** tab.

Four windows are now open, each showing a different sheet.

5 Click **Arrange All** in the Window group to display the dialogue box (Figure 1.47).

Figure 1.47 ▶

6 Choose the way you wish to view your worksheets. Figure 1.48 shows what happens when you select **Tiled**.

Figure 1.48 ▼

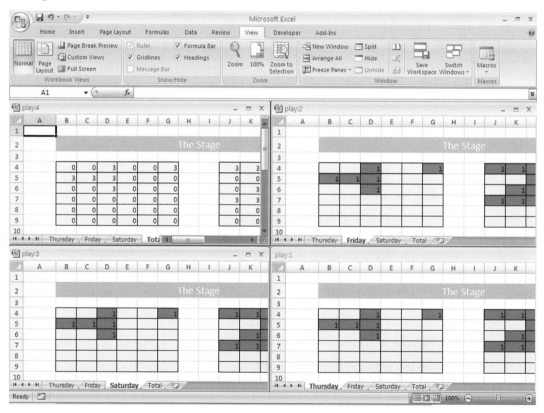

Using custom views

You may wish to return regularly and quickly to the tiled view previously used.

1 In the **Workbook Views** group, click **Custom Views** (Figure 1.49).

Figure 1.49 ▶

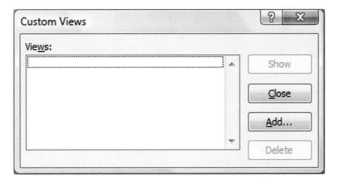

2 Click **Add** (Figure 1.50) and call the view **Overview**.

Figure 1.50 ▶

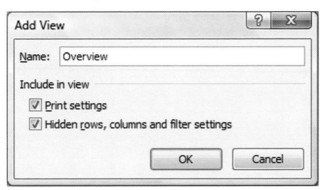

Whenever you wish to return to the custom view, click **Custom Views** and choose **Overview > Show**.

To return to the view showing one sheet, click the **Maximize** button on the active sheet.

Grouping sheets

If a number of sheets are going to contain the same headings, data and format it might be quicker to work with grouped sheets. Every operation carried out on the active sheet is copied across to the sheets in the selected group.

Select adjacent sheets as follows:

1 Click the tab of the leftmost sheet.
2 Hold down **Shift** and click the tab of the rightmost sheet.

To include non-adjacent sheets hold down CTRL while clicking the tabs of the sheets you wish to include.

Grouping is shown by the word 'Group' in the caption bar at the top of the screen (Figure 1.51).

Figure 1.51 ▶

Be careful because it is easy to overtype data in another sheet by accident when the sheets are grouped.

If you print when several sheets are selected, they will all be printed at once, but each sheet starts on a new page.

To turn off sheet grouping:

3 Right click the sheet tab of the sheet you wish to become active.
4 Select **Ungroup Sheets** from the short cut menu.

Spreadsheet starter 4: The dice experiment

Features used:
- INT
- RAND
- COUNT
- COUNTIF
- SUM
- AVERAGE
- MEDIAN
- MODE
- charts
- absolute references.

Katie Lewis is conducting an experiment with random numbers. She wants to roll a dice 100 times and count how many times each number appears.

Rather than actually rolling the dice, she wants to conduct the experiment on a computer using the RAND() function in Excel:

- **=RAND()** gives a random number between 0 and 1
- **=RAND()*6** gives a random number between 0 and 6
- **=RAND()*6+1** gives a random number between 1 and 6.9999
- **=INT()** takes the whole number part of a number – e.g. 8.73 becomes 8
- **=INT(RAND()*6+1)** gives a random whole number between 1 and 6

Note: Another way to do this is to use the RANDBETWEEN function.
- **=RANDBETWEEN(1,6)** gives a random whole number between 1 and 6.

1 Type **=INT(RAND()*6+1)** into cell A1. You will get a random whole number between 1 and 6.
2 Copy this formula down to A10 by dragging the fill handle of this cell down to cell A10.
3 Copy this formula across to column J by dragging the fill handle across with cells A1 to A10 highlighted.

You will have 100 random numbers – something like shown in Figure 1.52.

Figure 1.52 ▶

	A	B	C	D	E	F	G	H	I	J
1	2	6	2	3	4	3	2	1	3	5
2	4	3	4	6	2	6	4	1	4	1
3	3	2	6	2	5	2	6	5	1	5
4	1	4	4	3	2	1	4	1	4	1
5	2	3	5	5	4	3	3	5	3	3
6	3	4	2	3	3	3	4	4	3	5
7	4	6	2	4	3	6	1	6	3	6
8	5	6	3	2	2	2	4	3	1	4
9	3	5	3	3	1	6	4	6	3	1
10	6	4	1	2	3	6	3	2	1	5

Sheet1 / Sheet2 / Sheet3

4 We now want to count how many 1s there are. Enter 1 into cell A12, 2 into B12 ... up to 6 in F12. Do not worry if the random numbers change when you enter data.

5 In cell A13 type in **=COUNTIF($A$1:$J$10,A12)**

This formula counts the number of cells in A1 to J10 that have values equal to the value in A12.

The formula uses absolute references so that when you copy the formula to other cells, it always looks in the table from A1 to J10.

6 Drag this formula over to cell F13.
7 In cell G12 enter **Total**.
8 In cell G13 enter **=SUM(A13:F13)** – this should display 100.
9 Format the borders of cells of A12 to G13 to make the table stand out (Figure 1.53).

Figure 1.53 ▶

	A	B	C	D	E	F	G	H	I	J
1	2	3	5	3	1	2	2	1	3	2
2	2	1	4	4	5	4	2	6	5	2
3	5	4	6	5	5	1	6	3	3	4
4	5	2	2	3	1	2	1	6	5	6
5	3	4	5	2	1	3	2	5	5	2
6	2	2	3	6	2	4	1	3	1	3
7	2	4	4	5	2	2	2	2	3	5
8	1	4	5	1	5	6	2	6	4	1
9	4	3	5	6	5	6	3	5	4	6
10	2	1	1	2	2	3	1	2	2	2
11										
12	1	2	3	4	5	6	Total			
13	15	28	15	13	18	11	100			

Dice — Sheet1 / Sheet2 / Sheet3

10 Highlight cells A12 to F13. On the **Insert** tab in the **Charts** group, click **Column** and choose the first 2-D column graph (Figure 1.54).

Figure 1.54 ▶

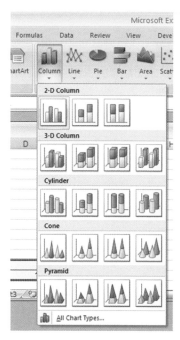

The chart is not the one wanted. It shows the totals for each number in red, but also shows the number on the dice in blue (Figure 1.55).

Figure 1.55 ▼

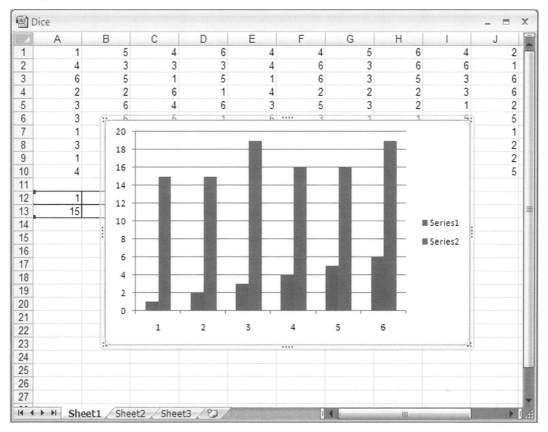

11 On the **Design** tab in the **Data** group, click **Select Data**.

Figure 1.56 ▶

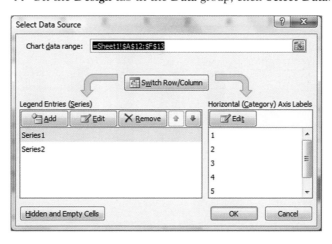

12 Select **Series1** (Figure 1.56) and click **Remove**.

13 Your chart will now look something like Figure 1.57.

Figure 1.57 ▶

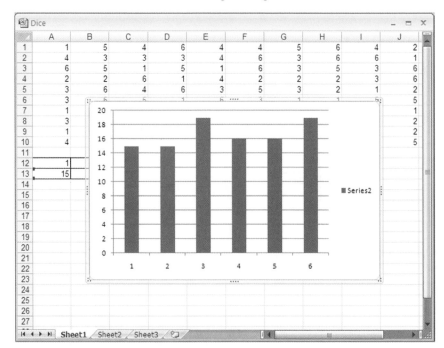

14 On the **Design** tab in the **Chart Layouts** group, click **Chart Layout 2** (Figure 1.58).

Figure 1.58 ▶

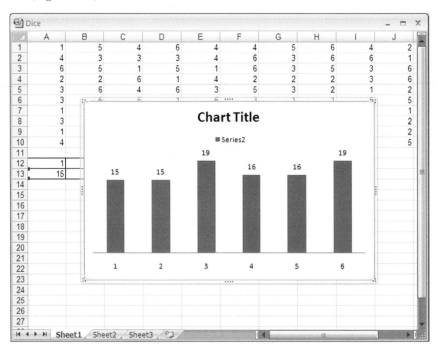

15 We do not need the key (called the legend) which says 'Series2'. Select the legend and press the **Delete** key.

16 Right click on **Chart Title**. Choose **Edit Text** and change the title to **Rolling Dice** (Figure 1.59).

Figure 1.59 ▶

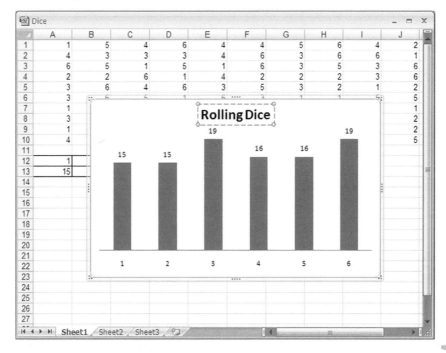

17 Position the chart as shown in Figure 1.60.

Figure 1.60 ▶

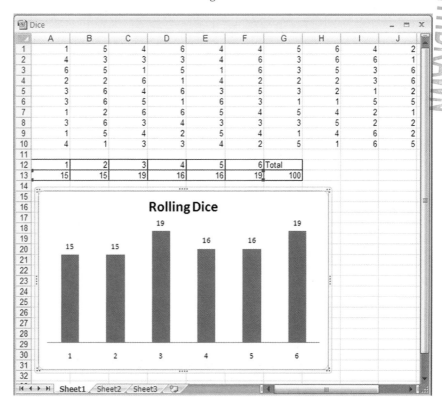

18 In cells I15 to I20 enter the headings **Average**, **Median**, **Mode**, **Count**, **Max** and **Min**. In cells J15 to J20 enter the formulas:

- =AVERAGE(A1:J10)
- =MEDIAN(A1:J10)
- =MODE(A1:J10)
- =COUNT(A1:J10)
- =MAX(A1:J10)
- =MIN(A1:J10)

Format the cell range as shown. If you press the F9 key, you will get a different set of random numbers. The totals and the graph will adjust automatically.

Extension exercises

1 Extend your spreadsheet to include the sum of two dice rolled at the same time. Can you make the spreadsheet 'roll' the dice 1000 times? See Figure 1.61.

 Hint You will need the formula: **=INT(RAND()*6+1) + INT(RAND()*6+1)**

Figure 1.61 ▶

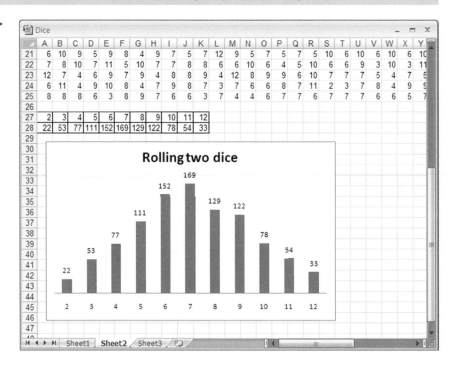

2 Investigate the various graph styles and layouts in Excel 2007. Select the graph and then click the **Design** tab. You can then choose from a variety of chart styles and layouts. See Figure 1.62

Figure 1.62 ▼

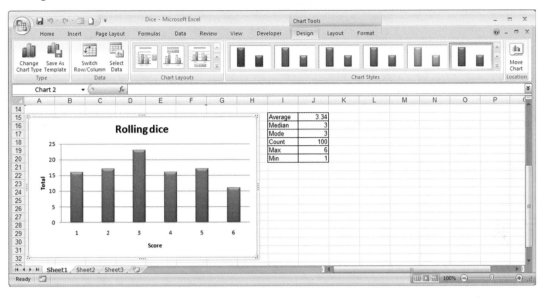

▪ Spreadsheet starter 5: Printing in Excel

There are many options available when printing in Excel. You can use features such as the following to customise your output:

- ▪ print areas
- ▪ landscape print
- ▪ headers and footers
- ▪ page breaks
- ▪ fitting a printout to a page.

Our aim is to produce a professional printout for the ticket sales, using colour and the whole of the page as shown in Figure 1.63.

Figure 1.63 ▼

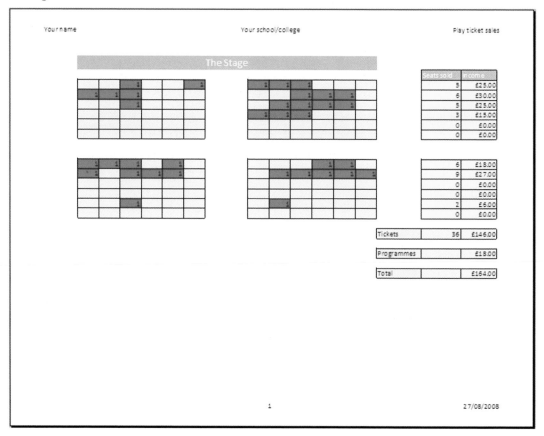

Setting the print area

1 Load the file **play.xlsx** from Spreadsheet starter 3 – The school play. Select the sheet called Thursday.

The first thing to do is decide what area you want to print.

2 Highlight the area to be printed, cells A1 to R23.
3 On the **Page Layout** tab in the **Page Setup** group, click **Print Area > Set Print Area**.

Only the selected area will be printed (Figure 1.63). A dashed line should appear around your print area. To clear this click **Print Area > Clear Print Area**.

Landscape or portrait printing

Printing in landscape mode is often more suitable in Excel because it reflects the shape of the screen. Set the Orientation to Landscape as follows:

1 Click the **Office Button** and click **Print > Print Preview**.
2 Click **Page Setup**, select **Landscape** and then click **OK**.

Adding a header and footer to your printouts

The header and footer are useful because they appear on every page of your printout, not just the first page. The sort of things that headers and footers are used for are:

■ titles of documents or sections of documents
■ the name of the creator of the document
■ their email address
■ page numbers
■ the date of creation.

1 On the **Insert** tab in the **Text** group, click **Header & Footer**. Enter the name of your school or college in the header as shown in Figure 1.64.

Figure 1.64 ▼

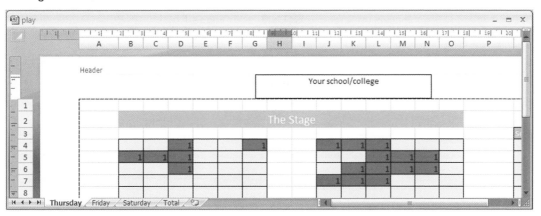

2 The header is in three sections – left, centre and right. Click to the left to enter text in the left-hand section as in Figure 1.65.

Figure 1.65 ▼

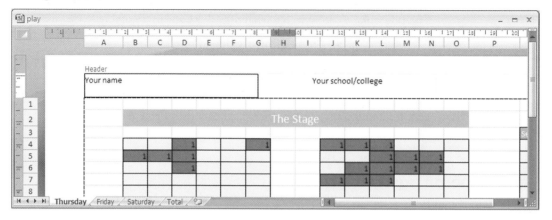

3 Enter your name in the left section.
4 Click to the right to select the right section and type in **Play ticket sales**.
5 Click **OK**.
6 Click **Go to Footer**.

In the centre section set up the page numbering by clicking the **Page Number** button (Figure 1.66).

Figure 1.66 ▼

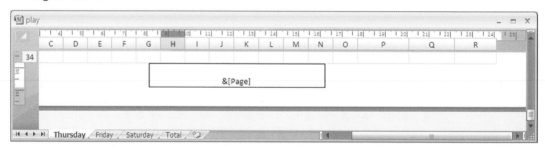

7 In the right section, enter the date by clicking the **Current Date** button. It appears on screen as **&[Date]** as in Figure 1.67.

Figure 1.67 ▼

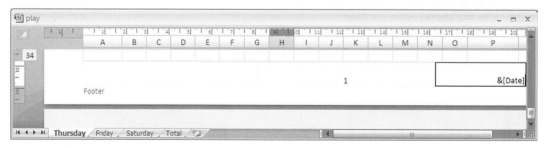

8 Customise the header and footer further if you wish.
9 Choose **Print Preview** by pressing the ESC key to see the effect.

Printing or not printing the gridlines and row and column headings

You can choose whether or not to print the row and column headings and the gridlines of your spreadsheet. This will depend on the purpose of your spreadsheet and the needs of the user, but it is always useful to show them when printing your formulas.

1 Press the **Ctrl** and **back tick** (the key left of 1) to show your formulas.
2 On the **View** tab in the **Show/Hide** group, uncheck **Gridlines** and **Headings** (Figure 1.68).

Figure 1.68 ▶

Another way to do this is to click the **Page Layout** tab. You can set whether or not to see and/or print the gridlines and headings, as shown in Figure 1.69.

Figure 1.69 ▶

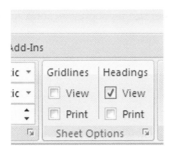

In formula view, you will probably need to adjust the width of columns so that the whole formula is visible.

To switch back to normal view, press CTRL and **back tick** again.

Note: If you want some gridlines to print but some others not, you will need to place a border around your cells:

- highlight the cells you want to have a border
- on the **Home** tab in the **Font** group, click the drop-down arrow next to the Borders button and choose **All Borders**.

To remove cell borders, click the drop-down arrow next to the Borders button and then click **No Border**.

Adjusting the size of your spreadsheet

You can make your printout bigger or smaller to fit onto your page.

1 Click the **Office Button** and choose **Print > Print Preview**. Click **Page Setup**.
2 Click the **Page** tab if it is not already selected.
3 The spreadsheet is a little smaller than the page so you can set the scaling to 105% as shown in Figure 1.70. It should still fit on the page. The printout will now be five per cent bigger than the normal size.

Figure 1.70 ▶

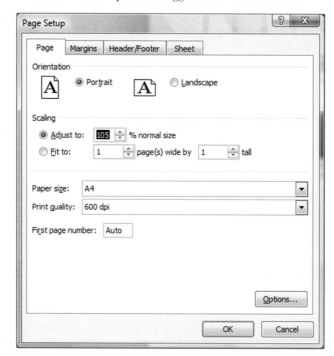

Click OK to check that it all fits on one page. If you choose 110%, it doesn't fit.

Automatically scaling the page

If your spreadsheet is slightly too big to fit on the page, you can select the **Fit to** option, **1 wide by 1 tall** as shown in Figure 1.71. Excel will reduce the worksheet by whatever percentage is needed to fit everything to the page.

Figure 1.71 ▶

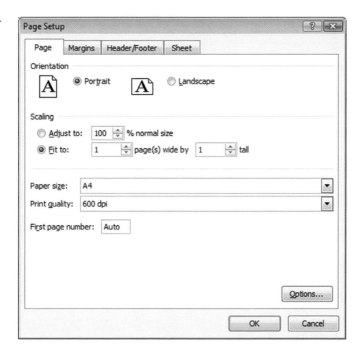

Print preview

Always preview before you print – it will save a lot of paper. You can check what will print by clicking **Office Button > Print > Print Preview**.

1 Check that your printout will be what you expect using **Print Preview**.
2 Click the **Show Margins** button in the Print Preview. You will see lines around the area to be printed, and small handles at the top of each column. Now you can adjust the column widths and the margins to improve the printout.
3 Print the page showing evidence of landscape printing, colour printing, headers, footers and resizing as shown in Figure 1.63.

2

Building a solution in Microsoft Excel 2007

In this part you will look at some more features of Excel 2007 that you might want to include in your spreadsheet through the scenario of a local newspaper.

The *Denton Gazette* is a weekly newspaper in the small town of Denton. Dozens of local businesses know that an advert in the *Gazette* gets a good response. Advertisements can be in colour or black and white and they can be a full page, a half page, a quarter page, an eighth of a page or a twelfth of a page.

The cost of an advertisement depends on:

- the size of the advertisement; a table of prices is given below
- whether the advertisement is in black and white or in colour
- the page on which the advertisement will be printed.

Size	Cost
Full page	£560.00
Half page	£300.00
Quarter page	£160.00
Eighth page	£85.00
Twelfth page	£60.00

This is the cost of a black and white advertisement on an inside page. A colour advertisement costs 30 per cent more.

If an advertisement is on the front page, it costs an extra 50 per cent. If the advertisement is on the back page it costs an extra 40 per cent. Advertisements on either the front page or the back page cannot be bigger than a quarter of the page.

Advertisers can book for up to 26 weeks. If they book for between four and nine consecutive weeks they get a discount of 10 per cent. If they book for ten or more consecutive weeks they get a discount of 20 per cent.

At present when someone places an order for an advertisement in the newspaper, the cost of the advertisement is calculated manually.

The owner of the *Denton Gazette*, Janice Peters would like an easy-to-use computer system that will calculate the price of placing advertisements in the newspaper.

The system must use:

- the company's house font, Verdana
- the company dove logo (Figure 2.1)
- the company's house colour scheme of
  - background – pale green;   Red 200, Green 237, Blue 234.
  - alternative background – mid green;   Red 176, Green 220, Blue 216
  - text – dark green;   Red 75, Green 112, Blue 105

Figure 2.1 ▶

Denton Gazette

Janice would like to have an easy-to-use system, where the user is able to:
- adjust prices easily
- store the name and address of the customer
- clear the screen for the next customer as required
- print the quotation at the touch of a button
- file the quotation away for future reference
- prevent full-page and half-page advertisements on the front page or the back page
- protect the file from accidental deletion of formulas
- create an automatic and user-friendly front-end for the system.

Unit 1: Named areas

In this unit you will learn how to name areas of your spreadsheet. It is not necessary to name these areas but it is good practice to name data in a table.

The first task is to enter the price data into a table.

1 Open a new file in Excel 2007.
2 Set the width of column B to 12 by clicking in B1. On the **Home** tab in the **Cells** group, click **Format > Column Width** and type in **12**.
3 Enter the data as shown in Figure 2.2 into Sheet1.

Figure 2.2 ▶

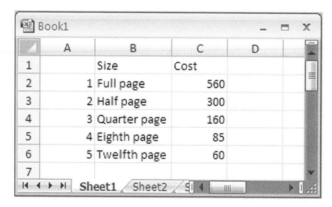

	A	B	C	D
1		Size	Cost	
2	1	Full page	560	
3	2	Half page	300	
4	3	Quarter page	160	
5	4	Eighth page	85	
6	5	Twelfth page	60	
7				

Sheet1 Sheet2

4 Highlight cells C2 to C6. On the **Home** tab in the **Number** group, use the **Number Format** drop-down list shown in Figure 2.3 to format the numbers in these cells to currency.

Figure 2.3 ▶

5 Rename the sheet **Prices** by double clicking the name on the Sheet tab (Figure 2.4).

Figure 2.4 ▶

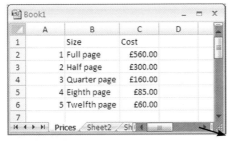

6 Highlight the cells A2 to C6. On the **Formulas** tab in the **Defined Names** group, click **Define Name**.

Figure 2.5 ▶

7 In the **New Name** box type in **Prices** and click **OK** (Figure 2.5).

Just below the ribbon on the left of the screen is the **Name**, which normally shows the reference of the selected cell, such as A1. But if you highlight a named area then the name of the area appears in the Name box as shown in Figure 2.6.

If you click the little arrow to the right of the Name box, you will get a list of all the named areas. At present there is only one named area in the list. If you click the name **Prices**, the named area will be selected.

Figure 2.6 ▶

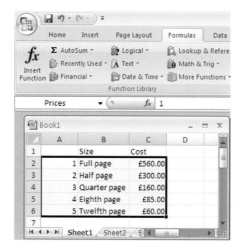

8 Save your file as **newspaper.xlsx**.

Unit 2: Check boxes

In this unit you will learn how to set up and use check boxes. A check box is a small square on the screen – if you click this square, a tick appears; if you click again the tick disappears. Use check boxes to turn options on or off.

You will use a check box to show whether an advertiser wants to have a colour advertisement or not.

1 Open the spreadsheet **newspaper.xlsx** from Unit 1 if it is not already loaded.
2 Go to Sheet2 and rename the sheet **Quotation**.
3 On the **Home** tab in the **Cells** group, click **Format > Column Width** to adjust the widths of each of these columns in turn:
   - column A: 5
   - column B: 16
   - column C: 45
   - column D: 5
   - column E: 19
   - column F: 6
   - column G: 11
   - column H: 5
4 For the next stage you need the **Developer** tab. If the Developer tab is not visible, click the **Office Button**. At the bottom of the drop-down menu, choose **Excel Options** as shown in Figure 2.7

Figure 2.7 ▶

Make sure that the **Show Developer tab in the Ribbon** is checked as in Figure 2.8.

Figure 2.8 ▶

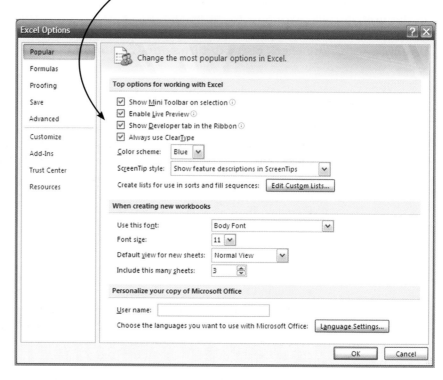

5 Click **OK**.

6 On the **Developer** tab in the **Controls** group, click **Insert**.

A drop-down box appears showing a number of buttons as shown in Figure 2.9

7 Click the **check box** button – it is the third button in the top row.

Figure 2.9 ▼

Note: You must choose the check box from the Form Controls and **not** from the Active X Controls.

8 Drag out a rectangle on the worksheet over cell E11 – it will look like Figure 2.10.

Figure 2.10 ▶

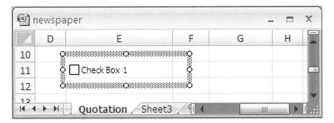

9 Right click the check box. Choose **Edit Text**, delete the text which says **Check Box 1** and replace it with the word **Colour** (Figure 2.11).

Figure 2.11 ▶

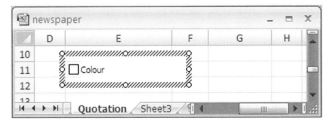

10 Right click again on the check box – click **Format Control**.
11 A dialogue box appears. Set the cell link to **F11** as in Figure 2.12 and click **OK**.

Figure 2.12 ▶

Click away from the check box.

12 Test that the check box works. When you click the box the tick appears and the word **TRUE** appears in F11. Click again – the tick is removed and the word **FALSE** appears in F11.
13 Save your work.

Unit 3: Using the IF function

In this unit you will learn how to set up and use the IF function. The IF function tests the value in a cell and does one thing if the test is true and another if the test is false.

IF statements have the form **=IF(A12=4,72,0)**

Suppose this formula is in cell A10. If the value in cell A12 is 4 then 72 will appear in cell A10. If the value in cell A12 is **not** 4 then 0 will appear in cell A10.

A colour advertisement costs 30 per cent more than a black and white one. That means that if an advertisement is in colour, we must multiply the price of a black and white advertisement by 1.3.

If an advertisement is in black and white, we multiply by 1.

1 Enter this formula in cell G11: **=IF(F11=TRUE,1.3,1)**
2 Save your work and test that as you click the check box the number in cell G11 changes from 1.3 to 1 and back again, as shown in Figure 2.13.

Figure 2.13 ▶

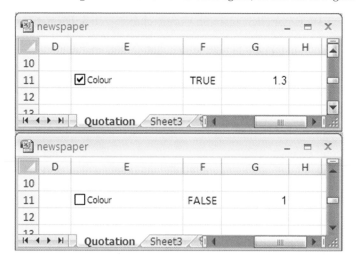

Unit 4: Option buttons

In this unit you will learn how to set up and use option buttons. Option buttons, sometimes called radio buttons, allow you to select one from a group of options.

You will use option buttons to make the choice of the front page, the back page or the inside pages because this is a factor that affects the cost of an advertisement.

1 On the **Developer** tab in the **Controls** group, click **Insert** and click **Option Button (Form Control)** – the right-most button in the top row (Figure 2.14).

Figure 2.14 ▼

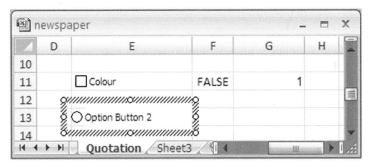

2 Drag out a rectangle over cell E13 (Figure 2.15).

Figure 2.15 ▶

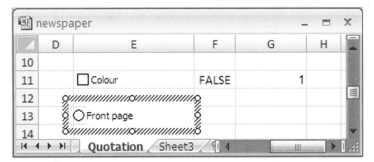

3 Right click the option button. Choose **Edit Text** and delete the text **Option Button 2** and replace it with **Front page** (Figure 2.16).

Figure 2.16 ▶

4 Right click again on the option button. Choose **Format Control**.
5 Set the cell link to **F15**.

6 Click **Insert > Option Button** again and drag out a rectangle over cell E15. Change the label of this button to **Back page**. You do not need to set the cell link again.

7 Then add a third option button over cell E17 and label this one **Inside pages** (Figure 2.17).

8 Test that as you click the Option buttons, F15 changes from 1 to 2 to 3.

Figure 2.17 ▶

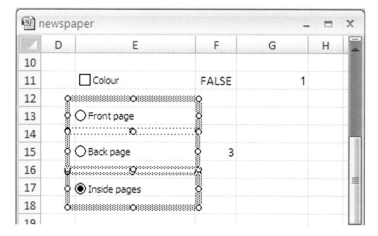

Hint   To make sure that all three buttons are in a neat straight line:
- Right click one of the option buttons.
- Hold down the **CTRL** key and click the other two option buttons in turn to select all three option buttons.
- On the **Page Layout** tab in the **Arrange** group, click **Align** and choose **Align Left**.
- Click **Align** again and click **Distribute Vertically**.

9 Save your work.

Note: All the option buttons on one sheet will link by default to the same cell. If you want two or more groups of option buttons, select the **Group Box** on the **Insert** drop-down menu and draw a box round each group of option buttons.

Unit 5: Nested IF statements

In this unit you will look at how you can use the nested IF function.

With an IF statement such as **=IF(F11=TRUE,1.3,1)** you have only two choices – TRUE and FALSE.

Nested IF statements increase the number of possible outcomes by placing one IF function inside another IF function. We want three choices – **Front page**, **Back page** or **Inside pages**.

Inside pages are the cheapest; back pages are 40 per cent more; the front page is even more expensive, 50 per cent more than inside pages.

So if F15 is 1 then the price is multiplied by 1.5.

If F15 is 2 the price is multiplied by 1.4.

If F15 is 3 the price is the same and we multiply by 1.

The formula for this is **=IF(F15=1,1.5,IF(F15=2,1.4,1))**

Here we have nested one IF function inside another. You can have more nested IFs – up to a maximum of 7.

This formula checks if F15 is 1. If it is then G15 is set to 1.5. If not then it checks if F15 is 2. If it is then G15 is set to 1.4. If not, it is set to 1.

1 Enter the formula above in cell G15.
2 Test that the IF statement is working correctly by clicking each option button in turn (Figure 2.18).
3 Save your work.

Figure 2.18 ▶

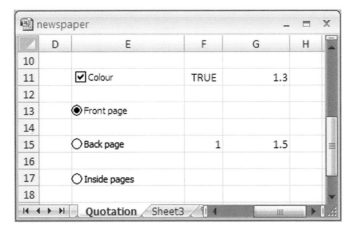

Unit 6: Combo boxes

In this unit you will look at using drop-down boxes to make a choice from a list.

'Combo box' is the term used in Excel for a drop-down box.

1 On the **Developer** tag, click **Insert**.
2 Select the **Combo Box (Form Control)** button – the second button from the left in the top row (Figure 2.19).

Figure 2.19 ▼

3 Drag out a rectangle over cell E9. A combo box will appear as shown in Figure 2.20.

Figure 2.20 ▶

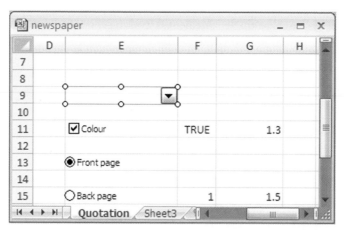

4 Right click the combo box and choose **Format Control**. A dialogue box appears on the screen.
5 Click in the **Input range** box. Click the **Prices** sheet tab to switch to the Prices worksheet and highlight cells B2 to B6.

6 Click in the **Cell link** box on the dialogue box and press **F9**. The dialogue box should look like the one in Figure 2.21.

Figure 2.21 ▶

7 Click **OK**.

8 Test that the choices on the combo box are as shown in Figure 2.22.

Figure 2.22 ▶

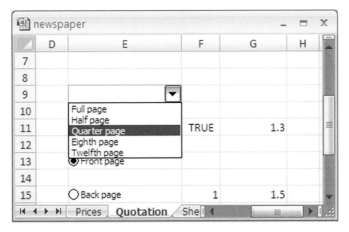

9 If you select the first item in the combo box, a number 1 will appear in cell F9 and so on. Check that as you choose a different selection from the combo box, the correct data appears in cell F9.

Note: If you type a value such as 2 into cell F9, it changes the information displayed in the combo box.

10 Save your file.

Unit 7: The VLOOKUP function

In this unit you will look at how to use the **VLOOKUP** function to look up data in a table. You will link the **VLOOKUP** to the combo box set up in **Unit 6** to look up the price of an advertisement for the size chosen.

There are three lookup functions – LOOKUP, VLOOKUP and HLOOKUP. We will concentrate on the most commonly used function, VLOOKUP (vertical lookup). HLOOKUP (horizontal lookup) and LOOKUP are very similar and may be worth investigating further later.

You will put the cost of the advertisement in cell G9.

1 Select cell G9 and format it to currency. On the **Home** tab in the **Number** group, click **Currency** from the drop-down list.
2 In this cell, enter the formula **=VLOOKUP(F9,Prices,3)**.

You should now see that when you select a different size advertisement using the combo box, you get the appropriate price in cell G9. For example the price of one-eighth of a page is £85 as shown in Figure 2.23.

Figure 2.23 ▶

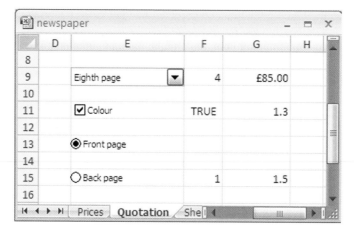

3 Test that it works by choosing different advertisement sizes using the combo box.

How does the formula work?

- **F9** is the cell whose value is to be looked up
- **Prices** is the named area storing the price data set up in Unit 1
- **3** is the number of the column in the table from which you want to take the data.

Figure 2.24 ►

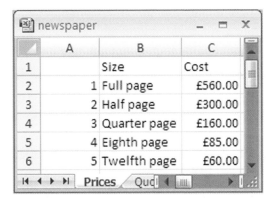

The software will look in cell F9 and find the value 4. It will then look in the first column of the prices table (Column A) until it finds 4 (Figure 2.24). Then it goes to the right until it reaches the third column (Column C). The value it finds here (£85.00) is displayed in cell G9.

Note: This will only work if the data in the first column is in ascending order.

4 Save the file.

You might want to experiment with typing impossible values – such as 0, 4.5 and 6 – into cell F9 to see what happens.

Unit 8: Spinners

In this unit you will learn how to set up and use spinner controls.

A **spinner**, or spin button, is a button with small up and down arrows that enable you to increase or decrease the value of a number in a cell by clicking the arrows.

1 Switch back to the **Quotation** sheet if not already selected. Enter **Number of weeks** into cell E19.
2 On the **Developer** tab in the **Controls** group, click **Insert**. The drop-down box appears as shown in Figure 2.25.
3 Select the fourth button from the left in the top row – it is called **Spin Button (Form Control)**.

Figure 2.25 ▶

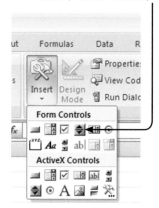

4 Drag out a small rectangle over part of cells F19 and F20. A spinner will appear like that shown in Figure 2.26.

Figure 2.26 ▶

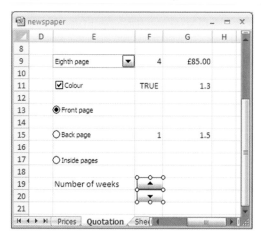

5 Right click the spinner and choose **Format Control**.

6 A dialogue box appears. Set the Minimum value to **1**, the Maximum value to **26**, leave the Incremental change at **1** and set the Cell link to **G19** as shown in Figure 2.27.

Figure 2.27 ▶

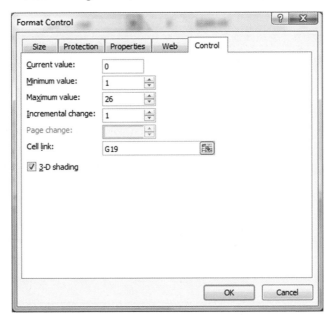

7 Click **OK**. Click off the spinner so that it is not selected and then click the spinner to test that it works.

8 Save your work.

Unit 9: Layout

In this unit you will learn to use Merge & Centre to merge cells and improve the layout of the page.

1 Still with the **Quotation** sheet selected, highlight cells B2 to G5 (Figure 2.28).

2 On the **Home** tab in the **Alignment** group, click the **Merge & Center** button.

Figure 2.28 ▼

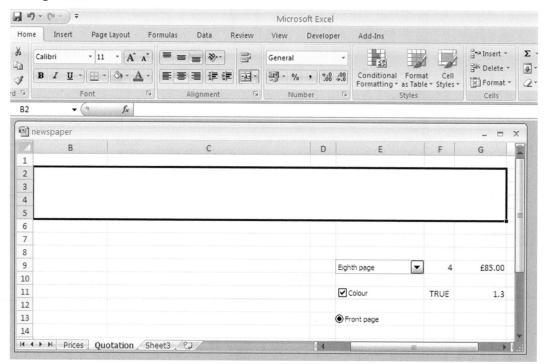

3 Set the font to size **48**.

4 Enter the title **Denton Gazette**.

Figure 2.29 ▼

5 Merge cells B6 to G6 in the same way.

6 Enter the address and phone number, **25 High Street, Denton, DN6 9AA (01976) 434343**

7 Merge cells B7 to G7.

8 Enter the company's website address, **www.dentongazette.co.uk**. If Excel formats the web address as a hyperlink click the **Undo** button on the **Quick Access** toolbar.

9 Format that cell to **bold**.

10 Save the file.

You are now ready to link all the information on the spreadsheet together to work out the price.

11 In cell E22 enter the wording **Basic price**.

12 In cell G22 enter the formula **=G9*G11*G15*G19**

This simply works out the price of the advertisement including colour and the page selected for the number of weeks chosen.

13 In cell E24 enter the wording **Discount**.

14 In cell G24 you need to enter a nested IF statement. If cell G19 is more than or equal to 10, there is a 20 per cent discount. If cell G19 is less than 4 there is no discount. Otherwise the discount is 10 per cent.

(If you can't work it out, the formula is given at the end of the unit.)

15 Format cell G24 to percentage. On the **Home** tab in the **Number** group, click the drop-down box and click **Percentage**.

16 In cell E26 enter the wording **Final price**.

17 Enter a formula in cell G26 to work out the price minus the discount. Again this is at the end of the unit if you can't work it out.

18 Format cell G26 to **bold** so that it stands out.

19 In cell B11 enter **Customer Details**. Format this cell to **bold**.

20 Enter the headings in B13, B15, B17, B19 and B21 as shown in Figure 2.30 and format these cells to **bold**. The customer's name and address will be entered next to these cells.

21 Format cells E22, E24 and E26 to **bold**.

Adding the date

A quotation like this will normally include the date.

1 Select cell **B9**.

2 Enter **=TODAY()**

You spreadsheet should look like that shown in Figure 2.30.

Figure 2.30 ▼

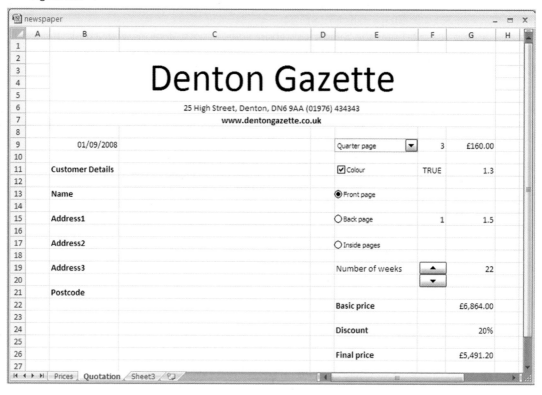

3 Save your work.

Testing your spreadsheet

It is important that you test your spreadsheet thoroughly – if it is not accurate it will be of little use.

The best way to check your spreadsheet is to test it for a number of different scenarios. You should work out the cost in your head or with a calculator and then check that the spreadsheet gives the correct amount.

For example you might choose the following scenarios:

- quarter page, colour, front page, 22 weeks
- full page, no colour, inside page, 3 weeks
- eighth page, colour, back page, 8 weeks.

For scenario 1, the price of the advertisement is £160. Colour is 30 per cent more. 30 per cent of £160 is £48. This gives £208.

The front page is 50 per cent more. 50 per cent of £208 is £104. This adds up to £312.

22 weeks will cost 22 times £312 = £6864 (Figure 2.31).

Figure 2.31 ▶

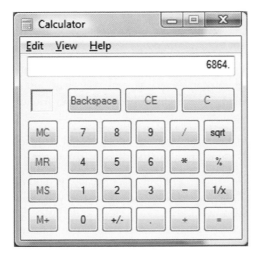

22 weeks qualifies for a 20 per cent discount. 20 per cent of £6864 = £1372.80. £6864 minus £1372.80 = £5491.20.

Figure 2.32 ▶

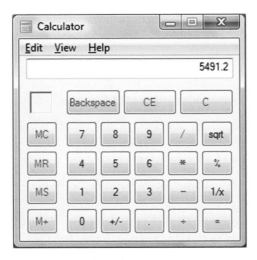

As you can see from Figure 2.30 and Figure 2.32, the spreadsheet gave the expected answer.

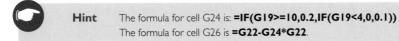

Hint   The formula for cell G24 is: **=IF(G19>=10,0.2,IF(G19<4,0,0.1))**
The formula for cell G26 is **=G22-G24*G22**.

Unit 10: Macros

In this unit you will learn about macros, why they are useful and how to create them.

A macro is a set of instructions. They are used to automate common procedures – this means that you can replace several clicks with just one click and so save time. Macros can also make spreadsheets more user-friendly for someone who is not an ICT professional.

Macros use a programming language called Visual Basic for Applications (VBA), often shortened to Visual Basic or VB. You can:

- Record macros – this is relatively easy because you do not need to know about Visual Basic coding. Most of the macros you will set up will be recorded in this way.
- Write the macros yourself in Visual Basic – this is more difficult because you need to know the various VB coding commands. However, some macros can **only** be set up in this way (see Unit 13).
- Edit the Visual Basic in macros you have recorded – again it is necessary to know about VB coding. You will edit a few macros in this way.

Having created a macro, you can then create a button on the spreadsheet or on the **Quick Access** toolbar to run it.

Recording macros

There are three common procedures that we want to automate using a macro:

- switching to the Prices worksheet (e.g. to change prices)
- switching back to the Quotation sheet
- clearing the data for the next customer.

You will start by recording a macro to switch to the Prices worksheet. Make sure that you are on the **Quotation** sheet.

1 On the **Developer** tab in the **Code** group, click **Record Macro**.
2 Call the macro **Prices** as in Figure 2.33 and click **OK**.

Figure 2.33 ▶

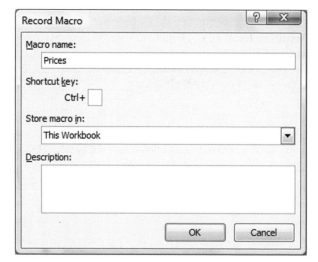

There is little on the screen to show that a macro is being recorded. You will notice a small button in the bottom-left of the screen as shown in Figure 2.34.

Figure 2.34 ▼

You may also notice that the words **Stop Recording** have replaced the words Record Macro in the ribbon, as in Figure 2.35.

Figure 2.35 ▼

3 Click the sheet tab to select the **Prices** sheet.
4 Click the **Stop Recording** button. Either the button in the bottom-left corner or the words 'Stop Recording' in the ribbon will work.

The macro has now been recorded. You can see the Visual Basic coding of the macro by clicking the **Developer** tab and in the **Code** group click **Macros**. Select **Module1.Prices. > Edit**. Figure 2.36 shows what it looks like.

Note: The Prices macro is sometimes labelled Prices or Module1.Prices. It will work whichever it is called.

Figure 2.36 ▶

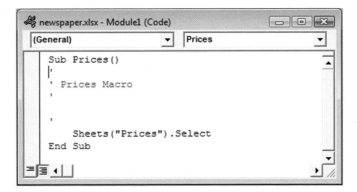

It is easy to see what is happening. The first line gives the name of the macro. The next five lines begin with a ' and are in green – they are just for information. The next line switches to the Prices sheet. All macros end with End Sub.

4 Return to Excel by clicking the **View Microsoft Excel** button or pressing ALT and **F11**.
5 Record a similar macro called **Quotation** to take you back to the Quotation sheet.
6 Don't forget to stop recording and save your work.

You should now test your macros.

7 Test the Prices macro by clicking **Macros > Module1.Prices > Run**. It should take you to the Prices sheet.
8 Test that the Quotation macro takes you back to the Quotation sheet; **Macros > Quotation > Run**.

Saving your macro

In Excel 2007 you cannot save a worksheet with macros unless it is stored as Macro-enabled worksheet.

1 Click the **Office Button**.
2 Select **Save As**.
3 Choose **Excel Macro-Enabled worksheet** as in Figure 2.37. Your file will be stored as **newspaper.xlsm**

Figure 2.37 ▶

Unit 11: Macro buttons

In this unit you will learn how to set up buttons to run macros. This means that you can run a macro with just one click.

You will now add two buttons – one to run each macro.

1 Go to the **Quotation** sheet of the **newspaper.xlsm** file if you are not already on it.
2 On the **Developer** tab in the **Controls** group, click **Insert**. Then click **Button (Form Control)** – the first button on the left in the first row.
3 Drag out a rectangle over cells B24 and B25 as shown in Figure 2.38.

Figure 2.38 ▶

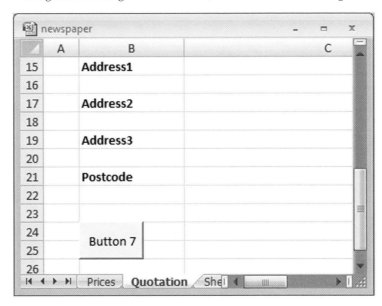

The button will be given a name such as Button 7.

4 The Assign Macro dialogue box will open. Assign the macro **Prices** (which will probably be called **Module1.Prices**) and click **OK**.

5 Right click the button. Choose **Edit Text** – delete the text on the button and replace it with **Prices** as shown in Figure 2.39.

Figure 2.39 ▶

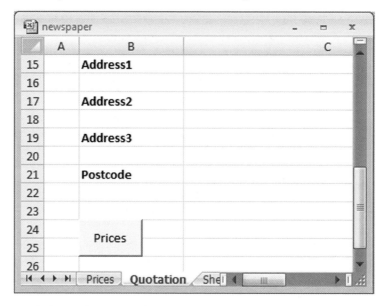

6 Click anywhere away from the button and then click the button to test that it works.

7 Add a similar button on the **Prices** sheet to run the **Quotation** macro – as in Figure 2.40.

Figure 2.40 ▶

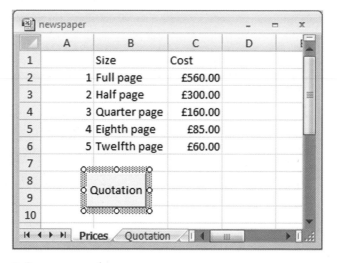

8 Save your work.

It is now easy to switch to the Prices sheet to adjust prices.

Unit 12: A macro to clear data

In this unit you will set up a macro to clear the sheet ready for the next customer.

The user needs to clear all the data after one quotation has been made so that another quotation can be given. This can also be done with a macro and a button.

1 Starting on the **Quotation** sheet, record a macro called **Clear**. On the **Developer** tab in the **Code** group, click **Record Macro**.
2 Select cell **F9** and press DELETE.
3 Select cell **F11** and press DELETE.
4 Select cell **F15** and press DELETE.
5 Select cell **G19** and press DELETE.
6 Select cell **C13** and press DELETE.
7 Select cell **C15** and press DELETE.
8 Select cell **C17** and press DELETE.
9 Select cell **C19** and press DELETE.
10 Select cell **C21** and press DELETE.
11 Click **C13** to make this cell the active cell.
12 Stop recording.

All the data has now been removed, although in some cells there may be the error message #N/A. You will learn how to remove these in Unit 16.

Add a button to run the Clear macro to the right of the Prices button. The best way to do this and get the second button the same size as the first is described next.

13 Right click the **Prices** button.
14 On the **Home** tab in the **Clipboard** group, click **Copy**.
15 Click **Paste**.

Slide the new button across so that it is exactly to the right of the first button. You can align the buttons in exactly the same way as you aligned the option buttons in Unit 4.

16 Right click the new button and edit the text to **Clear**.
17 Right click the new button and assign the macro to **Clear** (Figure 2.41).

Figure 2.41 ▶

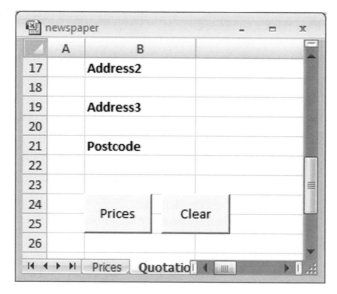

18 Enter some data and test that the Clear button works.
19 Save your work.

A print macro

One of the client's original requirements was to print a quotation at the touch of a button.

1 Set the page to Landscape – on the **Page Layout** tab in the **Page Setup** group, click **Orientation > Landscape**.
2 Highlight the area from A1 to H30. On the **Page Layout** tab in the **Page Setup** group, click **Print Area > Set Print Area**. The print area will be outlined by a dotted line.
3 On the **Insert** tab in the **Text** group, click **Insert > Header & Footer** to add your name, the date and the page number.
4 Record a macro called **PrintQuote** to print page 1 of the quotation sheet.
5 Add another button to run this macro and label this button **Print** as shown in Figure 2.42.

Figure 2.42 ▶

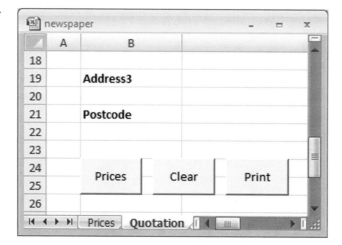

Unit 13: Message boxes

In this unit you will learn how to set up macros to display message boxes on the screen.

As explained in Unit 10, some macros can be created only by writing them yourself in Visual Basic or by editing the Visual Basic of an existing macro.

You need to know a little Visual Basic to put a message box on the screen like the one in Figure 2.43. Fortunately the code is not too difficult.

Figure 2.43 ▶

1 On the **Developer** tab in the **Code** group, click **Macros > Clear > Edit**.
2 This loads up the Visual Basic coding of the macro in Visual Basic Editor. Your code will be similar to that in Figure 2.44. You will learn more about Visual Basic Editor in Unit 21.

Figure 2.44 ▶

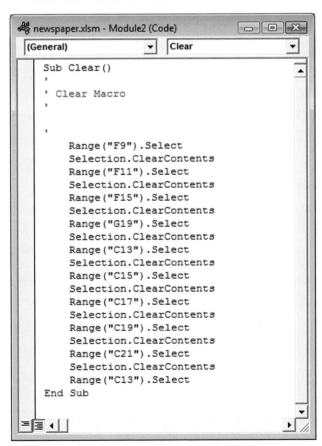

```
Sub Clear()
'
' Clear Macro
'

'
    Range("F9").Select
    Selection.ClearContents
    Range("F11").Select
    Selection.ClearContents
    Range("F15").Select
    Selection.ClearContents
    Range("G19").Select
    Selection.ClearContents
    Range("C13").Select
    Selection.ClearContents
    Range("C15").Select
    Selection.ClearContents
    Range("C17").Select
    Selection.ClearContents
    Range("C19").Select
    Selection.ClearContents
    Range("C21").Select
    Selection.ClearContents
    Range("C13").Select
End Sub
```

3 Click at the end of the line above End Sub. Press **Enter** and type in the code shown below. Remember that the coding has to be spelt exactly right for it to work.

```
response = MsgBox("Quotation cleared for next customer ", ,"Spreadsheet
Projects")
```

Figure 2.45 ▼

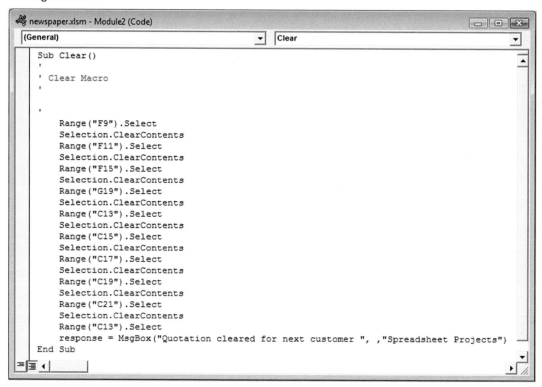

```
Sub Clear()
'
' Clear Macro
'

'
    Range("F9").Select
    Selection.ClearContents
    Range("F11").Select
    Selection.ClearContents
    Range("F15").Select
    Selection.ClearContents
    Range("G19").Select
    Selection.ClearContents
    Range("C13").Select
    Selection.ClearContents
    Range("C15").Select
    Selection.ClearContents
    Range("C17").Select
    Selection.ClearContents
    Range("C19").Select
    Selection.ClearContents
    Range("C21").Select
    Selection.ClearContents
    Range("C13").Select
    response = MsgBox("Quotation cleared for next customer ", ,"Spreadsheet Projects")
End Sub
```

4 Close the Visual Basic Editor program in the normal way, or press **Alt** and **F11**.

5 Run the **Clear** macro and make sure that the message box appears.

6 Save your work.

Sometimes people exit from a program in error. You can use a macro and a message box as a double check.

7 Load the Visual Basic code for the **Clear** macro as before. On the **Developer** tab in the **Code** group, click **Macros > Clear > Edit**.

8 Scroll down to the bottom and type in this code which creates a new macro called **Quit**:

```
Sub Quit()
response = MsgBox("Are you sure you want to quit?", vbYesNo)
If response = vbYes Then Application.quit
End Sub
```

See Figure 2.46.

Figure 2.46 ▼

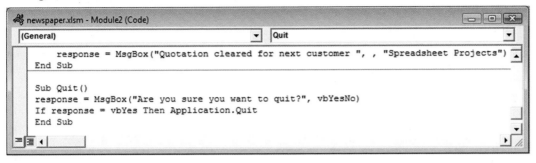

```
newspaper.xlsm - Module2 (Code)

(General)                                              Quit

        response = MsgBox("Quotation cleared for next customer ", , "Spreadsheet Projects")
   End Sub

   Sub Quit()
   response = MsgBox("Are you sure you want to quit?", vbYesNo)
   If response = vbYes Then Application.Quit
   End Sub
```

Hint   The computer will put the **End Sub** line in for you.

What does this macro do?

Line 1 says the macro is called **Quit**.

Line 2 **displays the message box** with the message and Yes and No buttons (see Figure 2.47).

Line 3 checks if the response is Yes and if it is exits from Excel.

Line 4 ends the macro.

Figure 2.47 ▶

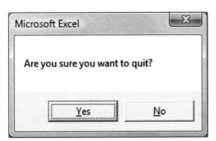

9 Save your file.
10 Close Visual Basic Editor (press **Alt** and **F11**) and test that the macro works for both the Yes button and the No button.
11 Add a button to run the **Quit** macro.

Unit 14: Further macros

In this unit you will learn how to set up a macro to file away quotation details.

In the original requirements, the client requested that the user should be able to file the quotation for future reference. You will do this by using a macro to copy data to a file in a different sheet.

1 Switch to **Sheet3** and rename the worksheet **QuoteFile** as shown in Figure 2.48.

Figure 2.48 ▶

Hint   Although it is possible to have a space in the name of a worksheet, it is easier when using certain features to avoid spaces.

2 Highlight columns A to K and set the column width to 10. On the **Home** tab in the **Cells** group, click **Format > Column Width > 10**.
3 Set the font size to 10 and enter the column headings as shown in Figure 2.49.

Figure 2.49 ▼

4 Highlight column A and set the date. On the **Home** tab in the **Number** group, click **Short Date** in the drop-down list.
5 Highlight column K and format to currency in the same way.
6 Switch back to the **Quotation** sheet.

You are now going to make a copy of all the data in row 31 at the bottom of the screen, ready to file.

7 Scroll down to cell A31. Enter the formula **=B9** (don't worry if the date does not fit in the cell and you see ######).
8 In B31 enter the formula **=C13**
9 In C31 enter the formula **=C15**
10 In D31 enter the formula **=C17**
11 In E31 enter the formula **=C19**
12 In F31 enter the formula **=C21**
13 In G31 enter the formula **=VLOOKUP(F9,Prices,2)**

14 In H31 enter the formula **=IF(F11=TRUE,"Colour","Not colour")**

15 In I31 enter the formula **=IF(F15=1,"Front Page",IF(F15=2,"Back page","Inside pages"))**

16 In J31 enter the formula **=G19&"weeks"**

This is called concatenation where two or more pieces of text are joined together in a cell.

Note: There is a space before the word *weeks*.

17 In K31 enter the formula **=G26**.

It will look something like Figure 2.50. If the details don't fit in the cells, it does not matter.

Figure 2.50 ▼

You are now ready to record the macro. It is quite complicated and you have to get all the commands in the right order. You may want to practise the sequence of tasks before you actually record the macro.

18 Switch to the **Quotation** sheet.

19 Start to record a macro called **FileQuote**. On the **Developer** tab in the **Code** group, click **Record Macro**.

20 Switch to the **QuoteFile** sheet.

21 Highlight cells A2 to K2.

22 On the **Home** tab in the **Cells** group, click **Insert > Insert Cells > Shift cells down > OK** (this makes a space to store the quotation).

23 Switch back to the **Quotation** sheet.

24 Highlight cells A31 to K31.

25 Click the **Copy** button.

26 Switch to the **QuoteFile** sheet again.

27 Click the **Paste** drop-down box > **Paste Values > OK** as shown in Figure 2.51. You cannot use Paste here because it won't work.

28 Switch back to the **Quotation** sheet again. Click cell **C13** and press the ESC key on the keyboard.

29 Stop recording.

30 We don't need to see the data in cells A31 to K31, so highlight these cells and set the font colour to be white. On the **Home** tab in the **Font** group, select the Font colour.

Figure 2.51 ▼

87

31 Add a button to run the **FileQuote** macro on the right of the other four buttons.

Align the tops of all five buttons and space them out evenly as follows.

32 Right click one button.

33 Hold down the CTRL key and click the edge of the other four buttons.

34 On the **Page Layout** tab in the **Arrange** group, click **Align > Align Top**.

34 Click **Align > Distribute Horizontally** as shown in Figure 2.52.

Figure 2.52 ▼

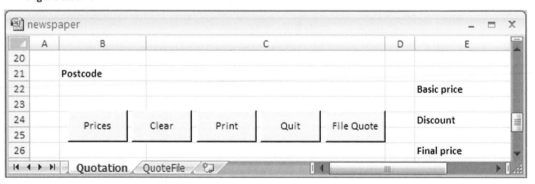

The buttons are now spaced evenly as shown in Figure 2.53.

Figure 2.53 ▼

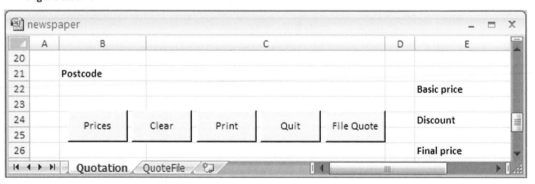

35 Test that the macro works by filing four or five additional quotations as shown in Figure 2.54.

Figure 2.54 ▼

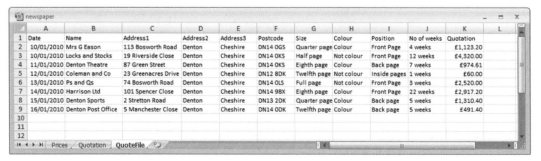

Unit 15: Data forms

In this unit you will learn how to use data forms to go back to previous quotations. You cannot load a data form from the Ribbon, but you can still use data forms in Excel 2007 by adding a button to the Quick Access Toolbar. So in this unit you will also look at how to modify the Quick Access Toolbar by adding a button.

1 Switch to the **QuoteFile** sheet. You should have several quotations as in Figure 2.55.

Figure 2.55 ▼

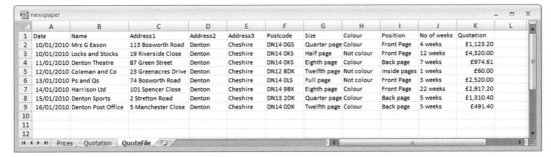

	A	B	C	D	E	F	G	H	I	J	K	L
1	Date	Name	Address1	Address2	Address3	Postcode	Size	Colour	Position	No of weeks	Quotation	
2	10/01/2010	Mrs G Eason	113 Bosworth Road	Denton	Cheshire	DN14 0GS	Quarter page	Colour	Front Page	4 weeks	£1,123.20	
3	10/01/2010	Locks and Stocks	19 Riverside Close	Denton	Cheshire	DN14 0KS	Half page	Not colour	Front Page	12 weeks	£4,320.00	
4	11/01/2010	Denton Theatre	87 Green Street	Denton	Cheshire	DN14 0KS	Eighth page	Colour	Back page	7 weeks	£974.61	
5	12/01/2010	Coleman and Co	23 Greenacres Drive	Denton	Cheshire	DN12 8DK	Twelfth page	Not colour	Inside pages	1 weeks	£60.00	
6	13/01/2010	Ps and Qs	74 Bosworth Road	Denton	Cheshire	DN14 0LS	Full page	Not colour	Front Page	3 weeks	£2,520.00	
7	14/01/2010	Harrison Ltd	101 Spencer Close	Denton	Cheshire	DN14 9BX	Eighth page	Colour	Front Page	22 weeks	£2,917.20	
8	15/01/2010	Denton Sports	2 Stretton Road	Denton	Cheshire	DN13 2DK	Quarter page	Colour	Back page	5 weeks	£1,310.40	
9	16/01/2010	Denton Post Office	5 Manchester Close	Denton	Cheshire	DN14 0DK	Twelfth page	Colour	Back page	5 weeks	£491.40	
10												
11												
12												

Prices / Quotation / **QuoteFile**

If you don't have many records on your sheet, you will need to add some more quotations.

2 Click any of the cells in the table.

3 Click the **Office Button** and choose **Excel Options** at the bottom of the menu.

4 A dialogue box will appear on the screen looking like Figure 2.56.

Figure 2.56 ▶

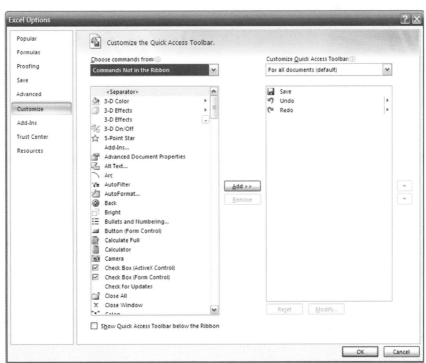

5 Click **Customize**.

6 In the **Choose Commands from** drop-down list, choose **Commands Not in the Ribbon** as in Figure 2.57.

7 Scroll down this list until you find Form. Select **Form** and click **Add**. Form will appear in the right-hand list as in Figure 2.57.

Figure 2.57 ▼

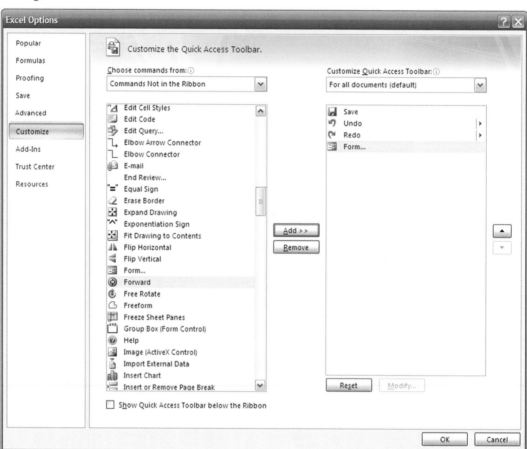

8 Choose **OK**. You will now see a new **Form** button in the **Quick Access** toolbar as in Figure 2.58.

Figure 2.58 ▶

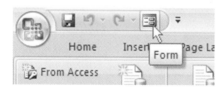

9 Click the **Form** button. A data form will load like the one shown in Figure 2.59.

Figure 2.59 ▶

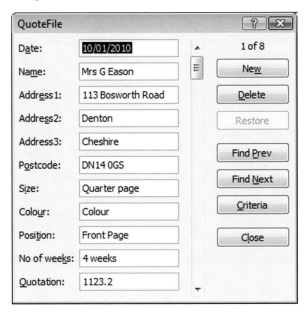

You can scroll through the records using the scroll bar.

Suppose you wanted to find the quotation for Harrison Ltd (or a company you have entered).

10 Click the **Criteria** button.
11 Enter the first few letters, such as **Harr**, in the Name box.
12 Click **Find Next**.

You should find the record for Harrison Ltd (Figure 2.60) or the one for your company.

Figure 2.60 ▶

QuoteFile   [?] [X]

Date:	14/01/2010	▲	6 of 8
Name:	Harrison Ltd		New
Address1:	101 Spencer Close		Delete
Address2:	Denton		Restore
Address3:	Cheshire		
Postcode:	DN14 9BX		Find Prev
Size:	Eighth page	≡	Find Next
Colour:	Colour		Criteria
Position:	Front Page		Close
No of weeks:	22 weeks		
Quotation:	2917.2	▼	

13 Record a macro called **Quotes** that will take you from the Quotation sheet to the QuoteFile sheet and display the data form. You will have to close the data form before you can stop recording, but the Close operation won't be recorded.

14 Add a new button on the Quotation sheet to run this macro. You now should have six macro buttons as shown in Figure 2.61.

Figure 2.61 ▶

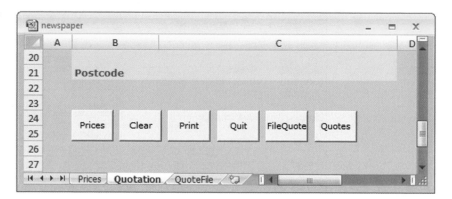

In this unit you will learn various ways of removing an #N/A error message.

If you run the **Clear** macro you get an #N/A error message in cells G22 and G26 of the Quotation sheet and 0.00% in G24.

This happens because a value in a formula is missing. In this case, it is missing because you have cleared the data.

For example, the formula in G22 is **=G9*G11*G15*G19**. There are no numbers in these cells, so we get an #N/A error message.

These #N/A messages are unsightly and unfriendly. You can remove it them follows.

1 Replace the formula in G22 with **=IF(F9="","", G9*G11*G15*G19)**.

This formula checks the value of F9. If it is blank (""), then G22 is also blank. Otherwise it looks up the value as before.

2 Test that the formula works. If you run the **Clear** macro, G22 is blank. As soon as you choose a size and a number of weeks, the price appears in G22.
3 There are also errors in cells G22 and G26. Enter the formulas to prevent these errors based on checking if F9 is blank. If you can't work them out for yourself, the formulas are given in the hint box below.

The error messages have now been removed (Figure 2.62).

4 Save your work.

Figure 2.62 ▼

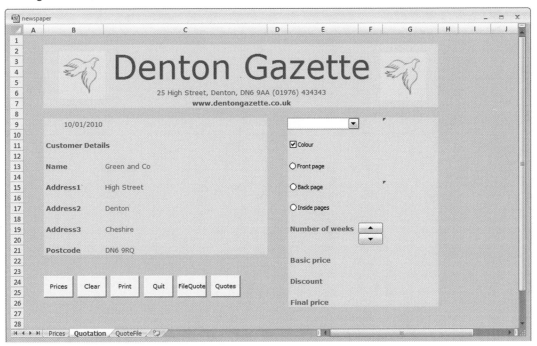

Error trapping – using the ISERROR function

An alternative method is to use the ISERROR function in Excel. This function tests if an error has occurred.

Again you use the IF function – and the command is even longer.

1 Replace the formula in G22 with **=IF(ISERROR(G9*G11*G15*G19),"", G9*G11*G15*G19)**.

This formula checks if there is an error in the calculation. If there is, it returns a blank. If not, it returns the value.

2 Test that the formula works. If you run the **Clear** macro, G22 is blank. If you choose a value from the combo box and spinner, the price appears in G22.

3 There is also an error in cell G26. Use the ISERROR formula to prevent this error based on checking if there is an error in the calculation G22-G24*G22.

It is possible to customise the screen to remove these features that might distract the user.

Record a macro called **Auto_open** to remove all these features.

1 Start recording the macro.
2 Click the **Office Button** and then click **Excel Options**.
3 Click the **Advanced** button and scroll down until you see **Display**.
4 Uncheck **Show formula bar**, **Show horizontal scroll bar**, **Show vertical scroll bar**, **Show sheet tabs** and **Show row and column headers** as shown in Figure 2.68.

Figure 2.68 ▼

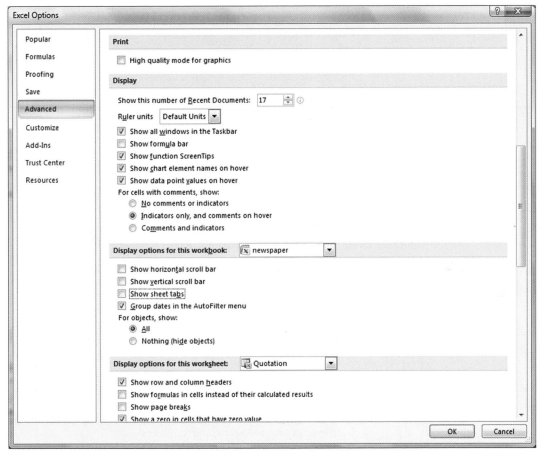

5 Remove the ribbon using CTRL and **F1**.
6 Stop recording by clicking on the **Stop recording** button at the bottom-left of the screen.

You now have improved the interface (Figure 2.69) by:

■ preventing deletion of formulas
■ preventing the user entering data in the wrong cell
■ removing clutter such as column headings and the ribbon.

Figure 2.69 ▼

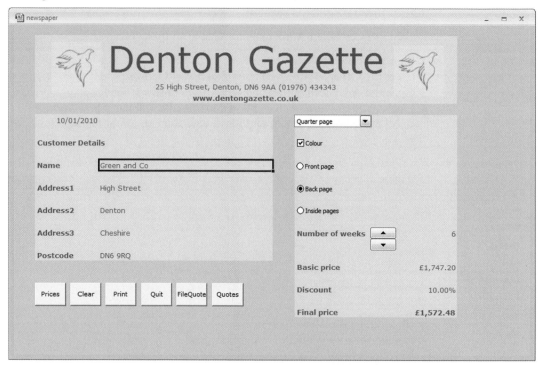

It's good idea to practise what you will record first before recording the macro.

This macro will run automatically when the spreadsheet loads. The macro coding will look like that shown in Figure 2.70.

Figure 2.70 ▶

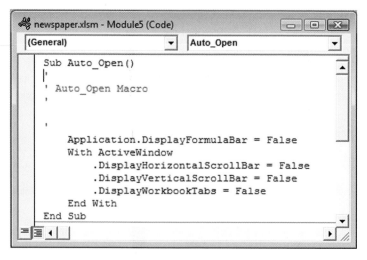

1 Record another macro called **Auto_close** to put all these features back when you close the spreadsheet.
2 Test that both macros work as expected.
3 Save the file.

Unit 19: Customising the spreadsheet and the screen

Now that your spreadsheet is nearly complete, there are a variety of things you can do to make the screen tidier and more user-friendly.

First, set up the foreground and background colours.

1 On the **Quotation** sheet, highlight cells A1 to J30.
2 On the **Home** tab in the **Font** group, click the **Fill Color** drop-down list (Figure 2.71).

Figure 2.71 ▶

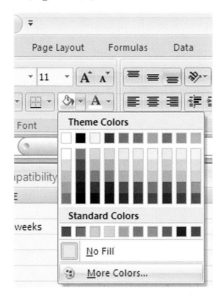

3 Select **More Colors**.
4 Click the **Custom** tab and choose the first house colour of the Denton Gazette – that's mid green: Red 176, Green 220, Blue 216 as in Figure 2.72 and click **OK**.

Figure 2.72 ▶

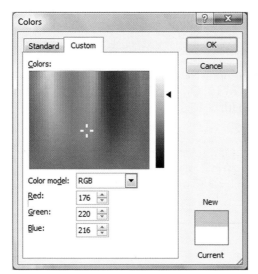

5 Highlight cells B2 to G7, B9 to C21, B23 to C26 and E9 to G26 – remember to use the CTRL key.

6 Set the **Fill Color** – this time to pale green: Red 200, Green 237, Blue 234.

7 You will need to resize and adjust the position of the macro buttons to allow for another button as shown in Figure 2.57.

8 Highlight cells A1 to J30 again. On the **Home** tab in the **Font** group, set the **Font color** to dark green: Red 75, Green 112, Blue 105.

9 Hiding the working – the data in the following cells does not need to be shown: F9, G9, F11, G11, F15 and G15. Set the font colour for these cells to be the same as the background colour (Red 200, Green 237, Blue 234) using the **Font Color** drop-down list.

10 Format the font to **Verdana, size 10** but leave the title at size 48.

11 Format the font of the buttons to **Verdana size 8**.

Your spreadsheet should look like that shown in Figure 2.73.

Figure 2.73 ▼

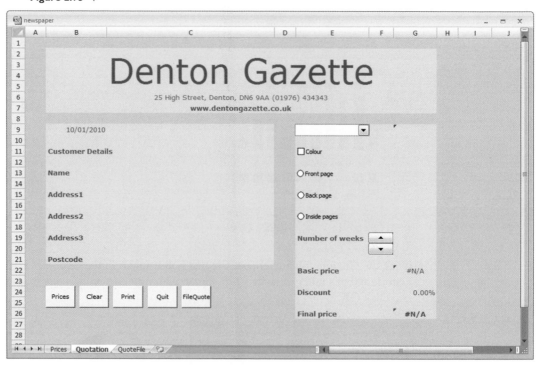

12 Column G is not wide enough to show every price so format the width of this column to **15**. On the **Home** tab in the **Cells** group, **Format > Column Width > 15**.

13 Add the company logo as shown in Figure 2.74.

Figure 2.74 ▼

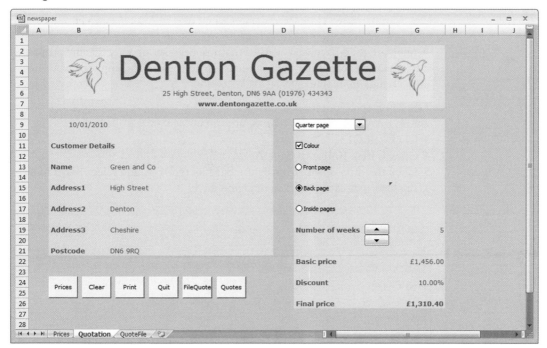

Unit 20: Templates

In this unit you will learn how to make the system reusable using templates.

A template is an Excel spreadsheet that has been set up for a specific purpose, into which you can enter data. It is easy to convert your completed worksheet into a template. It then can be loaded easily.

1 Start on the **Quotation** sheet.
2 Run the **Clear** macro to remove any data.
3 Click cell **C13**.
4 Click **Office Button > Save As…**
5 Click the drop-down arrow by the **Save as type** box and select **Excel Macro-Enabled template (*.xlt)** as in Figure 2.75.

Figure 2.75 ▶

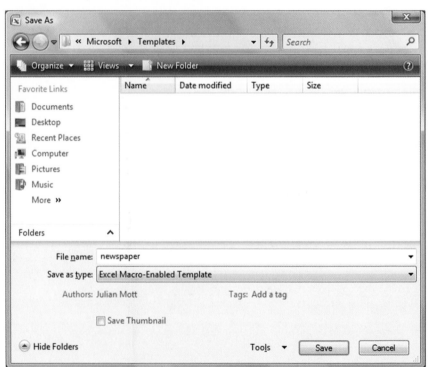

Your file will be saved as **newspaper.xlt**. It will be saved in your templates folder.

6 Close the file.

Loading a blank document

1 To load a document based on the template, click **Office button > New**. A menu appears as shown in Figure 2.76.

Figure 2.76 ▼

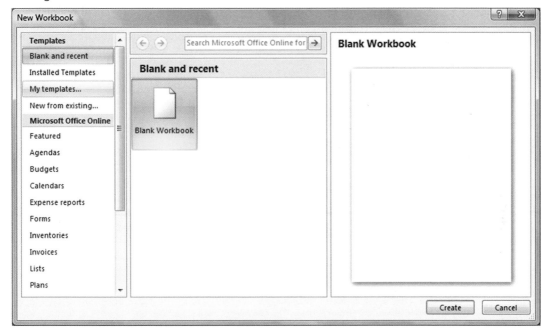

2 Click **My templates…**

Figure 2.77 ▶

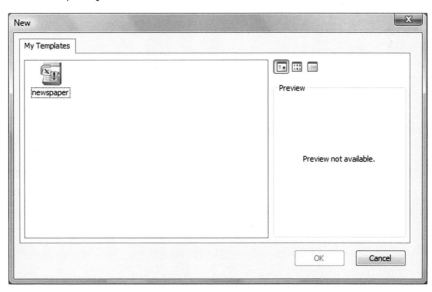

3 A dialogue box appears (Figure 2.77). Click **newspaper** and then **OK**.

Why use templates?

It is a good idea to use templates because when you start a document based on the template, it is a new file called Newspaper1, Newspaper2 etc. This means that each quotation is stored separately using different filenames.

Excel comes with some templates already installed. Click **Installed templates** to see these (Figure 2.78). Others are available online.

Figure 2.78 ▼

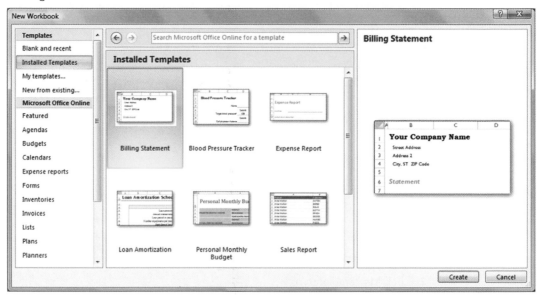

Unit 21: The Visual Basic Editor

In this unit you will learn how to use Visual Basic Editor to customise more features in Excel.

The Visual Basic Editor window is used for entering commands in Excel's programming language Visual Basic, sometimes called VBA (Visual Basic for Applications.)

You have already used VB Editor to set up macros such as to display a message box. You will also use it to set up UserForms.

Before this you need to familiarise yourself with Visual Basic Editor.

I Still using the same file as before (**newspaper.xlsm**), load **Visual Basic Editor**. On the **Developer** tab in the **Code** group, click **Visual Basic** or press **Alt** and **F11**.

The screen will look something like the one shown in Figure 2.79.

Figure 2.79 ▼

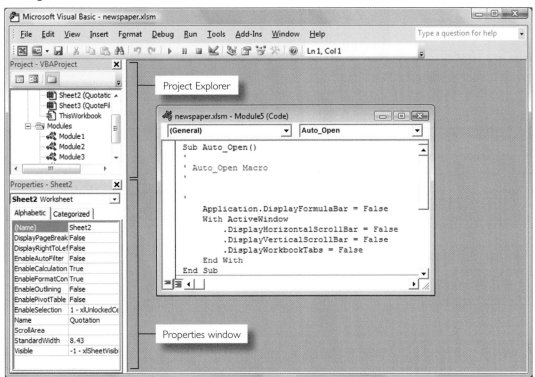

On the left of the screen is **Project Explorer** and the **Properties window**.

2 If either of these is not visible, click **View > Project Explorer** or **View > Properties Window**.

You can adjust the size of the windows and move them around the screen by dragging in the normal way.

Project Explorer displays a list of the projects. A project can be a worksheet, a module where macros are stored or a UserForm (see Unit 22).

3 Click the **+** sign to the left of the word 'Modules' in **Project Explorer** to display a list of all the modules. In Figure 2.80 five modules are shown.

Figure 2.80 ▼

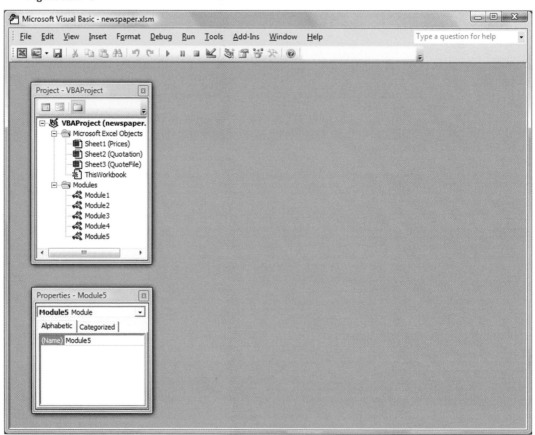

Why are there five modules?
When you first record macros in a file they will be stored in Module1. If you log off and log back on again later and record some more macros, they will be stored in Module 2 and so on. It will not affect the user wherever the macros are stored.

4 Double click **Module1** in Project Explorer. The coding for all the macros stored in Module 1 will appear in a new window on the right on the screen (Figure 2.81).

Figure 2.81 ▼

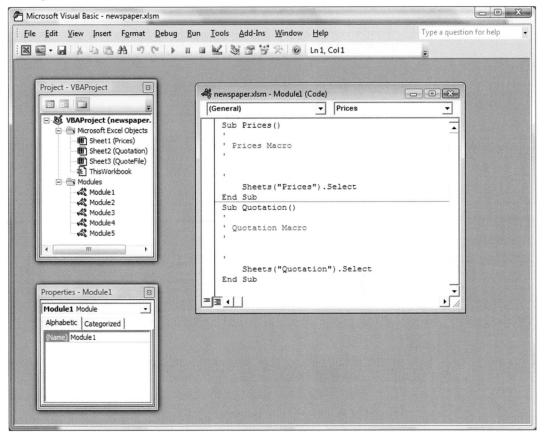

The **Properties window** displays the properties for the objects that make up the project – e.g. Modules, UserForms, Worksheets etc.

5 Close the Module1 window ready for the next unit.

Unit 22: UserForms

In this unit you will learn about UserForms and how they can be used as a user-friendly front-end for an Excel worksheet. Sometimes UserForms are called dialogue boxes.

A UserForm is a way of providing a customised user-interface for your system. A UserForm might look like the one shown in Figure 2.82, which you will set up in this unit.

Figure 2.82 ▶

Setting up a front-end UserForm

You will set up a front-end (menu system) that:

- loads automatically when the file is opened
- gives a choice of making a quotation, changing prices or looking at the quotation file.

1 Open the file **newspaper.xlsm** and load Visual Basic Editor. On the **Developer** tab in the **Code** group, click **Visual Basic** or press **Alt** and **F11**.
2 Make sure that Project Explorer and the Properties window are visible – click **View > Project Explorer** and **View > Properties Window** if necessary.
3 Click **Insert > UserForm** or click the **Insert UserForm** button.

A blank UserForm as shown in Figure 2.83 will appear in the main Visual Basic Editor window on the right-hand side.

Figure 2.83 ▼

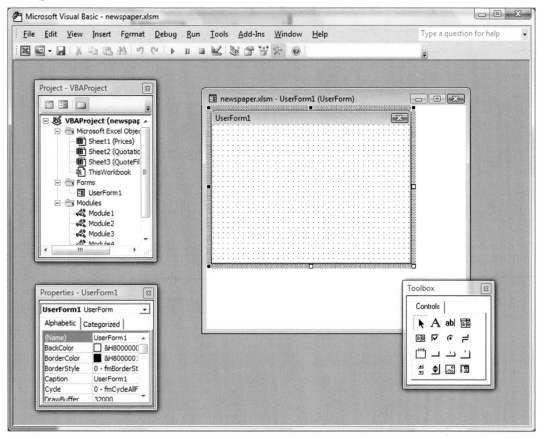

4 A set of buttons called the Toolbox will also appear (Figure 2.84). If it is not visible, click the blank UserForm and click **View > Toolbox**.

Figure 2.84 ▶

5 Click in the Properties window in the bottom left-hand corner of the screen – the Toolbox will disappear.

6 In the Properties window, set the height of the UserForm to **120** and set the width to **190** (Figure 2.85).

Figure 2.85 ▶

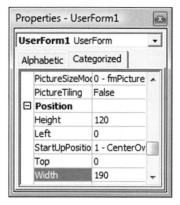

7 Click the blank UserForm – the toolbox will reappear.
8 In the Toolbox, click the **CommandButton** button and drag out a rectangle near the bottom-left of the UserForm as shown in Figure 2.86.

Figure 2.86 ▶

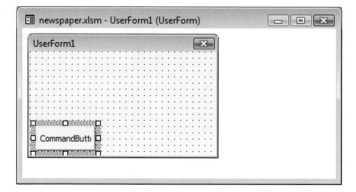

9 The text on the button will say **CommandButton1**. Edit this by clicking the button once, deleting and changing to **Quotation** as in Figure 2.87.

Figure 2.87 ▶

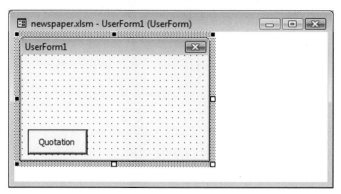

10 Double click the button. You will see the code shown in Figure 2.88.

Figure 2.88 ▶

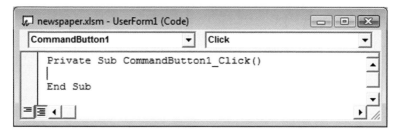

The cursor should be in the middle of these two lines. If it is not, click between the two lines.

11 Enter this text:

```
Sheets("Quotation").Select
UserForm1.Hide
```

It will now look like the script in Figure 2.89.

Figure 2.89 ▶

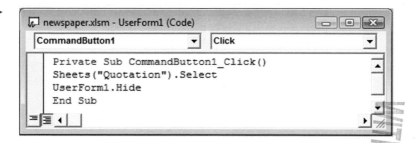

What it means

Sheets("Quotation").Select moves to the sheet called **Quotation.**

The command **UserForm1.Hide** removes the UserForm from the screen.

Note: The spelling and the punctuation must be exactly as above or it won't work. There are no spaces in the above commands.

12 Save the file.

13 Select UserForm1 in Project Explorer. Click **View > Object** or click the **View Object** button in Project Explorer (top-left of screen) shown in Figure 2.90 to go back to the plan of the UserForm.

Figure 2.90 ▼

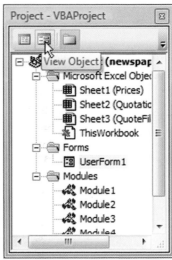

14 Add another button to the right of the first and the same size, as shown in Figure 2.91. The command here is exactly the same except it loads the **Prices** sheet (Figure 2.92).

Figure 2.91 ▶

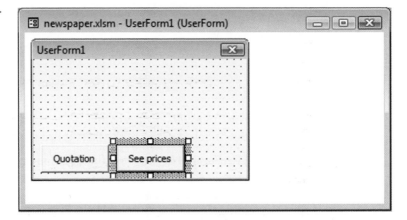

Figure 2.92 ▶

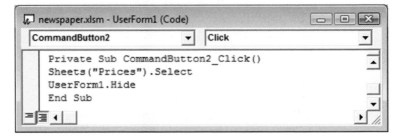

```
Private Sub CommandButton2_Click()
Sheets("Prices").Select
UserForm1.Hide
End Sub
```

15 Repeat this for a third button that will take you to the **QuoteFile** worksheet (Figure 2.93).

Figure 2.93 ▶

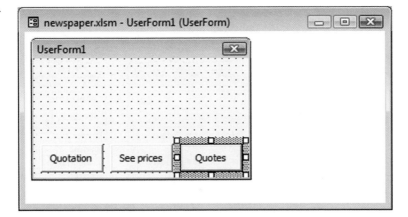

16 Click the **Label** button in the Toolbox.

17 Drag out a rectangle near the top-left of the UserForm and enter **Denton Gazette**.

The UserForm will now look like the one shown in Figure 2.94.

Figure 2.94 ▶

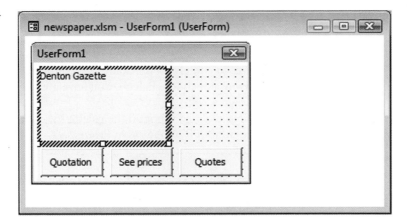

Using the Properties window

The Properties window at the bottom left-hand corner of the screen is used to set the properties of the UserForm. For example it is used to set the caption, the size, the colour, the font and any links to cells in the spreadsheet.

1 Select the label **Denton Gazette**. In the **Properties window** scroll down to **Font**, click the three dots button and set the font to **Verdana** and the size to **22**.

2 Scroll down to the **Text Align** property and select **2-fmTextAlignCenter** to centre the text as shown in Figure 2.95.

Figure 2.95 ▼

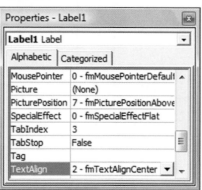

Figure 2.96 ▼

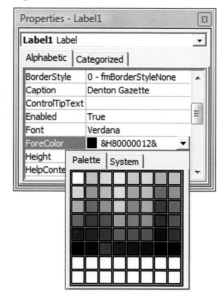

3 To edit the text colour, click **ForeColor** in the Properties window. Click the **drop-down arrow** and choose **Palette**. You have a variety of colours to choose from (Figure 2.96).

4 The green colour required is not on the palette so select **ForeColor** and enter the code **&H0069704A&** as in Figure 2.97.

Figure 2.97 ▶

5 Select all three buttons and set the text to **Verdana** font with the same ForeColor.

6 Select the label again and set the **BackColor** to **&H00EAF1C8&**. These numbers are in hexadecimal form.

7 Select the whole UserForm and set the **BackColor** to the same as the label. The UserForm will look like the one shown in Figure 2.98.

Figure 2.98 ▶

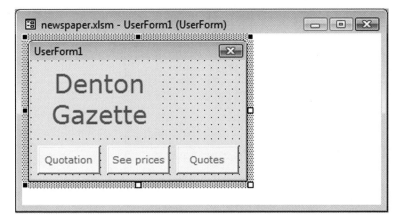

8 Select the **Caption** property to set the caption to **Denton Gazette**.
9 Choose appropriate colours, font and font size for the three command buttons.

Use the **Image button** in the Toolbox to add the image to your UserForm.

10 Click the **Image button** and drag out a rectangle on the UserForm.
11 Use **Picture** in the Properties window to select the image.
12 Use **PictureSizeMode** to set the picture size (choose **1-fm PictureSizeModeStretch**).
13 Set the **BorderStyle** to **0** (No border).
14 Save your file.

Figure 2.99 ▶

The UserForm is now set up (Figure 2.99). The finished UserForm is shown in Figure 2.82 at the beginning of this unit.

15 Test the UserForm by selecting it and clicking the **Run Sub/UserForm** button or by pressing **F5**. The UserForm will load as in Figure 2.100 – test the three buttons in turn.

Figure 2.100 ▶

Note: If, when you are in Visual Basic Editor, you insert a second UserForm by mistake, you can delete it by clicking **File > Remove UserForm**.

Setting up a macro to display your UserForm

Once you have created a UserForm, you will need to set up a macro to display it. The macro will be set up in Visual Basic.

1 If you are not already in VB editor, load **Visual Basic Editor**. On the **Developer** tab in the **Code** group, click **Visual Basic** or press **ALT** and **F11**.

2 Double click **Module1** in Project Explorer, as shown in Figure 2.83. If Module1 is not visible click the **+** sign next to **VBA project** in Project Explorer. Then double click **Module1**.

A new window opens with the coding of the macros you have already set up.

3 Scroll down to the bottom and underneath the last macro text, enter the following:

```
Sub Box()
Load UserForm1
UserForm1.Show
End Sub
```

This sets up a macro called **Box**. The two middle lines of code load the UserForm and display it on the screen. You will not need to type in the **End Sub** part because when you enter a line beginning with Sub, the End Sub line is automatically inserted below.

4 Click **File > Close and Return to Microsoft Excel** or press **Alt** and **Q** to close Visual Basic Editor and go back to Excel.

5 Check that the macro works. On the **Developer** tab in the **Code** group, click **Macros > Box > Run**. Test that the UserForm works for all three buttons.

When you are confident that the UserForm is working fully, you can include it in the Auto_open macro that runs when you load the file.

6 On the **Developer** tab in the **Code** group, click **Macros**. Select **Auto_open** and click **Edit**. This displays the Visual Basic coding of the macro.

7 Put the cursor at the beginning of the last line (End Sub).

8 Press ENTER.

9 Go up a line and enter the word **Box** as shown in Figure 2.101.

Figure 2.101 ▶

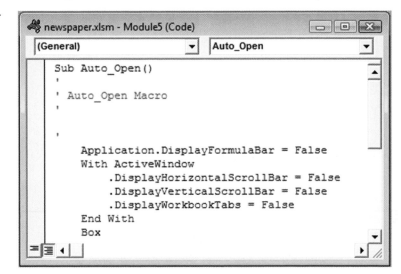

```
newspaper.xlsm - Module5 (Code)

(General)                          Auto_Open

Sub Auto_Open()
'
'  Auto_Open Macro
'

'

    Application.DisplayFormulaBar = False
    With ActiveWindow
        .DisplayHorizontalScrollBar = False
        .DisplayVerticalScrollBar = False
        .DisplayWorkbookTabs = False
    End With
    Box
```

10 Save your file and close Visual Basic Editor.

11 Add a button on the **QuoteFile** worksheet to run the **Box** macro. Put the button over columns L and M. Label the button **Menu**.

12 Copy this button and add it to the **Prices** worksheet.

13 Save and close the Excel file.

14 Reload the Excel file and test that the UserForm loads as expected.

Other functions of Excel 2007

In this part you will look at some other useful features of Excel. It is not necessary to use these features but you might find some of them useful in completing a project. These features include financial functions, scenarios, pivot tables and database functions.

■ Other functions 1: Financial functions

In this unit you will learn about financial functions, PMT, FV and RATE.

There are a number of useful financial functions in Excel. One example is the PMT function – PMT is short for 'payment'. This function works out the monthly repayments for a loan, given the amount of the loan, the interest rate and the term of the loan.

The formula is **=PMT(rate,nper,pv)** where:

- **rate** is the interest rate
- **nper** is the total number of payments
- **pv** is the amount of the loan.

You need to be careful because repayments are normally made monthly. In which case, the interest rate must also be a monthly rate. This is roughly but not exactly one twelfth of the annual rate.

Example: A loan repayment calculator

Figure 3.1 ▶

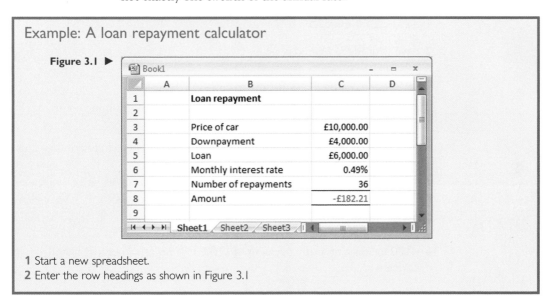

	A	B	C	D
1		Loan repayment		
2				
3		Price of car	£10,000.00	
4		Downpayment	£4,000.00	
5		Loan	£6,000.00	
6		Monthly interest rate	0.49%	
7		Number of repayments	36	
8		Amount	-£182.21	
9				

1 Start a new spreadsheet.
2 Enter the row headings as shown in Figure 3.1

3 Enter the data into cells C3, C4, C6 and C7.
4 Format cells C3 and C4 to Currency.
5 In C5 enter the formula **=C3–C4**
6 In C8 enter the formula **=PMT(C6,C7,C5)**
The monthly repayment (amount) is shown as a negative because it is being paid back. The repayment is £182.21.

Exercise I

Add a spinner to your spreadsheet to adjust the interest rate in steps of 0.01%.

Exercise 2

Add a scroll bar to your spreadsheet to adjust the downpayment in steps of £1000.

Note: A scroll bar works in a similar way to a spinner. On the **Developer** tab in the **Controls** group, click **Insert** and choose **Scroll Bar (Form Control)**.

Your finished spreadsheet should appear as in Figure 3.2.

Figure 3.2 ▶

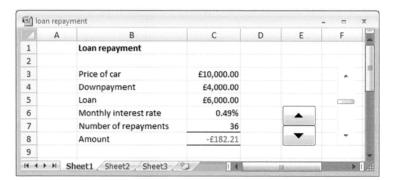

7 Save your file as **loan.xlsx**.

The Future Value (FV) function

This function returns the future value of an investment, assuming constant periodic payments and a constant interest rate.

Suppose you invest £100 per month for 2 years at 5% interest per annum. This is roughly 0.42% per month.
The formula to calculate the value of your money after 2 years is
=FV(0.42%,24,–100).

- **0.42%** is the interest rate
- **24** is the number of payments
- **–100** means a monthly payment of £100. It is negative because it is a payment.

Exercise 3

Add a future value calculator to your spreadsheet using a spinner to adjust the interest rate in steps of 0.01% and a scroll bar to adjust the payments in steps of £20.

The Rate function

This function works out the interest rate given the amount borrowed, the number of payments and the amount of each payment.

The formula **=RATE(24,−230,5000)** works out the interest rate for a loan of £5000, repaid at £230 a month for 24 months.

The result (which is the monthly interest rate) is 0.81%. If your computer gives this as 1%, click the **Increase decimal** button.

Multiply by 12 for a rough annual interest rate – the result is 9.7%.

Exercise 4

Add a rate calculator to your spreadsheet using a spinner to adjust the number of payments and a scroll bar to adjust the amount of payments in steps of £20 and the loan in steps of £1000.

Exercise 5

Use Excel's built-in online Help to investigate other financial functions.

Other functions 2: Scenarios

In this unit you will learn how to use scenarios to save different versions of the same worksheet.

The Hotel Manhattan wants to plan their cash flow. Their occupancy rates are around 70 to 80 per cent in summer and 50 to 60 per cent in winter. They can store various predictions for their income using **Scenarios**.

Figure 3.3 ▼

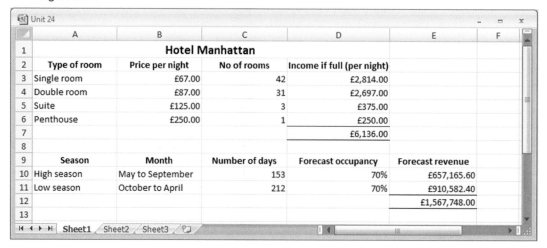

	A	B	C	D	E	F
1			Hotel Manhattan			
2	Type of room	Price per night	No of rooms	Income if full (per night)		
3	Single room	£67.00	42	£2,814.00		
4	Double room	£87.00	31	£2,697.00		
5	Suite	£125.00	3	£375.00		
6	Penthouse	£250.00	1	£250.00		
7				£6,136.00		
8						
9	Season	Month	Number of days	Forecast occupancy	Forecast revenue	
10	High season	May to September	153	70%	£657,165.60	
11	Low season	October to April	212	70%	£910,582.40	
12					£1,567,748.00	
13						

Sheet1 / Sheet2 / Sheet3

1 Load the spreadsheet **hotel.xlsx** (Figure 3.3).
Cells B3 to B6, D3 to D7 and E10 to E12 are formatted as currency. Cells D10 to D11 are formatted as percentages.

The hotel has decided to save predictions based on:

- 70 per cent occupancy all year round
- 60 per cent occupancy all year round
- 50 per cent occupancy all year round
- 70 per cent occupancy in high season and 50 per cent occupancy in low season.

You can set up four different scenarios to help them.

2 On the **Data** tab in the **Data Tools** group, click **What-If Analysis >
Scenario Manager**.
3 The Scenario Manager dialogue box appears as in Figure 3.4. Click **Add**.

Figure 3.4 ▶

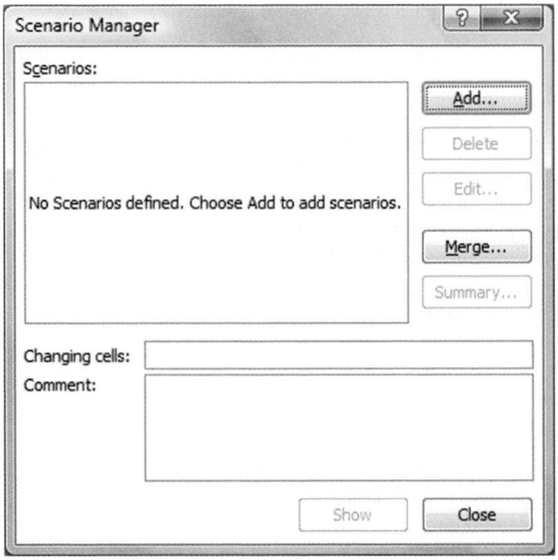

4 Enter the name of the scenario – **70 per cent occupancy** – and the names of the two changing cells into the dialogue box as in Figure 3.5.

Figure 3.5 ▶

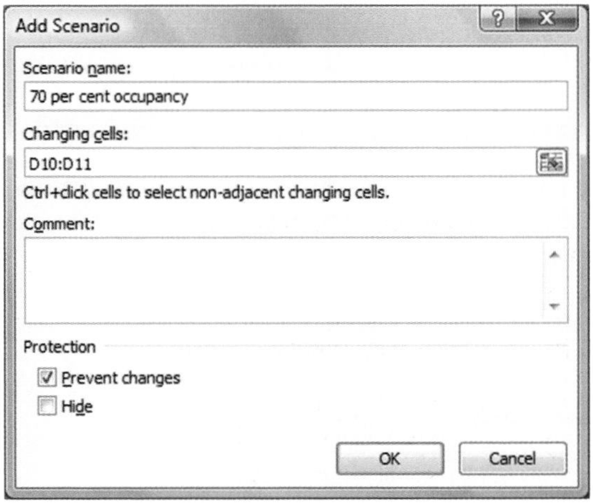

5 Click **OK**.

Figure 3.6 ▶

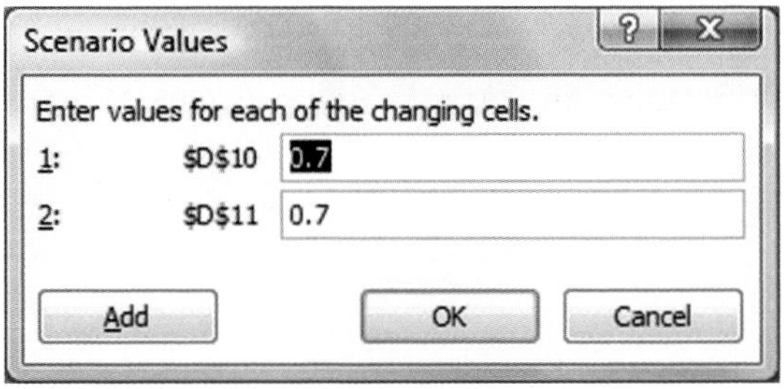

6 The scenario values box appears as in Figure 3.6. It has the value of 0.7, which is 70%.

7 Click **Add**. The next scenario is **60 per cent occupancy**. Click **OK** and then set the two changing cells to **0.6**.

8 Add two more scenarios with the appropriate data – **50 per cent all year round**, and **70 per cent summer and 50 per cent winter** (Figure 3.7). Then choose **OK**.

Figure 3.7 ▶

9 If you click **Summary...** you will set up a new worksheet with a summary of all the scenarios. First the Scenario Summary box appears as in Figure 3.8.

Figure 3.8 ▶

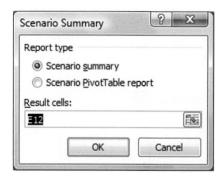

10 E12 is the cell with the total amount of the bill stored in it. This is the figure we want in the summary but we could click any cell. Click **OK**. The summary looks like Figure 3.9.

Figure 3.9 ▼

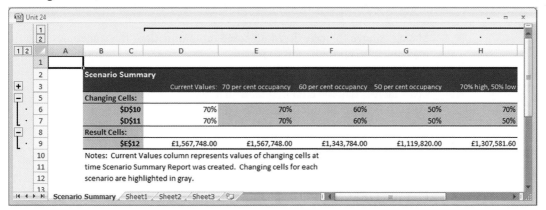

	Current Values:	70 per cent occupancy	60 per cent occupancy	50 per cent occupancy	70% high, 50% low
Scenario Summary					
Changing Cells:					
$D$10	70%	70%	60%	50%	70%
$D$11	70%	70%	60%	50%	50%
Result Cells:					
$E$12	£1,567,748.00	£1,567,748.00	£1,343,784.00	£1,119,820.00	£1,307,581.60

Notes: Current Values column represents values of changing cells at time Scenario Summary Report was created. Changing cells for each scenario are highlighted in gray.

11 To load any of the other scenarios:
- go back to Sheet1
- click **What-If Analysis > Scenario Manager**
- click the scenario required
- click **Show**
- click **Close**.

Other functions 3: Pivot tables

In this unit you will learn how to use pivot tables to group large amounts of data in an easy-to-read table.

Managers have to make decisions based on information. But sometimes they have too much information to take in – this is often called 'information overload'.

Pivot tables combine data in a table in a number of ways. This means it is easier to take in the information and decisions are more likely to be the correct.

Creating a pivot table

Download the file **salesdata.xlsx** and open it in Excel 2007. The file shows the sales of cuddly toys in a toy shop with three stores – in Sheffield, Leeds and Derby.

1 Highlight cells A2 to H1001.
2 On the **Insert** tab in the **Tables** group, click on **PivotTable**. The dialogue box shown in Figure 3.10 appears.

Figure 3.10 ▶

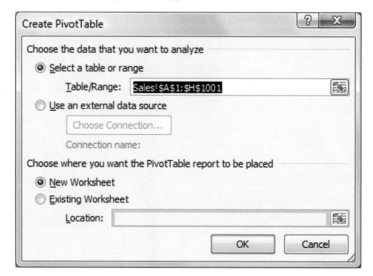

3 Click **OK**. The pivot table field list appears (Figure 3.11).

Figure 3.11 ▶

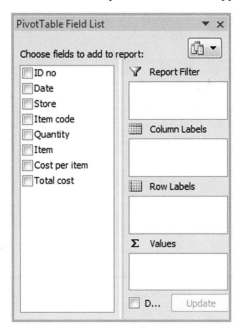

4 In the pivot table field list, drag the word **Store** into the **Column Labels** box.

5 Drag **Item** into the **Row Labels** box.

6 Drag **Quantity** the into **Values** box.

You can now see how many units of each item were sold in each store (Figure 3.12). For example, the Derby store sold 37 Cuddly cats.

Figure 3.12 ▶

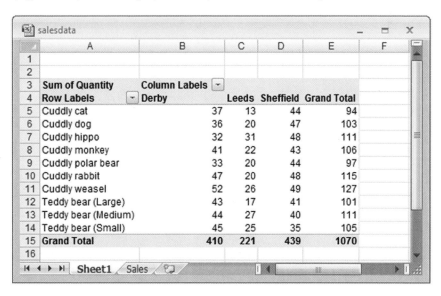

Note: If you click on a cell outside the table, the pivot table field list disappears. Click back on the table to make it reappear.

Grouping by date

Suppose you want to see monthly sales for each cuddly toy, such as sales in December.

1 In the pivot table field list, drag the word **Date** into the **Column Labels** box.

The sales on each day are now shown. You need to group sales by month.

2 Click on any one of the dates, such as the date in cell B5.
3 On the **Options** tab in the **Group** group, click **Group Selection**.

The dialogue box shown in Figure 3.13 will appear.

Figure 3.13 ▶

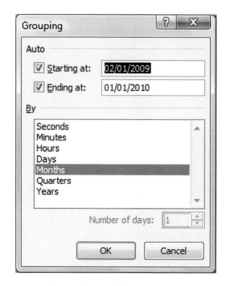

4 In the **By** list, click **Months > OK**.

The pivot table now shows monthly sales for each store, as shown in Figure 3.14.

Figure 3.14 ▼

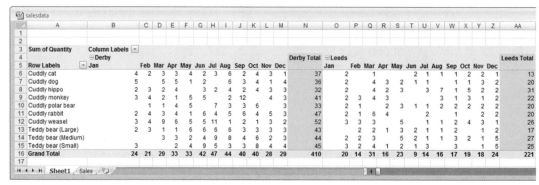

Row Labels	Derby Jan	Feb	Mar	Apr	May	Jun	Jul	Aug	Sep	Oct	Nov	Dec	Derby Total	Leeds Jan	Feb	Mar	Apr	May	Jun	Jul	Aug	Sep	Oct	Nov	Dec	Leeds Total
Cuddly cat	4	2	3	3	4	2	3	6	2	4	3	1	37	2		1			2	1	1	1	2	2	1	13
Cuddly dog	5		5	5	1	2		6	3	4	1	4	36	2		4	3	2	1	1		1	1	3	2	20
Cuddly hippo	2	3	2	4		3	2	4	2	4	3	3	32	2		4	2	3		3	7	1	5	2	2	31
Cuddly monkey	3	4	2	1	5	5		2	12		4	3	41	2	3	4	3			3	1	3	1	2		22
Cuddly polar bear		1	1	4	5		7	3	3	6		3	33	2	1		2	3	1	1	2	2	2	2		20
Cuddly rabbit	2	4	3	4	1	6	4	5	6	4	5	3	47	2	1	6	4		2		1		2	2		20
Cuddly weasel	3	4	9	6	5	5	11	1	2	1	3	2	52	3	3	3		5		1	1	2	4	3	1	26
Teddy bear (Large)	2	3	1	1	6	6	6	6	3	3	3	3	43	2	2	1	3	2	1	1	2		1	2		17
Teddy bear (Medium)		3	3	2	4	9	8	4	6	2	3		44	2	2	3		5	2	1	1	3	2	1	5	27
Teddy bear (Small)	3			2	4	9	5	3	3	8	4	4	45	3	2	4	1	2	1	3		3		1	5	25
Grand Total	24	21	29	33	33	42	47	44	40	40	28	29	410	20	14	31	16	23	9	14	16	17	19	18	24	221

5 To see only the sales for December, in the pivot table field list drag the word **Date** into the **Report Filter** box. **Date(All)** appears in cells A1 and B1.

6 Click the **All** drop-down box in B1, click **Dec** to choose December and click **OK** (see Figure 3.15).

Figure 3.15 ▶

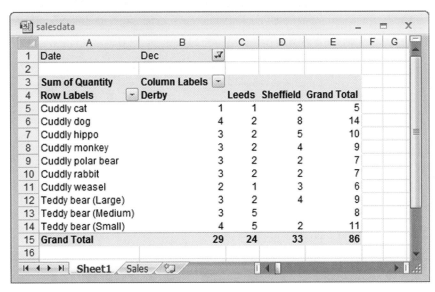

Showing only one store

I To show, say, only the Derby store, click the **Column Labels** drop-down list and make sure that only the Derby box is ticked (Figure 3.16).

Figure 3.16 ▶

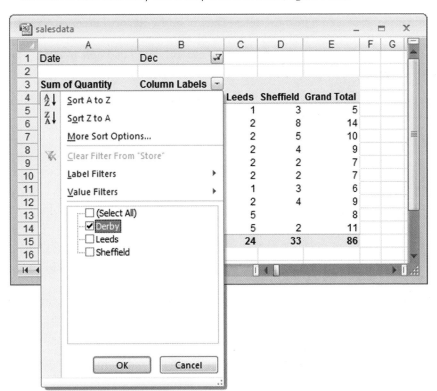

The resulting pivot table will look like as shown in Figure 3.17.

Figure 3.17 ▶

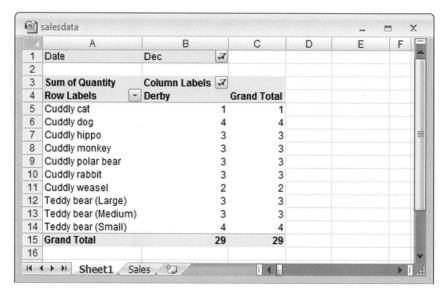

Showing income

You can show the income from these sales as follows.

1 Remove all filters so that you can show all months and all stores. Click **Select All** from the **Column Labels** drop-down list and in the pivot table field list delete **Date** from the **Report Filter** box – click the drop-down list and click **Remove Field**.

2 In the pivot table field list, drag **Total cost** into the **Values** box – it changes to **Sum of Total Cost** as shown in Figure 3.18.

Figure 3.18 ▼

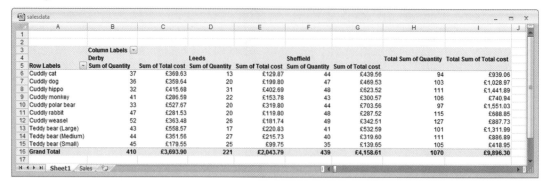

The pivot table should look like that shown in Figure 3.18. You will need to format columns C, E, G and I to **currency**.

You can you use this pivot table to answer questions such as:

- What was the total number of cuddly hippos sold in Derby in 2009?
- What was the grand total of sales of cuddly hippos in Derby in 2009?
- How many cuddly toys were sold in Sheffield in June?
- What was the grand total of sales in Sheffield in June?

Changing the PivotTable style

1 Click the pivot table.

2 On the **Design** tab, click on one of the styles in the **PivotTable Styles** group.

Updating data in a pivot table

Suppose the original data changes. How can you update the data in the pivot table? If the original data changes, the pivot table is *not* updated automatically.

1 On the **Options** tab in the **Data** group, click **Refresh** – or press ALT and **F5** together.

2 Experiment by changing the price of one cuddly toy to £20 and updating the data in the pivot table.

Drilling down

To see the data on which a pivot table is based, simply double click on the appropriate cell in the pivot table.

Pivot table exercises

Exercise 1

Download the file **invoices.xlsx** and open it in Excel 2007. The file shows the details of invoices sent from a small business to its customers.

1 Create a pivot table showing for each of the five areas Anslow, Horninglow, Rolleston, Stretton and Tutbury:

   a) the total amount paid

   b) the total amount outstanding.

2 Edit the pivot table to show the amount owed in each area broken down by month.

3 Edit the pivot table to show:

   a) the amount owed by residents with a **DE14** postcode from **April 2010**

   b) the number of people in each area who have paid their bill dated **May 2010**.

Exercise 2

Download the file **shareprices.xlsx** and open it in Excel 2007. A company has invested in a number of shares. The file shows the details of companies, the business sector, the value of each share and the number of shares held.

1 Create a pivot table showing the total value of the shares in each sector.

2 The different departments of a company are charged on the basis of hours of Internet use. The company has to distinguish between use for email and use for the worldwide web. Load the file called **pivotexercise.xlsx** as shown in Figure 3.19 and set up a pivot table to group the data, to show Internet use, intranet use and total use for each department split into www and email.

Figure 3.19 ▶

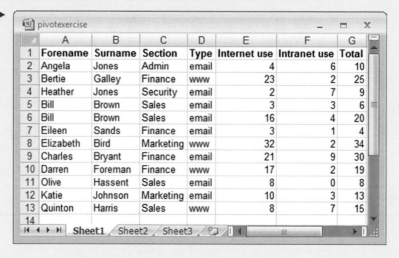

	A	B	C	D	E	F	G
1	**Forename**	**Surname**	**Section**	**Type**	**Internet use**	**Intranet use**	**Total**
2	Angela	Jones	Admin	email	4	6	10
3	Bertie	Galley	Finance	www	23	2	25
4	Heather	Jones	Security	email	2	7	9
5	Bill	Brown	Sales	email	3	3	6
6	Bill	Brown	Sales	email	16	4	20
7	Eileen	Sands	Finance	email	3	1	4
8	Elizabeth	Bird	Marketing	www	32	2	34
9	Charles	Bryant	Finance	email	21	9	30
10	Darren	Foreman	Finance	www	17	2	19
11	Olive	Hassent	Sales	email	8	0	8
12	Katie	Johnson	Marketing	email	10	3	13
13	Quinton	Harris	Sales	www	8	7	15
14							

Sheet1 Sheet2 Sheet3

Other functions 4: Using Excel as database software

In this unit you will cover how Excel can be used to create a database including:
- setting up, sorting and searching a database
- using Data Forms
- using AutoFilter
- using the Advanced Filter
- database functions.

A spreadsheet lends itself to storing and sorting lists of information such as employees, customers, cars, students and so on.

More commonly, files or lists such as this are called databases – Excel calls them **lists**.

Creating a data list

You are going to use a simple **file** containing a list of properties for sale.

Each **record** in the file, or **row** in the spreadsheet, will hold details about a property.

The **fields**, or **columns** in the spreadsheet, will be Agent, Area, Type, No of Bedrooms and Price – as shown in Figure 3.20.

Figure 3.20 ▶

	A	B	C	D	E
1	Agent	Area	Type	Bedrooms	Price
2	Raybould & Sons	Hulland Ward	semi-detached	5	590000
3	Bagshaws	Etwall	detached	4	495000
4	Bagshaws	Etwall	detached	4	479900
5	Hall & Partners	Mickleover	detached	3	440000
6	Raybould & Sons	Littleover	bungalow	3	364000
7	Raybould & Sons	Etwall	detached	4	354000
8	Raybould & Sons	Willington	semi-detached	3	335000
9	Bradford & Bingley	Littleover	detached	5	299900
10	Bradford & Bingley	Oakwood	detached	4	285900
11	Bradford & Bingley	Oakwood	detached	4	245900
12	Ashley Adams	Mickleover	bungalow	3	233900
13	Ashley Adams	Mickleover	bungalow	3	233900
14	Bradford & Bingley	Borrowash	detached	3	230000
15	Ashley Adams	Allestree	semi-detached	3	225000
16	Bradford & Bingley	Mickleover	detached	5	199900
17	Bradford & Bingley	Littleover	detached	3	191900
18	Halifax	Etwall	semi-detached	3	171000
19	Ashley Adams	Etwall	semi-detached	3	160000
20	Halifax	Littleover	semi-detached	3	150000
21	Halifax	Littleover	semi-detached	3	150000
22	Halifax	Littleover	semi-detached	3	150000
23	Hall & Partners	Egginton	detached	3	149998
24	Ashley Adams	Mickleover	semi-detached	3	149900

Unit 26 — Sheet1

135

Sorting the file

Sorting can be done on the whole file or on a named range of cells.

First you will produce a list of houses sorted by price.

1 Load the file **houses.xlsx**.
2 Click any cell in the table, such as A2. On the **Data** tab in the **Sort & Filter** group, click **Sort**. The Sort dialogue box shown in Figure 3.21 appears.

Figure 3.21 ▶

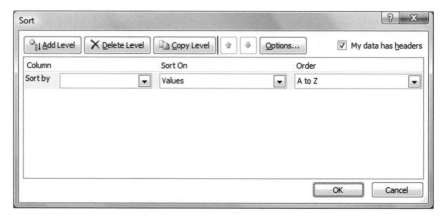

3 Click the down arrow on the **Sort by** box, choose **Price** and click **Smallest to Largest** in the **Order box**. Click **OK**.

It is also possible to sort on more than one field, for example in agent order and then in price order.

4 Click A2 or any other cell in the table. On the **Data** tab in the **Sort & Filter** group, click **Sort**.
5 Click the down arrow on the **Sort by** box, choose **Agent**. The order will be set automatically to **A to Z**.
6 Click **Add Level**.
7 Click the down arrow on the next **Sort by** box, choose **Price**. It will select **Smallest to Largest** for you (Figure 3.22). Click **OK**.

Figure 3.22 ▶

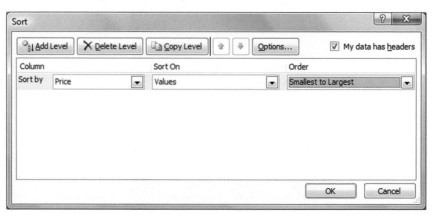

This will produce a list sorted by Agent and then by Price.

Using a Data form to search and edit a file

1 Click the **Form** button in the **Quick Access** Toolbar – you will see something like shown in Figure 3.23. (See Unit 15 if the Form button is not visible.)

Figure 3.23 ▶

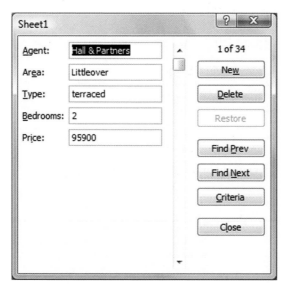

- Click **Find Next** to take you to details of the next house.
- Click **Find Prev** to take you to details of the previous house.
- Click **Delete** to remove a house from the file.
- Click **New** to enter details of a new property (press **Tab** between entering fields).

Using a Data Form to do simple searches

1 Click **Criteria** and a blank form loads.
2 Enter **Etwall** in the field area and click **Find Next** to scroll through the houses in Etwall.

You can narrow down the search.

3 Click **Criteria** again and enter **3** in the **Bedrooms** field. You can now scroll through the three-bedroomed houses in Etwall.

Data Exercise 1

Use a Data Form to answer the following questions.

1 Produce details of all houses for sale in Oakwood. How many are there?
2 A customer wants details of detached houses for sale in Mickleover. How many are there and what price are they?
3 A customer wants to purchase a house with three bedrooms in Littleover, search for details. How many are there and what price are they?

Using AutoFilter to search the database

1 Click any cell in the data table.
2 On the **Data** tab in the **Sort & Filter** group, click **Filter**. Drop-down boxes appear to the right of all the field names, as shown in Figure 3.24.

Figure 3.24 ▶

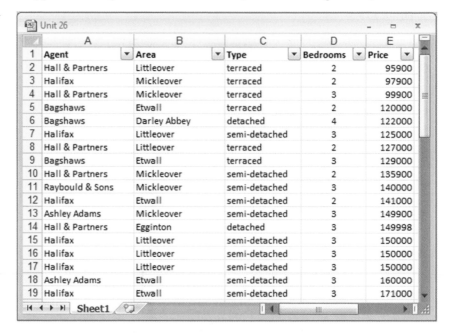

If you click an arrow it will give you a list of items in that field (Figure 3.25).

Figure 3.25 ▶

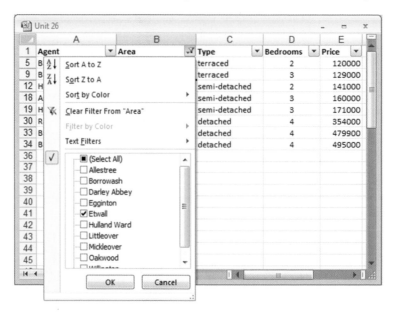

By checking and unchecking boxes, it is easy to build up quick searches – e.g. terraced houses in Mickleover.

3 Click the **Area** field drop-down arrow and choose only **Mickleover**.
4 Click the **Type** field drop-down arrow and choose **terraced**.

You should get the results shown in Figure 3.26.

Figure 3.26 ▶

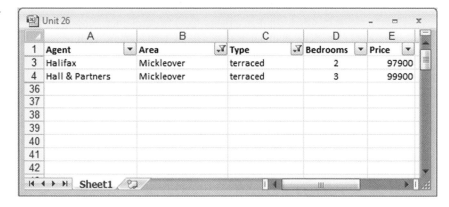

Excel hides the rows that do not meet the criteria and displays the row numbers in blue.

5 To remove all AutoFilters, click the **Clear** button.

It is possible to do more advanced searching by choosing the custom option.

Custom Filter I

Suppose you want to find properties in Mickleover or Littleover.

1 Clear any filters.
2 Choose the **Area** drop-down list and click **Text Filters > Custom Filter**. The dialogue box in Figure 3.27 appears – fill it in as shown.

Figure 3.27 ▶

3 Click **OK**. You can now see only the filtered records. In the bottom left-hand corner (Figure 3.28) you are told how many filtered records there are – 18 houses in this case.

Figure 3.28 ▶

Custom Filter 2

Suppose you want to find properties with a price between £150 000 and £200 000.

1 Clear any filters.
2 Click the **Price** drop-down list and click **Number Filters > Custom Filter**. The dialogue box in Figure 3.29 appears – fill it in as shown.

Figure 3.29 ▶

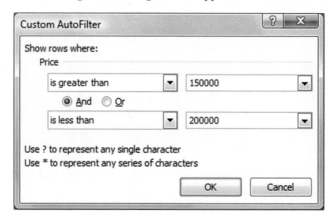

Four houses should be found, as shown in Figure 3.30.

Figure 3.30 ▶

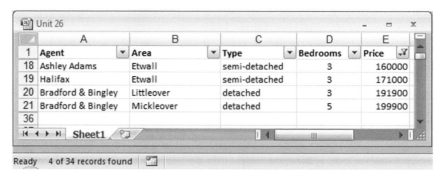

Data Exercise 2

Use **AutoFilter** and the file **Houses** to answer the following questions.
1 A customer wants details of houses for sale in Etwall. How many are there?
2 A customer wants to purchase a house with four bedrooms. How many are there?
3 A customer is interested in detached houses in Mickleover. Search for details.
4 A customer needs a three-bedroomed house in Littleover. Search for details.

The Advanced Filter

The advanced filter command allows you to search on more than two fields and offers increased options. The command can also be used to automate the moving of filtered data to another part of the worksheet.

Worked example

The first step is to define the cells that make up the database. This is called the **list range**.

1 Remove any filters. Highlight the cells A1 to E35 in the **Houses** file.

2 On the **Formulas** tab in the **Defined Names** group, click **Define Name**. Call the range **Database** and click **OK**.

The next stage is to set up and define the **Criteria range** – this is the range of cells which will store your search conditions.

1 Select the row **headings** in row 1 and copy and paste them into **row 39**.

2 In the rows below, enter the search conditions, as shown in Figure 3.31. This will produce a list of bungalows in Littleover.

Figure 3.31 ▶

Unit 26

	A	B	C	D	E	F
33	Bagshaws	Etwall	detached	4	479900	
34	Bagshaws	Etwall	detached	4	495000	
35	Raybould & Sons	Hulland Ward	semi-detached	5	590000	
36						
37						
38						
39	Agent	Area	Type	Bedrooms	Price	
40		Littleover	bungalow			
41						
42						

Sheet1

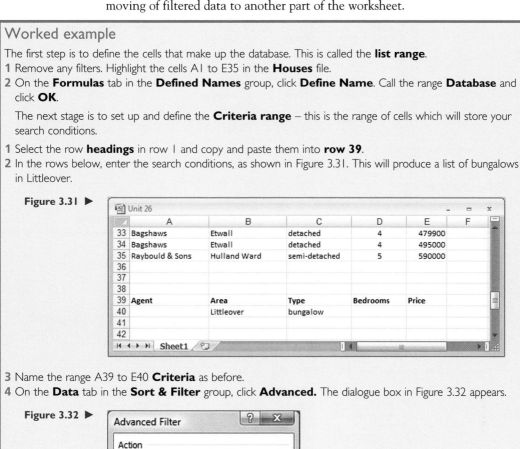

3 Name the range A39 to E40 **Criteria** as before.

4 On the **Data** tab in the **Sort & Filter** group, click **Advanced.** The dialogue box in Figure 3.32 appears.

Figure 3.32 ▶

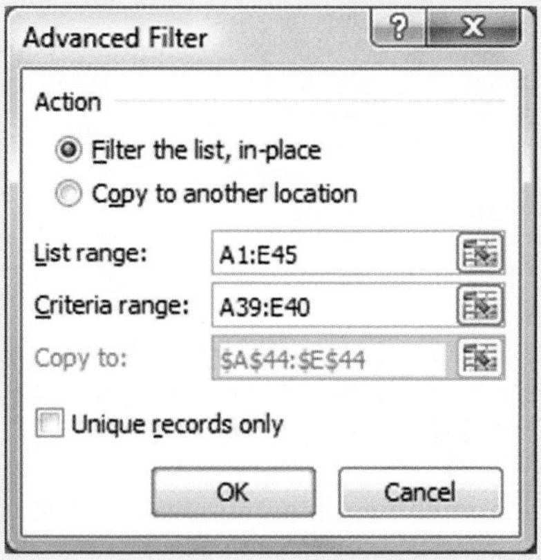

5 Enter the ranges shown in Figure 3.32.

6 Click **OK** to produce the filtered list shown in Figure 3.33 – the one property in the database that meets the criteria.

Figure 3.33 ▶

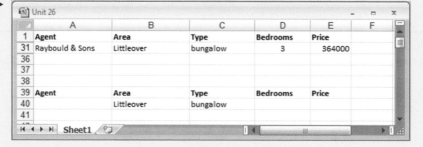

Searches can be built up in the same way. The search criteria shown in Figure 3.34 will list three-bedroomed properties in Mickleover or Etwall.

Figure 3.34 ▶

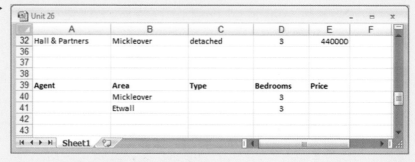

Note that the criteria range is now **A39:A41** (Figure 3.35).

Figure 3.35 ▶

Copying data to another location

1 Set up the search as shown in Figure 3.36 to find three-bedroomed properties in Etwall or Mickleover.

Figure 3.36 ▶

	A	B	C	D	E	F
34	Bagshaws	Etwall	detached	4	495000	
35	Raybould & Sons	Hulland Ward	semi-detached	5	590000	
36						
37						
38						
39	Agent	Area	Type	Bedrooms	Price	
40		Mickleover		3		
41		Etwall		3		
42						

Sheet1

2 On the **Data** tab in the **Sort & Filter** group, click **Advanced**.

3 In the dialogue box check **Copy to another location** and enter **A44** in the **Copy to** box. Make sure that the **Criteria range** is from **A39** to **E41** as shown in Figure 3.37.

Figure 3.37 ▶

Advanced Filter

Action

○ Filter the list, in-place

● Copy to another location

List range: $D$40:$D$41

Criteria range: $A$39:$E$41

Copy to: A44

☐ Unique records only

OK   Cancel

The search should produce the results shown in Figure 3.38.

Figure 3.38 ▶

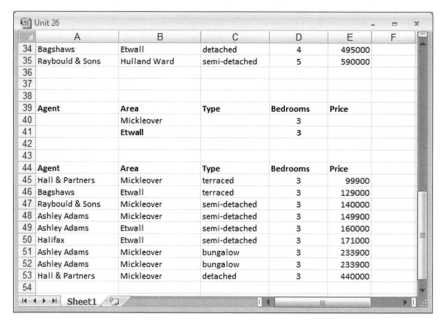

It is possible to vary the criteria in the criteria range. Try changing the criteria to produce the output shown in Figure 3.39.

Figure 3.39 ▶

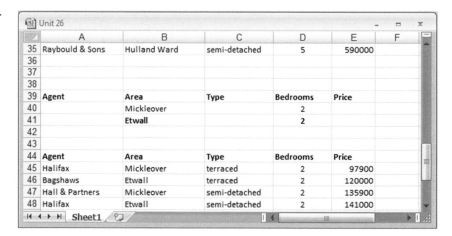

Using the Database functions

Excel provides a number of **D** or **database** functions – examples are **DCOUNT, DAVERAGE, DSUM, DMAX** and **DMIN**.

Database functions take the form **=Function(database,"field",criteria)** where:

- **database** is the name of database range you have defined
- **field** is the column you wish to operate on
- **criteria** is the criteria range you have defined.

Worked example

You are going to use the database functions to analyse house prices in the Mickleover area.

1 Set up the criteria and headings as shown in Figure 3.40.

Figure 3.40 ▶

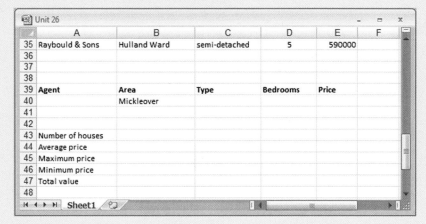

2 Make sure you have named the **Database** and **Criteria** ranges (**A1:E45** and **A39:E40**)

3 Enter the formulas shown in Figure 3.41.

Figure 3.41 ▶

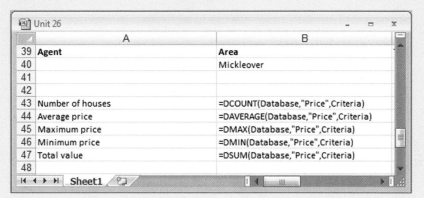

4 The results should be as shown in Figure 3.42.

Figure 3.42 ▶

	A	B	C	D
39	**Agent**	Area	Type	Bedrooms
40		Mickleover		
41				
42				
43	Number of houses	34		
44	Average price	224079.3529		
45	Maximum price	590000		
46	Minimum price	95900		
47	Total value	7618698		
48				

When you have it working, try varying the search criteria – for example, change the area to Littleover or narrow the search to houses with three bedrooms.

4 UserForm exercises

In this section you will learn how to run systems entirely from UserForms including entering data through the UserForm.

1: The ideal weight exercise

Problem statement

Fitness, diet and healthy eating magazines often present tables of ideal weights according to a person's gender and height as given in the file **weight.xlsm**. Load the file as shown in Figure 4.1.

Figure 4.1 ▶

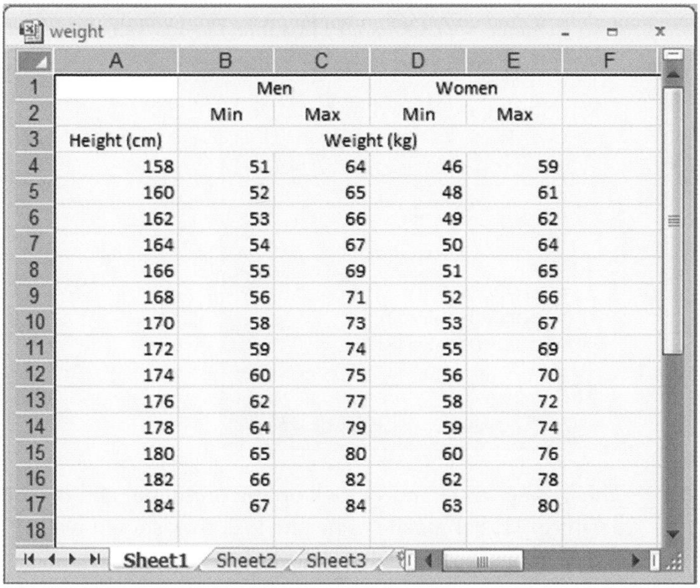

	A	B	C	D	E	F
1		Men		Women		
2		Min	Max	Min	Max	
3	Height (cm)		Weight (kg)			
4	158	51	64	46	59	
5	160	52	65	48	61	
6	162	53	66	49	62	
7	164	54	67	50	64	
8	166	55	69	51	65	
9	168	56	71	52	66	
10	170	58	73	53	67	
11	172	59	74	55	69	
12	174	60	75	56	70	
13	176	62	77	58	72	
14	178	64	79	59	74	
15	180	65	80	60	76	
16	182	66	82	62	78	
17	184	67	84	63	80	
18						

- You will produce a system to allow a user to enter their gender and height.
- The system will calculate, from tables, the user's ideal maximum and minimum weight range.
- The output will be to screen, with an option to print.

Brief design overview

A spinner will be used to enter a person's height in centimetres – it will be linked to cell J1.

Option buttons will be used to enter the user's gender. This will be linked to cell J2, which will store TRUE if male and FALSE if female.

Cell J3 will be used to decide which columns to look up based on whether the user is male or female. The minimum weight for a man is in column 2 – the minimum weight for a woman is in column 4. So if the user is a man, this cell will read 2 – if the user is a woman, the cell will display 4.

Cell J4 will be used to look up the minimum value from either column 2 or column 4.

Cell J5 will be used to look up the maximum value from either column 3 or column 5.

Setting up the worksheet

1 In cell J2 of the worksheet enter **TRUE** – TRUE represents male, FALSE represents female.
2 In J3 enter **=IF(J2=TRUE,2,4)**. This shows which column to look in for the minimum weight – column 2 for male, column 4 for female.
3 In J4 enter **=VLOOKUP(J1,table,J3)**. This looks up the minimum weight in either column 2 or column 4.
4 In J5 enter **=VLOOKUP(J1,table,J3+1)**. This looks up the maximum weight in either column 3 or column 5.

The formulas are shown in Figure 4.2.

Figure 4.2 ▶

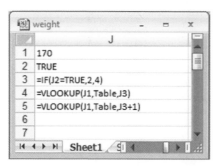

The lookups in J4 and J5 look up the minimum and maximum weights for the height in J1. For a male of height 170, they should read 58 and 73 respectively.

Setting up the UserForm

1 Load **Visual Basic Editor**. On the **Developer** tab in the **Code** group, click **Visual Basic** – or press **Alt** and **F11**.
2 Click **Insert > UserForm** or click the **Insert UserForm** button.
3 In the Properties window, set the Caption to **Your Ideal Weight**.

4 Also in the Properties window, set the background colour to **light grey** (Figure 4.3).

Figure 4.3 ▶

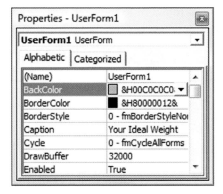

Note: Throughout this unit you can use the Properties window to format text and background colours as you wish.

I Use a Label to put the title **What is your Ideal Weight?** at the top of your UserForm.

2 In the Properties window, set the font size for the label to **14** – you may wish to set the background colour of the label too. The UserForm will look like the one shown in Figure 4.4.

Figure 4.4 ▶

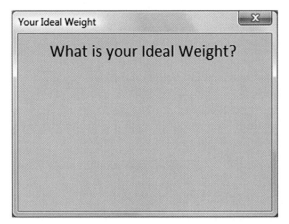

Setting up the Spinner to adjust the height

I Click **Spin Button** on the Toolbox and drag out a spinner near the top of the UserForm. If the spinner is pointing horizontally, hold down the **Alt** key and resize the spinner so that it points vertically.

2 With the spinner still selected, set **Max** in the Properties window to **184**, **Min** to **158**, **Small Change** to **2** and then set the **Control Source** to **J1**.

3 Double click the spinner and edit the text to read as follows:

```
Private Sub SpinButton1_Change()
Range("J1").Value = SpinButton1.Value
End Sub
```

This means that as you click the spinner, the value in cell J1 updates immediately.

4 Click the **Close** button to return to the UserForm.

5 Click the **Run Sub/UserForm** button to load the UserForm, as in Figure 4.5, and test the spinner. It should alter the numbers in J1, J4 and J5.

Figure 4.5 ▼

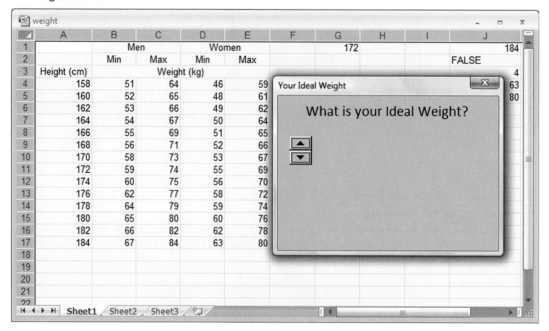

6 Close the UserForm by clicking the **Close** button.

7 Save your file.

8 Click the **Text Box** button in the Toolbox and drag out a small text box underneath the spinner as shown in Figure 4.6. Set the **Control Source** in the **Properties** window to **J1**.

Figure 4.6 ▶

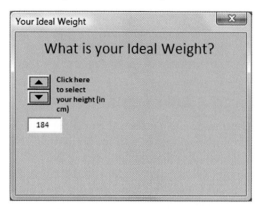

9 Add a label to your spinner as shown in Figure 4.6.

10 Click the **Run Sub/UserForm** button to test that the number in the text box goes up or down by 2 when the spinner is clicked.

11 Save your file.

Adding Option buttons for male and female

1 Click the **Option** button in the Toolbox and add an option button to your UserForm. Edit the label to **Male** as in Figure 4.7 and set the **Control Source** to **J2**.

Figure 4.7 ▶

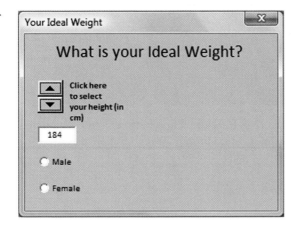

2 Add another option button labelled **Female**. You must not set the Control Source. Click the **Run Sub/UserForm** button to test that as you choose 'Female', the numbers change in J4 and J5.

3 Save your file.

Adding list boxes for the lookups

1 Click the **List Box** button in the Toolbox and add a **list box** to your UserForm as shown in Figure 4.8. Set the **Row Source** to **J4**.

Figure 4.8 ▶

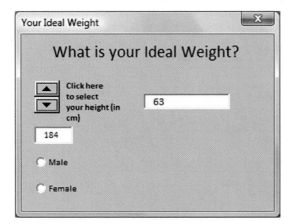

2 Add another list box with **Row Source J5** and add labels as shown in Figure 4.9.

Figure 4.9 ▶

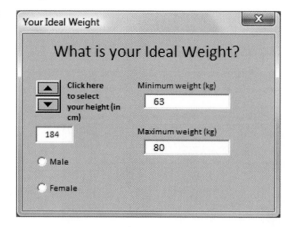

3 Click the **Run Sub/UserForm** button to test that as you click the spinner, the maximum and minimum weights change.

4 Save your file.

Note: When linking a UserForm box to a cell with a formula or a lookup, use a list box.

Adding Command Buttons

1 Click **CommandButton** in the Toolbox to add a command button as shown in Figure 4.10. Edit the text on the button to **Print**.

2 Double click the button – edit the text so that it reads as follows:

```
Private Sub CommandButton1_Click()
UserForm1.PrintForm
End Sub
```

3 Add another command button. Edit the text on the button to **Exit**.

4 Double click the second button – edit the text so that it reads as follows:

```
Private Sub CommandButton2_Click()
Application.Quit
End Sub
```

Figure 4.10 ▶

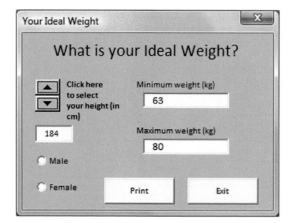

5 Click the **Run Sub/UserForm** button and test the buttons.

6 Save your file.

Finishing the system

1 Click **Insert > Module**. This opens a Visual Basic Editor window where macro coding is entered and stored.

2 Enter the following macro in Visual Basic Editor:

```
Sub Auto_open()
Load UserForm1
UserForm1.Show
End Sub
```

3 Go back to Excel by clicking the **View Microsoft Excel** button.

4 Remove the gridlines by clicking **Office Button > Excel Options > Advanced > Display options for this worksheet** and unchecking **Show Gridlines**.

5 Highlight all the cells and set the text colour to **white**.

6 Save your file.

7 Close the file. Reload it and test that the system works.

Ideas for further development

You can develop the system further by:

- removing row and column headings
- removing the toolbars
- removing the scrollbars
- removing the status bar, formula bar and tabs
- adding a second sheet storing the heights and weights in Imperial units
- setting up a UserForm for the user to select either Imperial or metric units.

2: The invoice exercise: formulas

A common use of Excel is to set up and calculate invoices. In this unit you will set up an invoice and use UserForms like the one in Figure 4.11 to enter data.

Figure 4.11 ▶

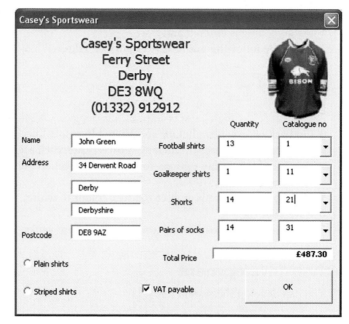

A sportswear shop supplies kits to football clubs.

You will set up a spreadsheet to calculate and display the cost of kit and work out the total cost, including VAT at the current rate.

1 Enter the data into a new macro-enabled spreadsheet as shown in Figure 4.12 – or load the file **caseys.xlsm.** Don't forget to format the prices to **Currency**.

Figure 4.12 ▼

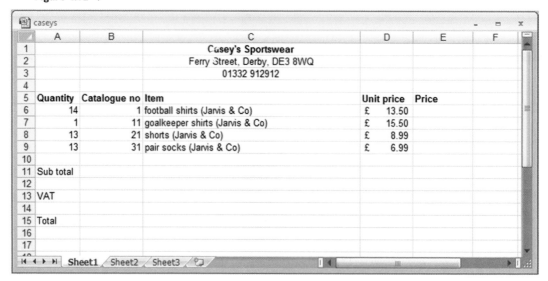

2 Enter the formula **=A6*D6** into cell E6. It should generate £189.00.
3 Copy the formula in E6 into cells E7 to E9. There are various ways of doing this:
   ■ Highlight the cells E6 to E9. On the **Home** tab in the **Editing** group, click **Fill >Down**.
   ■ Click E6. On the **Home** tab, click **Copy**. Highlight the cells E7 to E9 and click **Paste**.
   ■ Click E6 and drag the formula down to E9 using **Drag Copy Short Cut**.

Note: As the formula is copied, it changes. In row 7 it is =A7*D7, in row 8 =A8*D8 and so on.

4 Click E11. On the **Home** tab in the **Editing** group, click **AutoSum** button and then press ENTER. This will add up the costs of the items.
5 Enter the formula for calculating the VAT due in **E13**.
6 Enter the formula for the calculating total in **E15**.
7 Format the totals in E11 and E15 to stand out.

Your spreadsheet should now look like the one shown in Figure 4.13.

Figure 4.13 ▼

	A	B	C	D	E	F
1			Casey's Sportswear			
2			Ferry Street, Derby, DE3 8WQ			
3			01332 912912			
4						
5	Quantity	Catalogue no	Item	Unit price	Price	
6	14	1	football shirts (Jarvis & Co)	£ 13.50	£ 189.00	
7	1	11	goalkeeper shirts (Jarvis & Co)	£ 15.50	£ 15.50	
8	13	21	shorts (Jarvis & Co)	£ 8.99	£ 116.87	
9	13	31	pair socks (Jarvis & Co)	£ 6.99	£ 90.87	
10					£ -	
11	Sub total				£ 412.24	
12						
13	VAT				£ 72.14	
14						
15	Total				£ 484.38	
16						
17						

Sheet1 / Sheet2 / Sheet3

8 Save your work as **caseys.xlsm**.

3: The invoice exercise: lookups

Casey's Sportswear sell three different makes of football kit, all at different prices.

You will set up your spreadsheet so that when the catalogue number is entered into column B, the item name and unit price automatically appear in columns C and D.

1 On Sheet2 enter the details of the items and prices as shown in Figure 4.14 – if you loaded the file caseys.xlsm, this data will already be stored.

Figure 4.14 ▶

	A	B	C	D
1	Catalogue no	Item	Unit price	
2	0	-	£ -	
3	1	football shirts (Jarvis & Co)	£ 13.50	
4	2	football shirts (Skinner Bros)	£ 14.00	
5	3	football shirts (BCW)	£ 16.00	
6	11	goalkeeper shirts (Jarvis & Co)	£ 15.50	
7	12	goalkeeper shirts (Skinner Bros)	£ 17.50	
8	13	goalkeeper shirts (BCW)	£ 20.00	
9	21	shorts (Jarvis & Co)	£ 8.99	
10	22	shorts (Skinner Bros)	£ 8.50	
11	23	shorts (BCW)	£ 10.00	
12	31	pair socks (Jarvis & Co)	£ 6.99	
13	32	pair socks (Skinner Bros)	£ 7.50	
14	33	pair socks (BCW)	£ 8.00	
15				

Sheet1 **Sheet2** Sheet3

2 Define the area from A2 to C14 as **items**. On the **Formulas** tab in the **Defined Names** group, click **Define Name**.
3 Switch back to Sheet1. In cell C6 enter the formula **=VLOOKUP(B6,items,2)**. This picks up the Catalogue number in B6, finds that number in column A of the named area **items** and returns what is in the second column on that row.
4 In cell D6 enter the formula **=VLOOKUP(B6,items,3)**. This looks up the Unit Price for the Catalogue number returned in B4.
5 **Copy** and **Paste** these two formulas down as far as cells C9 and D9. Check that if you enter a catalogue number in column B, the correct information appears in columns C and D.
6 Test that the lookups work. Investigate what happens if you type in a false product number in this workbook:
   ■ try one that is too big, like 35
   ■ try one that is too small, like −5
   ■ try one that doesn't exist, like 7.

7 To avoid such errors you can use validation. Click B4 and use Data Validation so that only 1, 2 or 3 can be entered into this cell, as shown in Figure 4.15. On the **Data** tab in the **Data Tools** group, click **Data Validation** (Figure 4.15).

Figure 4.15 ▶

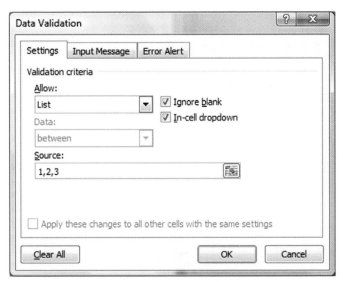

8 Similarly only 11, 12 or 13 can be entered into B7; 21, 22 or 23 into B8 and 31, 32 or 33 in B9.

9 To use the spreadsheet, enter the catalogue number in column B and the quantity in column A. If a line is not being used, leave column B blank.

10 Check the lookups work for all possible values.

11 Save your work.

4: The invoice exercise: option buttons

Football shirts are available in two types – plain or striped. Striped shirts cost an extra £1.00 per shirt.

1 Add option buttons to the bottom-left of the spreadsheet (see Unit 4). Link the buttons to cell A17.
2 Use the **IF** function in cell E10, so that if A17 is equal to 2, this cell is equal to A4 – else it is 0.
3 Make sure that the formula in E11 is **=SUM(E6:E10)**.
4 Save the file.

Your spreadsheet should look like the one in Figure 4.16.

Figure 4.16 ▼

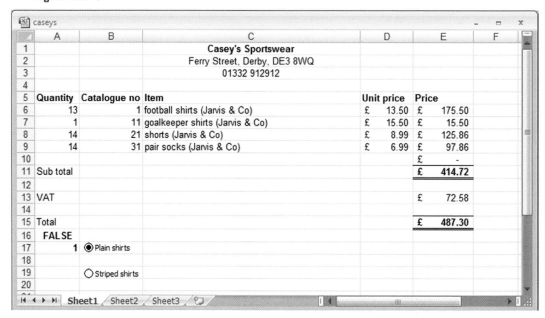

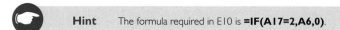 **Hint**   The formula required in E10 is **=IF(A17=2,A6,0)**.

5: The invoice exercise: using a macro to clear data

A very important use of a macro is to clear data from a sheet ready for new data entry – for example, the invoice may need to be cleared for a new customer. The steps are to clear all the data in cells A6 to B9 and A17. For example, see Figure 4.16 – the data in there will be cleared ready for another customer, as shown in Figure 4.17.

Figure 4.17 ▼

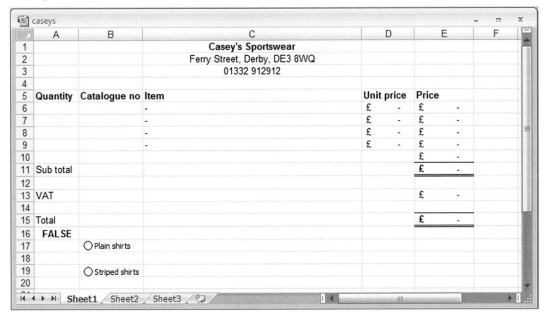

1 Start recording a new macro called **Clear**. On the **Developer** tab in the **Code** group, click **Record Macro**).
2 Highlight cells A6 to B9.
3 On the **Home** tab in the **Editing** group, click **Clear > Clear All**.
4 Click cell A17.
5 On the **Home** tab in the **Editing** group, click **Clear > Clear All** and stop recording.

6: The invoice exercise: setting up a message box

1 On the **Developer** tab in the **Code** group, click **Visual Basic** to load Visual Basic Editor.

2 Double click **Module1** in **Project Explorer**.

3 Scroll down to the bottom of the macro coding in the main Visual Basic Editor window.

4 Enter this text to set up a macro called Message1:

```
Sub Message1()
MsgBox "Our helpline is 01332 912912.", vbOKOnly, "Casey's Sportswear"
End Sub
```

Note:

■ As with recorded macros, the macro must begin with Sub and end with End Sub.

■ You will not need to type in the End Sub part because when you enter a line beginning with 'Sub', the End Sub line is automatically inserted below.

■ You can define the title (in this case 'Casey's Sportswear'), the message (the helpline details) and the buttons. 'vbOKOnly' means you get just an OK button.

5 Go back to Excel by clicking the **View Microsoft Excel** button.

6 Run the macro **Message1** – on the **Developer** tab in the **Code** group, click **Macros > Message1 > Run** and you will see the message box shown in Figure 4.18.

Figure 4.18 ▶

7 Add a button to the worksheet to run this macro.

7: The invoice exercise: UserForms

In this unit you will use a UserForm as a user-friendly front-end for an Excel worksheet.

A UserForm is a way of providing a customised user interface for your system – sometimes it is called a dialogue box. A UserForm might look like the one shown in Figure 4.19 which you will set up in this exercise.

Figure 4.19 ▶

1. Rename Sheet1 as **Invoice** and Sheet2 as **Data**.
2. Record a macro called **Data** to switch to the Data worksheet.
3. Record a macro called **Invoice** to switch to the Invoice worksheet.
4. Load **Visual Basic Editor.** On the **Developer** tab in the **Code** group, click **Visual Basic** – or press **Alt** and **F11**.
5. Click **Insert > UserForm** or click the **Insert UserForm** button. A blank UserForm will appear in the main Visual Basic Editor window as shown in Figure 4.20.

Figure 4.20 ▶

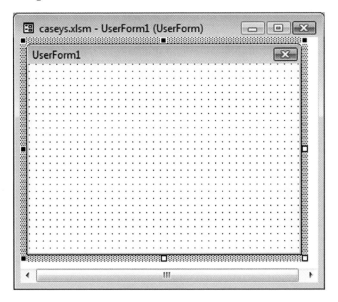

6 A set of buttons called the Toolbox will also appear, as shown in Figure 4.21. If it is not visible, click the blank UserForm and click **View > Toolbox**.

Figure 4.21 ▼

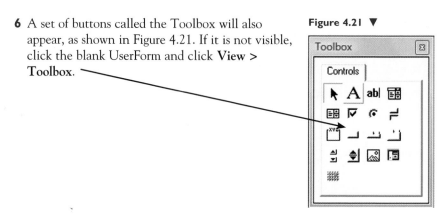

7 On the Toolbox, click **CommandButton** and drag out a rectangle on the UserForm just below the middle on the left-hand side as shown in Figure 4.22.

8 The text on the button will say **CommandButton1**. Edit this by clicking the button once – delete the text and change it to **View invoice**.

Figure 4.22 ▶

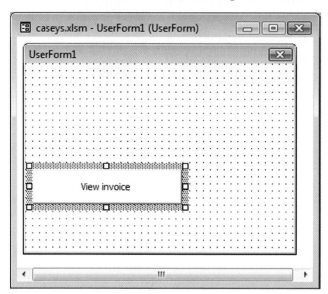

9 Double click the button. You will see the code shown in Figure 4.23.

Figure 4.23 ▶

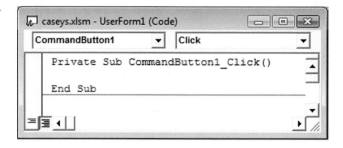

The cursor should be in the middle of these two lines. If not, click between the two lines.

10 Enter this text:

```
Invoice
UserForm1.Hide
```

It will now look like Figure 4.24.

Figure 4.24 ▶

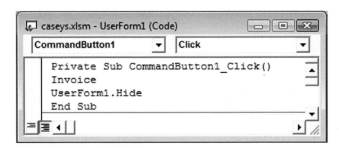

Invoice is the name of the macro that will run when you click this button.

The command **UserForm1.Hide** removes the UserForm from the screen.

Note: The spelling and the punctuation must be exactly as above or the macro won't work.

11 Click **View > Object** or click the **View Object** button in Project Explorer as shown in Figure 4.25 to go back to the plan of the UserForm.

Figure 4.25 ▼

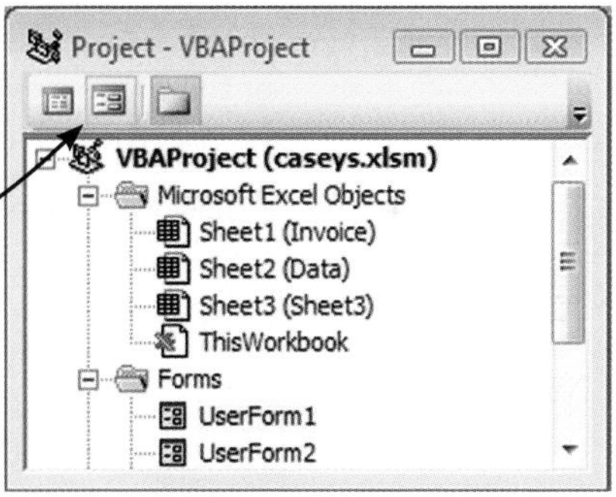

12 Add one more button as shown in Figure 4.26 to run the other macro called **Data**.

13 Click the **Label** button in the Toolbox. Drag out a rectangle near the top of the UserForm and enter the name of the company. The UserForm will now look like Figure 4.26.

Figure 4.26 ▶

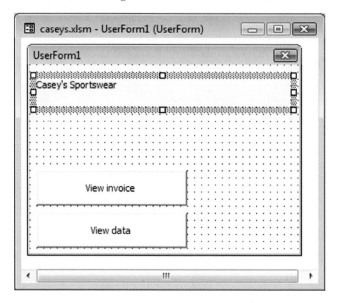

Using the Properties window

The Properties window at the bottom left-hand corner of the screen is used to set the properties of the UserForm. For example, it is used to set the caption, the size, the colour, the font and any links to cells in the spreadsheet.

1 Select the label **Casey's Sportswear**. In the **Properties window** scroll down to **Font.** Click the three dots button and set the size to **18**.
2 Scroll down to the **Text Align** property and select **2-fm TextAlignCenter** to centre the text as shown in Figure 4.27.

Figure 4.27 ▶

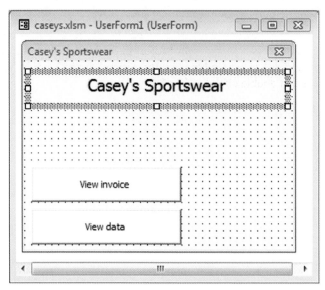

3 Click off the label and on the **UserForm**. Select the **Caption** property to set the caption to **Casey's Sportswear**. The UserForm will now look like Figure 4.28.

Figure 4.28 ▶

The UserForm is now set up – but it is not very attractive.

4 Save your file.
5 Test the UserForm by clicking the **Run Sub/UserForm** button or by pressing **F5**. The UserForm will load.
6 Click the **Close** button (the **X** in the top right-hand corner of the UserForm) to go back to Visual Basic Editor.

Note: If when you are in Visual Basic Editor, you insert a second UserForm by mistake, you can delete it by clicking **File > Remove UserForm**.

Setting up a macro to display your UserForm

Once you have designed a UserForm, you will need to set up a macro to display it. The macro will be set up in Visual Basic and, once again, exact syntax is vital.

1 On the **Developer** tab in the **Code** group, click **Visual Basic**.
2 Double click Module1 in Project Explorer as shown in Figure 4.29. (If Module1 is not visible click the **+** sign next to **Modules** in Project Explorer. Then double click **Module1**.)

Figure 4.29 ▶

3 You should see the coding of the macros you have already set up. Scroll down to the bottom and underneath the last macro text, type in the following:

```
Sub Box()
Load UserForm1
UserForm1.Show
End Sub
```

The middle two lines of code load the UserForm and display it on the screen.

You will not need to type in the 'End Sub' part because when you enter a line beginning with 'Sub', the End Sub line is automatically inserted below.

4 This sets up a macro called **Box**. Click the **View Microsoft Excel** button to go back to Excel.
5 Check that the macro works. On the **Developer** tab in the **Code** group, click **Macros**. Click **Box > Run**.
6 Test that the UserForm works for both buttons.

 Tip   Set up a button on the toolbar to run the **Box** macro – this will save time.

7 Go back to Visual Basic Editor. Load the UserForm by double clicking **UserForm1** in Project Explorer.
8 In the Properties window set the **Height** of the UserForm to **220** or extend the UserForm just by dragging downwards. Add an extra button, as shown in Figure 4.30. Edit the text on the button to read **Cancel**. Double click the new button and make the text read as follows:

```
Private Sub CommandButton3_Click()
End
End Sub
```

Figure 4.30 ▶

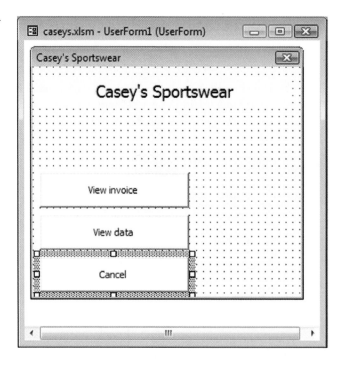

9 Save your file.

Each item on a UserForm – such as a command button, a combo box or a text box – is an object.

Each object has a unique name such as CommandButton1, TextBox6 or ComboBox4.

If you double click the UserForm, you will see the code for each object. It will appear as follows:

```
Private Sub CommandButton1_Click()
Invoice
UserForm1.Hide
End Sub

Private Sub CommandButton2_Click()
Data
UserForm1.Hide
End Sub

Private Sub CommandButton3_Click()
End
End Sub
```

8: The invoice exercise: customising your UserForm

You can develop your UserForm in a number of ways, for example by:

- editing background colours
- changing the font
- adding an image
- resizing the UserForm.

The properties of each object are set up in the Properties window.

1 Go back to **Visual Basic Editor** and load the UserForm by double clicking **UserForm1** in Project Explorer as shown in Figure 4.31.

Figure 4.31 ▶

2 To edit the background colour, click the UserForm. In the **Properties** window, click **BackColor**. Click the drop-down arrow and choose **Palette** as in Figure 4.32 – you have a variety of colours to choose from.

3 Click one of the command buttons on the UserForm. Use the **Properties** window to change the colour of the button, the colour of the text (**ForeColor**) and the **font** as required. Repeat this for the other buttons and the label.

4 To add a picture, click the **Image** button in the Toolbox and drag out a rectangle on the UserForm. Click the row called **Picture** in the Properties window. Double click the button with three dots to select

Figure 4.32 ▼

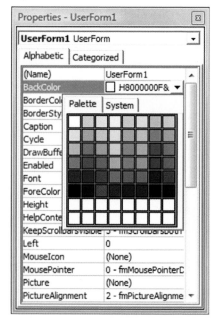

a picture. Find the picture you require. Choose **PictureSizeMode** 3 so that the picture resizes to fit.

5 Add a control tip text to your buttons using the **Control Tip Text** row of the Properties window. Whatever you type in here appears on the screen as help text when you move the mouse over a control like a text box.

6 Resize the UserForm and the command buttons by dragging the controls in the normal way.

7 Save your file.

UserForms can be made to look eye-catching as shown in Figure 4.33.

Figure 4.33 ▶

Hint   To add an extra line in your label, press **CTRL** and **ENTER**.

9: The invoice exercise: using UserForms to enter data

In this unit you will learn about how UserForms can be used to enter data into an Excel workbook.

Text boxes on a UserForm can be linked to cells in a spreadsheet and can be used for entering data. List boxes can be used to display data from the spreadsheet in the UserForm.

Obviously you can just type the data straight into the cells, but a UserForm can make it easier for a user and gives greater control.

You can include other controls in a UserForm such as command buttons, combo boxes and option buttons as shown in Figure 4.34 which you will set up in this unit.

Figure 4.34 ▶

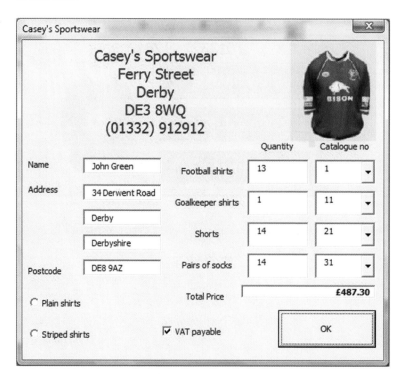

Setting up the UserForm

You will set up the UserForm to enter the customer's name and address and details of purchases – catalogue number, quantity, if VAT is payable and whether the shirts are plain or striped. The total price will be displayed.

1 Load **Visual Basic Editor** by pressing ALT and **F11**. Insert a UserForm by clicking **Insert > UserForm.** This will be called UserForm2.
2 Enlarge the UserForm so that it is 360 wide and 330 high. These can be set using the **Width** and **Height** properties in the Properties window.

3 In the Properties window, set the caption to **Casey's Sportswear**. Add a label with the company address (use font size 12) and a picture for a logo as shown in Figure 4.35.

Figure 4.35 ▶

Hint   To go onto a new line in the label, press **CTRL** and **ENTER**.

---

4 Add a Command Button at the bottom-right on the UserForm as in Figure 4.36. Edit the text to **OK**.

Figure 4.36 ▶

5 Double click the button and add the text **UserForm2**. Hide as shown in Figure 4.37.

Figure 4.37 ▶

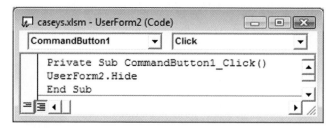

6 Double click **Module1** in Project Explorer. Scroll down to the bottom and add this macro:

```
Sub Details()
Load Userform2
Userform2.Show
End Sub
```

This sets up a macro called **Details** to load the UserForm.

7 Switch back to Excel to test that running the macro displays the UserForm.

Adding text boxes

1 Switch back to Visual Basic Editor. Double click **UserForm2**. Click the **TextBox** button in the Toolbox. Drag out a box on the right-hand side of the UserForm as shown in Figure 4.38.

Figure 4.38 ▶

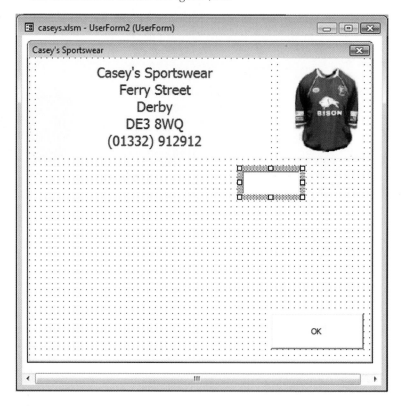

2 With the box selected, set the **Control Source** in the **Properties window** to **A6** as in Figure 4.39.

Figure 4.39 ▼

3 Click the **Label** button and drag out a box above the text box. Enter the text **Quantity** into the Label as shown in Figure 4.40. Change the font, the colour of the text and the text alignment if required.

Figure 4.40 ▶

4 You now need to add extra text boxes and labels as shown in Figure 4.41.

Figure 4.41 ▶

5 Set the control source for each text box as follows:
- football shirts catalogue number – **B6**
- goalkeeper shirts quantity – **A7**
- goalkeeper shirts catalogue number – **B7**
- shorts quantity – **A8**
- shorts catalogue number – **B8**
- pair of socks quantity – **A9**
- pair of socks catalogue number – **B9**

6 Switch back to Excel. Make sure that Sheet1 is showing and run the **Details** macro. Test that you as you enter data into the text boxes the data entered goes into the correct cell as in Figure 4.42.

Figure 4.42 ▶

7 Save your file.

Adding a check box to your UserForm

Now add a check box to the UserForm to choose if VAT is payable.

I Switch back to **Visual Basic Editor**. Load UserForm2 by double clicking **UserForm2** in Project Explorer.

2 Click the **CheckBox** button in the Toolbox and drag out a rectangle near the middle of the bottom of the UserForm. Edit the text to read **VAT payable** as in Figure 4.43.

Figure 4.43 ▶

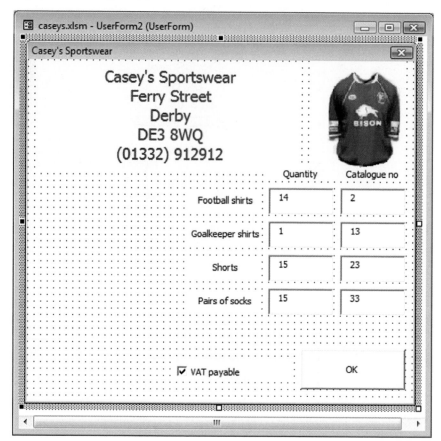

3 In the Properties window set the control source to **A23**.
4 Switch to Excel and change the formula in cell E13 to
=IF(A23=FALSE,0,E11*17.5%).
5 Run the UserForm again. Test that the check box works by running the **Details** macro.
6 Save your file.

Adding option buttons

Now add option buttons to the UserForm to choose striped or plain shirts.

1 In **Visual Basic Editor**, use the **Option** button in the Toolbox to add two option buttons as shown in Figure 4.44. Set the control source for plain shirts to **A14.**

Figure 4.44 ▶

2 In Excel enter the formula **=IF(A16=TRUE,1,2)** into cell A17.
3 Run the **Details** macro and test that the option buttons work.

10: The invoice exercise: adding combo boxes to speed up data entry

The catalogue number for football shirts can only be 1, 2 or 3, so we can replace the top-right text box on the UserForm with a combo box (drop-down box) giving a choice of 1, 2 or 3. This will speed up data entry and avoid mistakes.

1 In **Visual Basic Editor**, load UserForm2 by double clicking **UserForm2** in Project Explorer.
2 Click the top-right text box – it is in the football shirts row and the catalogue number column. Press **Delete** on the keyboard.
3 Click the **ComboBox** button in the Toolbox.
4 Drag out a box on the UserForm to replace the deleted text box as shown in Figure 4.45.

Figure 4.45 ▶

5 With the Combo box still selected, set the **Control Source** in the Properties window to cell **B6** and the **Row Source** to **Data!A3:A5**.

6 To test that it works, click in the UserForm and then press **F5**. The items in the drop-down list should be as shown in Figure 4.46.

Figure 4.46 ▶

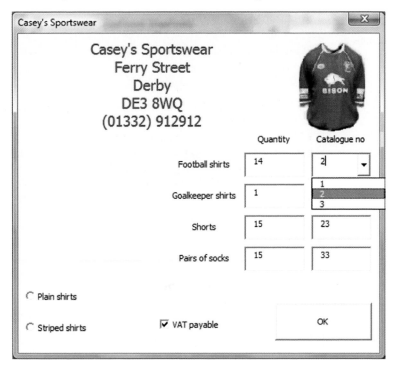

7 Develop the UserForm further by adding a combo box for the other three catalogue numbers as shown in Figure 4.47.

Figure 4.47 ▶

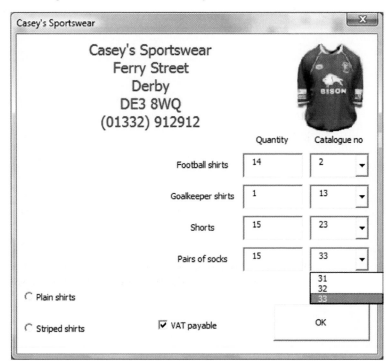

Completing the design

1 Add five text boxes on the left of the UserForm, as shown in Figure 4.48.
2 Add three labels as shown.

Figure 4.48 ▶

3 In the Properties window set the **Control Source** for these text boxes to **A24** to **A28** respectively. This enables the name and address of the customer to appear on the UserForm.

4 Still in Visual Basic Editor, click the **ListBox** button in the Toolbox. Drag out a box above the OK button, as shown in Figure 4.49.

5 Add a label **Total Price** as shown.

Figure 4.49 ▶

6 Select the list box. In the Properties window, set the **Row Source** to **E15**, set the font to **bold** and align the text to the **right**.

7 Create a new macro called **Auto_open** as shown below so that UserForm2 is displayed when the file loads. Load Module1 and type in this coding:

```
Sub Auto_open()
Sheets("Invoice").Select
Load UserForm2
UserForm2.Show
End Sub
```

8 Save your file and test it thoroughly.

5   Project ideas

Here are some potential spreadsheet projects. You could adapt a problem or undertake a similar problem to meet the demands of a real user.

■ 1: The stock controller

Client: Ron Wilson

Organisation: Wilson's Builders' Merchant – a small builders' merchant specialising in selling small quantities of materials to the building trade.

Client's position: Owner

The problem: Ron would like a system that will keep control of his stock, particularly to warn him when stocks get low. As an item is sold, he wants to create an invoice and automatically adjust the stock levels. Stock figures should also be updated as deliveries arrive.

The items sold, the prices and minimum stock levels are shown in the table below.

Item	Quantity	Price	Minimum stock level
Building sand	1 tonne	£15.00	25
Grit sand	1 tonne	£10.00	10
Gravel	1 tonne	£40.00	10
Yorkshire flagstones	1 square metre	£50.00	10
Concrete paving blocks	1 square metre	£10.00	100
Yorkshire stone blocks	1 square metre	£65.00	25
Cement	25 kg	£5.00	50
Concrete common bricks	each	£0.25	1000
Red bricks	each	£0.45	5000
Blue engineering bricks	each	£0.80	1000

Ron wants to be able to be able to set up a blank invoice for the next customer. He needs to be able to change prices easily. He also wants the spreadsheet set up so that you cannot accidentally delete formulas and data by mistake.

The system must prevent anyone from ordering an item if it is not in stock.

(See *Tips and tricks 44* and *45*.)

2: Print 4U

Client: Harry Price

Organisation: Print 4U – a printing company in Bradford.

Print 4

Client's position: Owner

The problem: Print 4U print leaflets and flyers for customers, in all sizes from A0 to A7.

They can print in colour or in only one colour (usually black). This is called monochrome.

They print on various thickness of paper from 70 gram per square metre up to 250 gram per square metre. The thicker the paper, the more it costs.

At present, Harry works out all his quotes with a calculator and writes out quotations by hand. Harry has asked you to use spreadsheet software to set up an easy-to-use quotation system which will automatically work out the cost of a printing and create a professional-looking quotation displaying the quote. He wants to be able to print this quote at the click of a button.

The prices per 1000 copies in monochrome are:

Paper size	70 gsm	80 gsm	100 gsm	150 gsm	200 gsm	250 gsm
A0	£756	£860	£1121	£1225	£1616	£1955
A1	£398	£453	£590	£645	£851	£1,029
A2	£209	£238	£310	£339	£448	£542
A3	£110	£125	£163	£179	£236	£285
A4	£58	£66	£86	£94	£124	£150
A5	£32	£37	£48	£52	£69	£83
A6	£18	£20	£27	£29	£38	£46
A7	£10	£11	£15	£16	£21	£26

Full colour is 50 per cent extra. Glossy paper is 20 per cent extra. The printed work can be folded once or twice at an extra cost of £10 per 1000 copies per fold.

Prices for more than 1000 copies are on a pro rata basis – this means to find the price of 3000 multiply by 3 and so on. Print 4U do not accept orders of quantities fewer than 1000.

Harry wants to be able to clear the quote at the click of a button and to be able to change prices easily. He also wants the spreadsheet set up so that he cannot accidentally delete formulas and data by mistake or enter data which is unacceptable.

He also wants to store the invoices and the names of the customers in a table, and for the system to have an automatic front-end.

3: Carla's salon

Client: Carla Jenkinson

Organisation: Carla's Beauty Salon

Client's position: Owner

The problem: Carla Jenkinson runs a beauty salon in South Wales. The services that she offers and the prices are shown in the table below.

Service	Price
Nails:	
■ Polish change	£10.00
■ Press-on nails (professional application)	£15.00
■ Manicure	£15.00
■ Pedicure	£25.00
Hair:	
■ Wash and style	£10.00
■ Haircut with wash and style	£25.00
■ Colour	£45.00
■ Highlights	£55.00
■ Perm	£60.00
Waxing:	
■ Eyebrows	£18.00
■ Arms	£25.00
■ Legs	£45.00
■ Lips	£10.00
Ear piercing:	
■ Ear piercing, with studs	£10.00 per ear

Prices are reduced on some days of the week – Monday and Tuesday 20 per cent off, Wednesday and Thursday 10 per cent off.

At present, Carla works out all prices with a calculator and writes out receipts by hand. Carla has asked you to use spreadsheet software to set up a pricing system which will automatically work out the cost of a beauty treatment and create a professional-looking receipt. She wants to be able to print this receipt at the click of a button.

Carla wants to be able to clear price calculations at the click of a button and to be able to change the prices easily. She also wants the spreadsheet set up so that you cannot accidentally delete formulas and data by mistake or enter data which is unacceptable.

She would like an automatic front-end for the system.

4: Foreign exchange calculator

Client: Simon Smith

Organisation: Go Fast Travel

Client's position: Assistant

The problem: Simon Smith works in a travel agent's office. Many customers want to be able to convert the local currency where they are going on holiday into UK pounds.

At present, Simon carries out all calculations by hand but he realises that this is slow and may be inaccurate. He would like a computer system that will allow him to choose the country to be visited (e.g. Italy) from a list. The system will then display the currency in that country (e.g. Euros) and also the up-to-date exchange rate. Simon wants to be able to enter an amount in UK pounds and for the system to convert this into the corresponding amount in the foreign currency. He also wants to be able to enter an amount of the foreign currency and then convert this into UK pounds. All the details will be printed out at a touch of a button.

Simon wants to be able to clear the calculations at the click of a button ready for the next customer. He also wants the spreadsheet set up so that he cannot accidentally delete formulas and data by mistake or enter data which is unacceptable, such as negative amounts of money.

Simon wants to be able to change exchange rates easily – in fact he would like the system to operate so that the exchange rates are automatically updated from a website.

(See *Tips and tricks 40.*)

5: Recording studio

Client: MC Slim Janie

Organisation: A recording studio called MC *Slim's* in Brighton. There are four different rooms that can be hired out by local musicians for up to four hours at a time.

Client's position: Owner

The problem: MC Slim Janie owns a recording studio in Brighton. She has four different rooms that she hires out to local musicians for up to four hours at a time.

At present MC works out all prices with a calculator and writes out invoices by hand. MC wants you to use spreadsheet software to make an invoicing system that will work out the cost of using the studio and print an invoice at the click of a button.

MC also wants to be able to clear a quote easily and to be able to change the prices. She also wants the spreadsheet set up so that you can't delete formulas and data by mistake and she also wants to prevent impossible data being entered.

MC Slim Janie wants to store all the invoices and the names of the customers in a table.

All the details of rooms, prices and optional extras are given in the table below:

Rooms are:

Studio 1	Eight track	£20 per hour
Studio 2	16 track	£50 per hour
Studio 3	32 track	£100 per hour
Studio 4	48 track	£150 per hour

Additional charges are as follows:

- use of session musicians   £50 per musician per hour
- video sessions   £30 per hour
- use of grand piano   £60
- either 24HD system   £25 per hour
- or RADAR IZ 24   £35 per hour
- UREI graphic equaliser   £30 per hour
- Sound technician   £20 per hour
- Instrument hire   from £10 per hour.

6: Golf scoreboard

Client: Debbie Green

Organisation: North Dunbar Golf Club

Client's position: Secretary

The problem: A number of tournaments are held every year at the club. Most tournaments are held over one round of 18 holes.

During tournaments players like to know how well they are doing compared to other players.

Debbie would like to use a spreadsheet system to record the scores. The system would need to:

- store the names of the players and their handicap
- allow the score for each player to be entered for each hole
- store the par score for each hole
- calculate each player's total score so far (e.g. 63 after 14 holes)
- calculate each player's total score compared to par (e.g. 3 over par)
- display the leaderboard for current leading players
- calculate the final gross score for everyone's round and take off any handicap
- sort scores in increasing order.

Debbie wants a template that can be used for any tournament.

She also wants the spreadsheet set up so that she can't delete formulas and data by mistake or enter any impossible data.

Client: Lisa McClure

Organisation: Green Valley Car Hire

Client's position: Owner

The problem: Green Valley Car Hire rent cars to local businesses for periods from one day to two weeks. They have around 15 different cars on their books and hire to 12 different businesses. The prices are:

1	Fiesta (LH06PTH)	£45.00
2	Fiesta (LH06PTQ)	£45.00
3	Fiesta (WQ57KHB)	£45.00
4	Fiesta (LL08WWA)	£45.00
5	Ka (LH06PTX)	£35.00
6	Ka (LH06PTY)	£35.00
7	Focus (LH06PTK)	£55.00
8	Focus (LH56PPP)	£55.00
9	Focus (LH56PPK)	£55.00
10	Focus (LH57PAV)	£55.00
11	Mondeo (LH06PTB)	£60.00
12	Mondeo (LH06PTC)	£60.00
13	Mondeo (LH08JYJ)	£60.00
14	Scorpio (LH06PKJ)	£75.00
15	Scorpio (LH06PKR)	£75.00

The charge is per day – any 24 hour period
Cars can be hired for up to 14 days
25 per cent discount for more than 3 days

Additional charges are as follows:	
• Insurance – no excess	£7 per day
• Additional driver	£10 per day
• Bring back with fuel empty	£35
• International insurance	£12 per day
• AA cover	£5 per day
• RAC cover	£4.50 per day
• Green Flag cover	£4.65 per day

The owner, Lisa McClure calculates prices with a calculator. Now she wants a computer system to work out the charges. She has asked you to help.

Lisa wants you to use spreadsheet software to make an invoicing system that will work out the cost of hiring a car and print an invoice at the click of a button. She also wants to be able to clear a quote at the click of a button and to be able to change prices easily. She also wants the spreadsheet set up so that you can't delete formulas and data by mistake.

She would like the system to have an automatic front-end.

8: Shed orders

Client: Alan Rivers

Organisation: Alan Rivers Sheds

Client's position: Owner

The problem: Alan makes garden sheds and sells them through eBay. He makes eight different sheds.

He works out the cost of a shed on scraps of paper in his workshop. He knows this is not good enough and wants a computer system to calculate the costs and store all the orders. He has asked you to help.

The prices are given in the table below.

1	Warwick	£ 99.00
2	Stafford	£115.00
3	Leicester	£125.00
4	Derby	£145.00
5	Nottingham	£165.00
6	Lancaster	£175.00
7	Lincoln	£199.00
8	York	£225.00

Additional charges are as follows:	
Yale door lock	£10
Three-lever lock	£30
Five-lever lock	£50
Shed insurance	£32 (12 months)
Fire extinguisher	£24.99
Sooper-dooper roof felt	£43.99
Maxi-guttering	£48.99

Alan Rivers wants you to use spreadsheet software to make an invoicing system that will work out the cost of a shed and print an invoice at the click of a button. He would like to store the invoices and the names of the customers in a table.

He wants to be able to clear a quote at the press of a button and to be able to change the prices easily. He also wants the spreadsheet set up so that you can't delete formulas and data by mistake.

9: Departmental stationery account

Client: Marian Wilkins

Organisation: Snetterton High

Client's position: Head of English Department

The problem: The English department has a stationery budget to be spent on items such as A4 lined paper, white board pens and document wallets. All these items are ordered through the education authority. Items have a stock number and a set price.

Marian would like a spreadsheet where she can put in the stock number and the quantity of the order – the computer system will then calculate the cost and the remaining balance. Details of items ordered are to be stored along with the starting balance. Marian would like to predict year-end figures.

She wants the system to look professional and to be able to produce meaningful graphs.

She also wants the spreadsheet set up so that she cannot accidentally delete formulas and data by mistake or enter data that is unacceptable.

10: Orders for a joke shop

Client: James McKay

Organisation: Jim's Jokes is a shop in Nottingham that sells fun items by mail order, mainly to smaller joke shops around England.

Client's position: Owner

The problem: The work of the shop has expanded in recent months and they can no longer cope with storing sales on paper. They have asked you to help.

Jim's Jokes sell twenty different items.

1	Big squeaky spider	£1.50
2	Cockroach	£0.75
3	Exploding lighter	£6.99
4	Exploding pen	£9.50
5	Fake fried egg	£2.50
6	Fake parking ticket	£1.25
7	False teeth	£2.50
8	Fake sick	£5.00
9	Fang caps glow in dark	£1.99
10	Fly in ice cube	£2.00
11	Fun blood	£3.99
12	Glow in the dark spider	£3.50
13	Loaded dice	£3.00
14	Long fangs	£10.00
15	Monster teeth	£1.25
16	Rubber snake	£4.29
17	Stink bombs (5)	£9.99
18	Tarantula	£1.50
19	Vampire teeth	£2.25
20	Vicar's teeth	£1.45

Jim's Jokes want you to use spreadsheet software to make a professional invoicing system that will work out the cost of an order and print an invoice.

James wants to be able to clear a quote at the press of a button and to be able to change the prices easily. He also wants the spreadsheet set up so that you can't delete formulas and data by mistake.

He would like to store the invoices and the names of the customers in a table and have an automatic front-end for the system.

11: Carpets 'R' Us

Client: Richie Fitzsimons

Organisation: Carpets 'R' Us – who sell carpets throughout the country.

Client's position: Store manager

The problem: At present Carpets 'R' Us work out all prices with a calculator and write out invoices by hand. The cost of a carpet depends on its area in square metres, although all carpets start as a rectangular shape. As a result, the area is the length (in metres) times the breadth (in metres).

The types of carpet available are shown in the table below.

Type	Price per square metre
Berber	£12.99
Wool	£19.99
Nylon	£11.99
Olefin	£9.99
Polyester	£10.99
Acrylics	£12.99
Sisal	£7.99

Optional extras include:

- Underlay   £3.99 per square metre
- Fitting   £50.00 per room
- Carpet gripper   £17.99 per door in the room
- Stainmaster treatment £60.00
- Extended 5-year warranty £119.

All carpets are subject to VAT ay the current rate.

Carpets 'R' Us have asked you to use spreadsheet software to set up an invoicing system that will automatically work out the cost of a carpet and create a professional-looking invoice. They want to be able to print invoices at the click of a button.

Carpets 'R' Us want to be able to clear a quote at the press of a button and to be able to change the prices easily. They also want the spreadsheet set up so that you can't delete formulas and data by mistake.

The VAT must be shown on the invoice.

12: Rugby scoreboard

Client: Reg Winter

Organisation: Netherton Rugby Club

Client's position: Club secretary

The problem: Reg Winter is responsible for the scoreboard that keeps the score during rugby union matches. He employs a young student to operate the scoreboard, putting up the numbers when a try or goal is scored.

Reg thinks that an electronic scoreboard linked to a scoring system on his laptop would make it much easier. Essentially he wants the solution to be mouse-driven, automatic and remove the need for paying a helper.

Reg has suggested that there are different buttons on the screen to represent, for example, scores for Netherton and scores for visitors – tries (5 points), conversions (2 points), penalties (3 points) and drop goals (3 points).

The solution must display the name of the visiting team, be able to reset scores back to 0 – 0 at the end of a game and prevent accidental deletion of any data. It must also store the final results and the dates of matches in a table.

More project ideas can be downloaded from www.dynamic-learning-student.co.uk

Practice assignments

1: Happy Days

Client: Sandra Welsh

Organisation: Happy Days is a specialist company that designs and produces invitations to events such as weddings, christenings, house warming parties, 40th birthday parties etc. Prices are not cheap but this reflects the high quality of the invitations.

Mr and Mrs Steven Robins
request the honour of your presence
at the marriage of their daughter
Megan Elizabeth
to
Mr Charles Henderson
at St Mary's Church, Netherfield
on Saturday 28 September 2008
at 2 p.m.

Client's position: Accounts clerk

The problem: Sandra wants a reliable way of calculating the costs of printing invitations and printing invoices.

Invitations are normally A6 size. The company uses three different thicknesses of card – standard, luxury and superior. Happy Days will produce any number of cards from 20 to 1000.

The prices per invitation are given in the table below.

Quality	Price per card
Standard	£0.57
Luxury	£0.95
Superior	£1.35
Gold leaf print	£0.25 extra
Gold leaf edging	£0.30 extra
Crinkle edge	£0.10 extra
Embossed	£0.35 extra

At present, Happy Days work out all quotes on a calculator and write out quotations by hand. Happy Days have asked you to set up a system that will automatically work out the cost of invitations and create a professional-looking invoice displaying the number of cards to be printed, the choices made, the type of party and the amount of the quote. They want to be able to print this quote at the click of a button.

Happy Days also want to be able to clear a quote at the click of a button and to be able to change prices easily. They also want the system set up so that they cannot delete formulas and data by mistake or enter data which is unacceptable.

They would like an automatic front-end for the system.

2: Planet Fireplace

Client: Sally McLeish

Organisation: Planet Fireplace is a shop that sells fireplaces. The shop is at 67 High Street, Wilmington, WN3 8KW. The phone number is (0119) 451 1122.

Client's position: Proprietor

The problem: When customers buy a fireplace, they have to buy a fire, a surround and a fret (the decorative front of the fire).

Sally would like a computer system that will allow her to enter customers' choices easily, automatically calculate the total cost including VAT, easily produce and print a delivery note, easily produce and print a professional invoice for the customer and allow her to edit the prices of all the products.

The prices are given in the tables below.

Fires

Name	Manufacturer	Price	Type
Airflame Convector 16	Wonder Fires	£324.00	Coal effect
Airflame Convector 18	Wonder Fires	£345.00	Coal effect
Atlanta Chimney glass front	Flavel Leisure	£349.99	Pebble
Belvedere Gas brass	Robinson Willey	£270.00	Coal effect
Blenheim C1 Hotbox	Valor	£189.99	Log effect
Blenheim Slimline	Valor	£199.99	Coal effect
Ceram 60	Matchless	£350.00	Coal effect
Class I/II Hotbox	Real Cozy Fires	£189.99	Pebble
Crystal Sunrise	Crystal Fires	£528.00	Pebble
Designer Elegance black	Focal Point	£320.00	Log effect

The surround can be 42, 48 or 54 inches wide but this makes no difference to the cost. For an extra £100, the customer can have a remote control for their fire. The customer can collect the fireplace themselves or get it delivered for £25. If required, Planet Fireplace will install the fireplace for £100. All costs (price, delivery and installation) are subject to VAT at the current rate.

Surrounds

Name	Manufacturer	Price
Adelaide	Antique pine	£219.99
Barcelona	Marble	£615.00
Belmont	Light oak	£327.00
Celtic	Cast iron	£328.00
Cranborne	Limestone	£599.00

Some frets are free, others must be paid for.

Frets

Name	Manufacturer	Price
Blenheim Black Front	Sirocco	£0.00
Blenheim Brass Front	Sirocco	£0.00
Blenheim Silver Front	Sirocco	£0.00
Royal Black	Sirocco	£10.00
Royal Chrome	Sirocco	£10.00
Style Front	Sirocco	£30.00

6 Documenting your project

An ICT project is much more than just setting up a system using Microsoft Excel. You must also include documentation covering:

- user requirements
- design
- implementation
- testing
- a user guide
- technical documentation
- evaluation.

The following pages show you how to document your system by looking at some of the documentation provided with the *Denton Gazette* system.

Remember: This documentation is not complete, but each section offers examples, pointers and hints as to what is considered to be good practice.

1: Contents

A contents page is very useful – both for you in checking that every part of your documentation is present, but also for the person who will mark your project by helping them to find the various sections.

Denton Gazette

Contents

2: Introduction

In this section you need to give some of the background to your proposed system and its requirements. You will need to answer questions such as:

■ Who is the client?
■ Who is the user?
■ What is the problem?
■ Why do they want a spreadsheet solution?

Who is the client?

The *Denton Gazette* is a weekly newspaper published in the small town of Denton. The client is the owner of the *Denton Gazette,* Janice Peters.

What is the problem?

Dozens of local businesses advertise in the *Gazette*. Advertisements can be in colour or black and white, they can be full page, half page, quarter page, an eighth of a page or a twelfth of a page.

The cost of an advertisement depends on:

■ the size of the advertisement – table of prices is given below
■ whether the advertisement is in black and white or in colour
■ the page on which the advertisement will be printed.

Size	Cost
Full page	£560.00
Half page	£300.00
Quarter page	£160.00
Eighth page	£85.00
Twelfth page	£60.00

These are the costs of black and white advertisements on an inside page. A colour advertisement costs 30 per cent more.

If an advertisement is on the front page, it costs an extra 50 per cent. If the advertisement is on the back page it costs an extra 40 per cent. Advertisements on either the front page or the back page cannot be bigger than quarter page.

Advertisers can book for up to 26 weeks. If they book for between 4 and 9 consecutive weeks they get a discount of 10 per cent. If they book for 10 or more consecutive weeks they get a discount of 20 per cent.

At present, when someone places an order for an advertisement in the newspaper, the cost of the advertisement is calculated manually.

The owner of the *Denton Gazette,* Janice Peters is worried about errors in the calculations and would like an easy-to-use computer system that will calculate the price of placing advertisements in the newspaper. The system must use the company's colour scheme of green and light green, use Verdana their house font and use the company dove logo.

The system will be used by Katie Walker, the accounts clerk at the *Gazette* who currently deals with all advertisements, calculates the costs, sends out the invoices and files details in the filing cabinet.

Katie is highly IT literate and has a computer on her desk that she uses for word processing. However, she will need a comprehensive user guide to show her how to use the new system.

Such a system would be faster and more reliable than the present manual system.

3: User requirements

In this section you need to make a list of all of the requirements of the client and the end-users. You may need to interview your client to find out these requirements – everything they require must be listed. When you have set up the system, you will need to check that you have met all of these requirements. It is a good idea to number them.

Once you have made a list of the user requirements, you will need to work out the inputs, processes and outputs for your solution.

You may find it easiest to start with the outputs – what information must the solution provide? From here work backwards to find out what data must be entered to get these outputs. Then specify what processes must take place to turn the inputs into outputs.

Give as much detail as possible about the outputs. What format are they in? Give some examples.

What are the user requirements?

The user requirements for the *Denton Gazette* system are as follows.

1 The system should be user-friendly and easy to understand.

2 The system must be able to calculate the cost of an advertisement given the size, position, number of weeks and colour of the advertisement.

3 The user must be able to select the different options easily.

4 The price must be calculated automatically for the customer.

5 The new system must save the user time compared with the current method in which this is all done manually.

6 There must be a file within the system in which quotations can be stored in sufficient detail so they can be easily located and referred back to if necessary. This will stop paperwork being misplaced and will help the company to become more organised in processing quotations.

7 Filing the quotations must be automated to make it quicker and easier for the user.

8 It must be easy to clear quotations automatically once they have been filed ready for another customer. This will save the user's time.

9 It must be easy to quit the system – e.g. at the end of the day – but there must be a double check in case the user quits accidentally. This will aid the user when using the system.

10 A printed quotation is required giving the customer a guaranteed price for their advertisement at the touch of a button. This should look professional and be easy to understand so the customer can query any problems. This can be done by breaking down each section of the quotation so that the customer can see how the price is calculated.

11 Calculations must be automatic in the system. Examples are the total price, which will also involve looking up data from a table. This will aid the user and reduce the number of mistakes.

12 It must be easy to access the price details and amend them when necessary.

13 All of the outputs – the display screen and the quotation – must be of high quality and look professional.

14 The font Verdana must be used.

15 The company's colours – green and light green – must be used.

16 There must be clearly labelled buttons to perform operations – such as filing quotations or clearing data.

17 Invalid combinations must be prevented.

18 There must also be alert boxes to warn the user of any errors that have occurred.

19 Unexplained error messages – such as #N/A – must be avoided.

20 Deletion of formulae from the spreadsheet by accident must not be possible.

4: Inputs, processing and outputs

Defining the inputs – tips

Some solutions may require that the user enters data like a name, a date of birth and a price.

Don't just say that the input data will be the name, date of birth and price – state exactly what format the data will be in and give an example.

Input examples

- Title (one of Mr, Mrs, Miss, Ms) – e.g. Ms
- Surname maximum 20 characters – e.g. Brown
- Forename maximum 15 characters – e.g. Kathryn
- Date of birth in dd/mm/yyyy format – e.g. 17/06/1992
- Price in pounds to 2 decimal places – e.g. £5.99
- If the input data is chosen from a list (such as the Title above) give all the possible choices.

Inputs

The user needs to choose/input the:

- customer name – e.g. Denton Carpets
- customer address in four fields, the last field is the postcode
- date from the computer's clock in dd/mm/yyyy format
- size of the advertisement – full page, half page, quarter page, eighth page or twelfth page
- colour of the advertisement – colour or black and white
- position of the advertisement – front, back or inside page
- number of weeks – 1 to 26
- standard prices for advertisements – particularly if there is any change.

Defining the processing – tips

Examples of processing that you might use in other solutions include:

- calculations
- lookups
- IF statements
- sorting
- searching
- grouping information
- validating input data.

Again, make sure that you say exactly what the processing involves, no matter how obvious it may seem.

Processes

The system needs to be able to:

- Look up the cost of each size of advertisement from a table.
- Calculate the cost.
- Calculate any discount.
- Subtract the discount to work out the final cost.
- Clear the calculations for the next user using just one button.
- Store the information on a separate sheet.
- Check if an invalid combination has been chosen.
- Check if the error message #N/A will appear.
- Prevent deletion of formulas by having cell protection.
- Ask if the user really wants to quit.

Defining the outputs – tips

If the output is a quotation or an invoice, you must describe what will appear on the invoice. For example, if the output is a printed A4 invoice then the invoice needs to include:

- company details – name, address, postcode, phone number, fax number, email address
- customer details – name, address, postcode
- the date
- the invoice number
- the word 'Invoice'
- a list of all the items purchased
- the quantity of each item
- the total cost of each item
- the sum of the total costs
- the VAT at the current rate
- the grand total
- payment details.

Outputs

The system should produce:

- an on-screen quotation that is clear and easy to understand, including the final total and the discount in Verdana font
- a printed version of this quotation
- error messages if an invalid combination is chosen
- an on-screen file of the quotations supplied to customers including the company name and address, the date the quotation was issued in dd/mm/yyyy format, the choices made and the total costs. For example:

Denton Hair	15/04/2008	Quarter page	Not colour	Back page	2 weeks	£ 446.00

5: Design

The project should be broken down into clear sub-tasks or modules, which should relate to the user's requirements. Produce design plans for each sub-task.

It usually takes much longer to produce designs on computer than by hand so it is best to hand draw your design plans. Use one side of A4 for each worksheet and use a ruler. It is a good idea to draw your designs on a blank grid from an Excel spreadsheet.

Good spreadsheet designs will include details of:

- sheet naming, named cells and cell ranges
- validation and cell protection
- labels and formulae used
- links between sheets
- general sheet layouts
- interfaces and screen designs
- macros and macro buttons
- any customised outputs.

Design do's

- Present your plans in a format such that a reasonably competent person could take them and make a start on setting up your system.
- Make them legible and neat – this person must be able read them.

Design don'ts

- Don't use screenshots from the actual system as part of your design plans.

Sub-tasks

I will break the *Denton Gazette* problem down into the following sub-tasks.

1 The Quotation worksheet

2   The Prices worksheet

3 The QuoteFile worksheet

4   Macros are needed to:
   a) file the quotations
   b) clear the screen
   c) print the quotation
   d) quit Excel with a warning
   e) navigate the system

5   Check for invalid combinations

6 Activate the start-up screen

The designs for the sub-tasks highlighted in **bold** are shown below.

Sub-task 1 – the Quotation worksheet

Figure 6.1 ▼

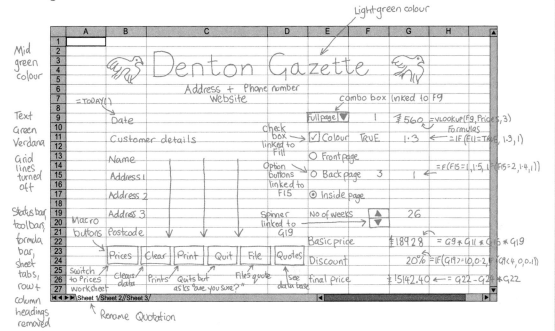

Sub-task 3 – the QuoteFile worksheet

Figure 6.2 ▼

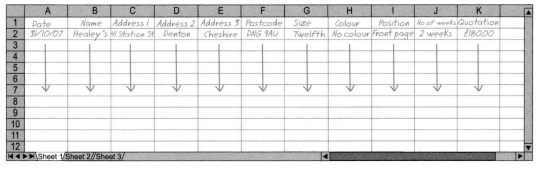

Sub-task 4(a) – macro to file the quotations

The macro must:

- go to the QuoteFile worksheet
- select row 2
- insert a row
- go back to Quotation worksheet
- select cells A30 to G30
- copy them
- paste Special > Paste Values
- go back to the Quotation worksheet
- end.

Sub-task 4(b) – macro to clear the screen

The macro must:

- select the Quotation worksheet
- select cells C11, H9, H14, I19 and A13 using **CTRL** and click
- clear the contents
- display a message box to say that 'The old data has been cleared'
- end.

Sub-task 6 – design of the start-up screen and options

Figure 6.3 ▶

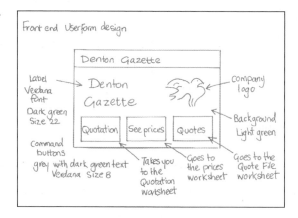

6: Implementation report

This section should contain clear evidence that you have implemented each part of your system.

This is likely to include the following as evidence of work done:

- an annotated screenshot of every worksheet
- printouts from the system
- a screenshot in formula view of any worksheet containing formulas
- annotated coding of any macros used
- screenshots of any UserForms and message boxes used
- commentary on the work you have done.

Implementation do's

- Be clear and concise.
- Use screenshots to support your explanation.
- Describe clearly the features of the software you have used.
- Describe any validation you have included.

Implementation don'ts

- Don't undersell the work you have done and remember that the person marking the project can only give credit for what they can see.
- Don't submit self-generating code and claim it as work done by you.
- Don't reproduce large tracts of Excel manuals.

Implementation report

In setting up the system, I have done the following tasks.

1 **Set up the Prices worksheet with details of the prices of advertisements**.

2 **Set up the Quotation worksheet with the input controls to enter the details of the advertisement**.

3 Set up a LOOKUP function on the Quotation worksheet to bring in the price data.

4 Set up the Quotation worksheet by entering formulas used in calculating the quotation.

5 **Set up formulas to calculate the final price of the quotation**.

6 Set up the QuoteFile worksheet to store details of the quotations issued.

7 Automated the filing of quotations using a macro and saved my file as a macro-enabled workbook.

8 **Automated clearing the current screen to enter a new quotation using a macro**.

9 Added navigation buttons for the system.

10 **Prevented invalid combinations**.

11 Protected the sheet from accidental deletion.

12 Customised the interface and added finishing touches.

13 Added the front-end.

Six of the steps (**bold**) are documented in this section as examples of documentation.

The implementation report would go on to explain and illustrate how each of the other sub-tasks was implemented.

1. Set up the Prices worksheet with details of the prices of advertisements

I named this worksheet **Prices**. I entered the sizes and prices. Each size has a number attached in column A which will be used later to look up the price.

I named the area A2 to C6 **Prices** (Figure 6.4).

Figure 6.4 ▶

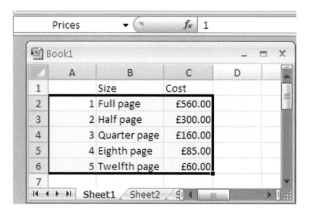

2. Set up the Quotation worksheet with the input controls to enter the details of the advertisement

This part of the system deals with the part of the worksheet where the advertisement options are entered as in Figure 6.5. I named this worksheet **Quotation**.

Figure 6.5 ▶

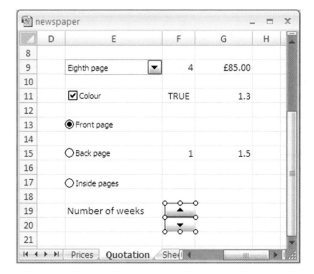

I dragged a combo box over cells A9 to C9 and linked it to cell C11. I set the input range to Prices!B2:B6. This will make the drop-down box display the sizes listed in column B on the Prices worksheet.

In cell F9 I placed a check box linked to cell H9. It returns TRUE when checked and FALSE when not.

Three option buttons were placed over cells F12 to F16 and linked to cell H14. The number returned in H14 gives the position of the advertisement – 1 for front page and 2 for back page and 3 for inside pages.

I set a spinner control over cells H19 and H20 linked to cell I19, setting the minimum value to 1 and maximum to 26 to allow for up to 26 weeks.

5. Set up formulas to calculate the final price of the quotation

The basic price of the quotation is calculated by multiplying the numbers in D11, I9, I14 and I19 of the Quotation worksheet.

The discount is calculated using the formula **=IF(I19>=10,0.2,IF (I19<4,0,0.1))**.

The final price is then the basic price minus the discount. The formulas are shown in Figure 6.6.

Figure 6.6 ▼

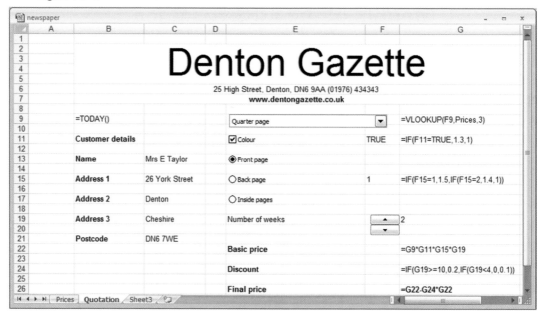

8. Automatically clearing the current screen to enter a new quotation with a macro

The cells on the screen that need clearing are cells C11, H9, H14, I14 and I19 of the Quotation worksheet.

I recorded a macro called Clear. I highlighted in turn the cells C11, H9, H14, I14 and I19 using **Ctrl** and click. I then clicked **Edit > Clear > Contents**

I finished the macro by adding a message box to say that the data has been cleared. The macro code generated is shown in Figure 6.7.

Figure 6.7 ▼

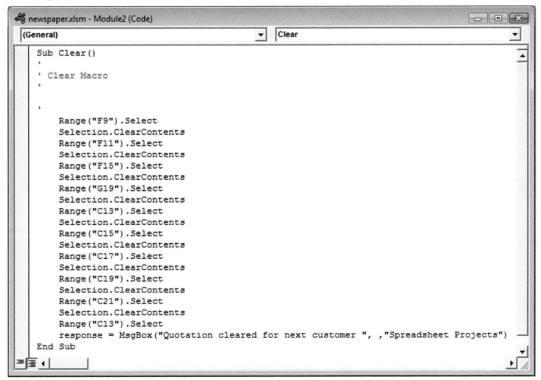

```
newspaper.xlsm - Module2 (Code)
(General)                                    Clear

Sub Clear()
'
' Clear Macro
'

'
    Range("F9").Select
    Selection.ClearContents
    Range("F11").Select
    Selection.ClearContents
    Range("F15").Select
    Selection.ClearContents
    Range("G19").Select
    Selection.ClearContents
    Range("C13").Select
    Selection.ClearContents
    Range("C15").Select
    Selection.ClearContents
    Range("C17").Select
    Selection.ClearContents
    Range("C19").Select
    Selection.ClearContents
    Range("C21").Select
    Selection.ClearContents
    Range("C13").Select
    response = MsgBox("Quotation cleared for next customer ", ,"Spreadsheet Projects")
End Sub
```

The message box looks like the one shown Figure 6.8.

Figure 6.8 ▶

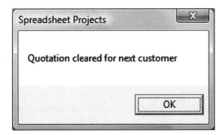

10. Prevented invalid combinations

It is not possible to have a full page or half page advertisement on the back or front pages. So I have written the macro code shown in Figure 6.9 to prevent this from happening.

Figure 6.9 ▼

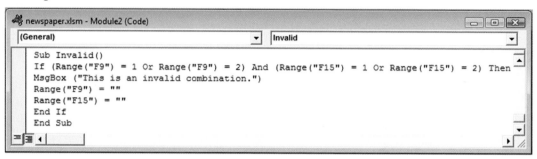

```
newspaper.xlsm - Module2 (Code)

(General)                                      Invalid

Sub Invalid()
If (Range("F9") = 1 Or Range("F9") = 2) And (Range("F15") = 1 Or Range("F15") = 2) Then
MsgBox ("This is an invalid combination.")
Range("F9") = ""
Range("F15") = ""
End If
End Sub
```

The macro is called **Invalid** and is run whenever a user clicks on an option button. I have done this by assigning it to the option buttons using **Assign macro**.

The second line of the macro checks if the value of C11 is 1 or 2 and if the value of H14 is 1 or 2. These are the invalid combinations.

If an invalid combination has been chosen, the message box in Figure 6.10 appears and C11 and H14 are cleared. Acceptable combinations are allowed, of course.

Figure 6.10 ▶

13. Added the front-end

I have set up a UserForm as shown in Figure 6.11 using the Visual Basic Editor.

Figure 6.11 ▶

I have added commands to the three buttons. The coding for the second button is given in Figure 6.12.

Figure 6.12 ▶

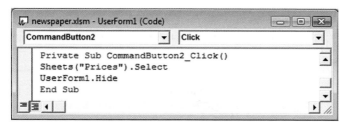

Click on the top button to get to the Quotation worksheet and close the UserForm. Click on the middle button to get to the Prices worksheet and close the UserForm. Click on the bottom button to get to the QuoteFile worksheet and close the UserForm.

I then wrote a macro called **Box** (Figure 6.13) to load this UserForm.

Figure 6.13 ▶

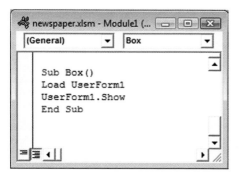

I then recorded a macro called **Auto_open** to remove the sheet tabs, row and column headings, scroll bars etc. This macro will run automatically when the file loads. I added a line at the end with the command Box (Figure 6.14) to run the Box macro when the file loads.

Figure 6.14 ▶

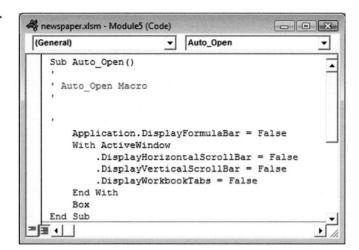

```
newspaper.xlsm - Module5 (Code)

(General)                          ▼    Auto_Open                  ▼

Sub Auto_Open()
'
' Auto_Open Macro
'


'
    Application.DisplayFormulaBar = False
    With ActiveWindow
        .DisplayHorizontalScrollBar = False
        .DisplayVerticalScrollBar = False
        .DisplayWorkbookTabs = False
    End With
    Box
End Sub
```

When you load the file the UserForm shown in Figure 6.11 appears. Note that there is an **Auto_close** macro that replaces the toolbars etc. when the file is closed.

7: Testing

Making a test plan

Testing is an integral part of developing an IT system. You should create a test plan and follow it.

The test plan should cover every aspect of your solution, saying exactly what will be tested, what the test (input) data will be and what the expected output data should be. Particular attention should be paid to checking that the output from the system (in this case the advertisement price quotation) is correct.

Test plans should include a range of suitable test data together with expected outcomes. Your test plan should include tests that will ensure that:

- output is 100 per cent accurate
- output is clear
- data input is validated
- printed output is as expected – such as it all fitting on one side of A4
- the solution meets the requirements of the client
- the solution is useable by the end-user and/or intended audience.

The test plan might say that the process of calculating the quotations will be tested for several different customers. The amount will also be calculated by the old method and the results compared.

Extreme data, for example, high but acceptable numbers or long double-barrelled surnames should be used to test that they fit. For example, you should work out the cost of the most expensive quotation and see if it fits in the column.

Erroneous test data, such as invalid combinations, will also be used in the tests and it is to be expected that they will be rejected. The system will also be tested by staff of the *Denton Gazette* (user testing).

Tests in the test plan should:

- be numbered
- state the purpose of the test
- specify the test data to be used
- outline the expected result.

You may want to set the tests out in a table.

Include sets of test data – data that you will enter and check that the outputs are as expected.

It is not necessary to perform dozens of similar tests. For example, if data validation has been applied to many cells, it is not necessary to repeat the same test on each cell.

Test plan

Setting up the Quotation worksheet – testing the input controls for entering the details of the advertisement

Test	Purpose of test	Test data used	Expected outcome	Actual outcome and comments
I	Contents of combo box	–	Should be full page, half page, quarter page, eighth page, twelfth page	
2	Combo box	Eighth page	Returns 4 in C11	
3	Test Check box returns TRUE/FALSE	Check the check box and uncheck it	Returns TRUE/FALSE in H9	
4	Test Option buttons	Back page	Returns 2 in H14	
5	Test the Spinner control	Increment spinner	Number in I19 should vary from 1 to 26.	

Preparing the quotations – testing the VLOOKUP, discount, cost of colour etc

Test	Purpose of test	Test data used	Expected outcome	Actual outcome and comments
6	Test VLOOKUP in D11 returns correct price	Twelfth page	Price should be £60	
7	Test VLOOKUP in D11 returns correct price	Full page	Price should be £560	
8	Test IF function in I9 returns correct value	Check colour	1.3 is returned in I9	
9	Test nested IF function in I14 returns correct value	Check front page	1.5 is returned in I14	
10	Test discount – boundary test	Spinner set at 10 weeks	Discount is 20%	
11	Test discount – boundary test	Spinner set at 9 weeks	Discount is 10%	
12	Test discount – boundary test	Spinner set at 4 weeks	Discount is 10%	
13	Test discount – boundary test	Spinner set at 3 weeks	Discount is 0%	

Calculating the total cost of the quotation

Test	Purpose of test	Test data used	Expected outcome	Actual outcome and comments
14	Test the formulas in I22 and I26 calculate bill correctly	Data set 1 (see below)	Bill worked out on calculator. Total cost = £1123.20	

Data set 1

Quarter page, front page, colour, 4 weeks

Data set 2

Full page, inside page, no colour, 3 weeks

Data set 3

Twelfth page, back page, colour, 20 weeks

Automating the filing of quotations

Test	Purpose of test	Test data used	Expected outcome	Actual outcome and comments
15	Test the Filequote macro to see if data is transferred correctly to the QuoteFile worksheet	Routine data – i.e. short name plus advertisement details	On running the macro, details should appear in the QuoteFile sheet	
16	Test the Filequote macro to see if data is transferred correctly to the QuoteFile worksheet and within the column widths set	Routine data BUT the longest name (Shelley and Reeves) plus advertisement details	On running the macro, details should appear in the QuoteFile sheet	
17	Test the Filequote macro when no data is entered	No data entered	A blank row should appear in the QuoteFile sheet	

Clearing the current screen to enter a new quotation

Test	Purpose of test	Test data used	Expected outcome	Actual outcome and comments
18	Test Clear macro	Routine details	Screen should be clear of data	
19	Test Clear macro after it has been run once	No data	Screen should be clear of data	

Testing the Quit macro

Test	Purpose of test	Test data used	Expected outcome	Actual outcome and comments
20	Test the 'Are you sure?' message of the Quit macro		Message box appears. Choose Yes – exits program; choose No – returns to program	

Testing invalid combinations

Test	Purpose of test	Test data used	Expected outcome	Actual outcome and comments
21	Checks invalid combinations are rejected	Front page, full page	Rejected – error message appears and data is cleared	
22		Back page, full page	Rejected – error message appears and data is cleared	
23		Front page, half page	Rejected – error message appears and data is cleared	
24		Back page, half page	Rejected – error message appears and data is cleared	
25		Inside pages, half page	Accepted	
26		Front page, quarter page	Accepted	

Customising the interface and finishing touches

Test	Purpose of test	Test data used	Expected outcome	Actual outcome and comments
27	Test the **Auto_open** macro starts the system correctly	Start the system up	System loads, removes Excel standard features and displays UserForm	
28	Test the **Auto_close** macro closes down the system properly	Close the system down	System closes and restores Excel standard features	

Testing the front-end

Test	Purpose of test	Test data used	Expected outcome	Actual outcome and comments
29	Test the 'Make a quotation' button	None, test button	Quotation worksheet loads UserForm closes	
30	Test the 'See prices' button	None, test button	Prices worksheet loads UserForm closes	
31	Test the 'See quotations' button	None, test button	QuoteFile worksheet loads UserForm closes	

User testing

Test	Purpose of test	Actual outcome and comments
32	Install the system in the office of the *Denton Gazette* for a week for the staff to see if it meets their requirements	

Testing

You now need to follow your test plan to test that your spreadsheet is fully working. The purpose of testing is to try to provoke failure. Better to find mistakes now than when installed at the user's office.

Try to make your system go wrong! Remember that you are testing if the data is processed correctly, not just whether a button works or not.

You must provide evidence in the form of screenshots and printouts. Number any output items and cross-reference them to the number of the test that it refers to. Try to present the evidence next to the test plan because it is much easier for the marker to handle. Try to avoid appendices which make it harder to mark. Examples are shown below.

Check that the actual results match the unexpected results. Provide screenshots and outline any corrective action needed or taken.

The end-user should also be involved in testing – if there is no real end-user get a colleague to go through your system. You could use a questionnaire and analyse the results. They may comment on:

- its ease of use
- consistencies of layout, fonts, buttons, colours used
- the look and feel of the interface
- simple vocabulary, spelling and grammar used.

Test results

Here is a selection of test results for the *Denton Gazette* system.

Test	Purpose of test	Test data used	Expected outcome	Actual outcome and comments
I	Contents of combo box	–	Should be full page, half page, quarter page, eighth page, twelfth page	Full page, half page, quarter page, eighth page, twelfth page

Figure 6.15 ▶

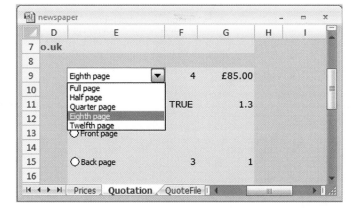

| 2 | Combo box | Eighth page | Returns 4 in C11 | Returns 4 in C11 |

Figure 6.16 ▶

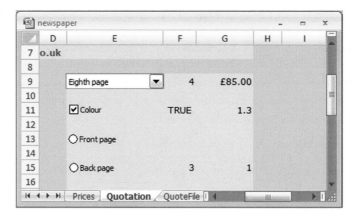

Test	Purpose of test	Test data used	Expected outcome	Actual outcome and comments
6	Test VLOOKUP in D11 returns correct price	Twelfth page	Price should be £60	The price is £60

Figure 6.17 ▶

10	Test discount – boundary test	Spinner set at 10 weeks	Discount is 20%	Discount is 20%

Figure 6.18 ▶

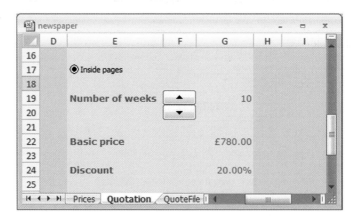

8: User guide

user guide is just that — a guide for the **user** or **users** of your system. It should include details

- the purpose of the system
- the minimum hardware and software requirements needed to run your system – you can find these at the Microsoft website
- how to install the system
- getting started
- the main menu options
- how to perform each of the routine tasks that make up your system
- common problems or error messages and possible solutions
- security measures, back-up procedures and passwords needed.

ser guide do's

- It should contain simple, clear, step-by-step instructions about using your system.
- It should be jargon-free and well illustrated.
- It might form or be part of online help built into the system.

ser guide don'ts

- It should not be a guide to using the software, but a guide to your system.
- Don't include large tracts of text from user manuals.
- Try to avoid using jargon.

rt of a user guide is given below.

User guide to the *Denton Gazette* quotation system

4 Getting started

4.1 To start the system double click the file icon called **newspaper.xlsm**. You will see the menu shown in Figure 6.23.

Figure 6.23 ▶

Calculating the total cost of the quotation

Test	Purpose of test	Test data used	Expected outcome	Actual outcome and comments
14	Test the formulas I22 and I26 calculate bill correctly	Data set I (see below)	Bill worked out on calculator. Total cost = £1123.20	Total cost is £1123.20

Data set 1

Quarter page, front page, colour, 4 weeks

Figure 6.19 ▶

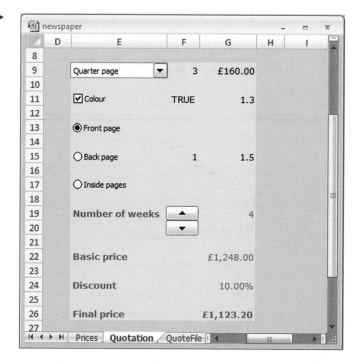

Test	Purpose of test	Test data used	Expected outcome	Actual outcome and comments
20	Test the 'Are you sure?' message of the **Quit** macro		Message box appears. Choose Yes – exits program; choose No – returns to program	Message box appears. Choose Yes – exits program; choose No – returns to program

Figure 6.20 ▶

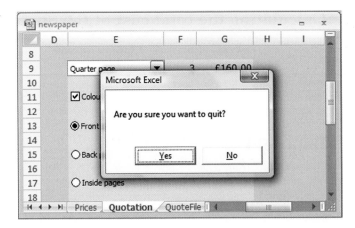

Test	Purpose of test	Test data used	Expected outcome	Actual outcome and comments
21	Checks invalid combinations are rejected	Front page, full page	Rejected – error message appears and data is cleared	Error message appears (Figure 6.21) and data is cleared when OK is clicked (Figure 6.22)

Figure 6.21 ▶

Figure 6.22 ▶

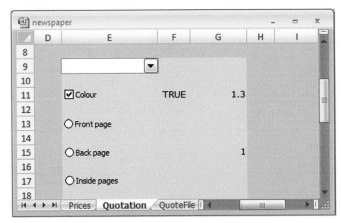

Test	Purpose of test	Actual ou
32	Install the system in the office of the *Denton Gazette* for a week for the staff to see if it meets their requirements	System wo

User testing

The system was tested by Katie Walker, a clerk at the had used the system for a few days she made the follow

The system issued quotations easily and quickly, which when dealing with phone enquiries.

She would have liked the system to produce carbon co automatically, as opposed to clicking **Print** a number

She thought the system was potentially user-friendly b the need for a start-up screen. All she wanted to do wa slowed her down – and eventually became irritating du day.

She said that it was difficult to enter a new customer a much space she had to enter the customer name in. Sh quotation would have had more of a professional feel i footer.

As she used the system, the file of customer quotations eventually going off the screen. She found she needed search for a particular quotation or to sort them into a

She was worried about how to back-up the system and in case of computer breakdown. She also forgot to save wondered if this could be built in to the system.

4.2 To make a quotation click on the first button

4.3 To see and edit prices, click on the second button.

4.4 To see past quotations, click on the third button.

5 Using the system

5.1 Making a quotation (see Figure 6.24).

Figure 6.24 ▼

5.1.1 To make a quotation, enter the customer details – name, address etc.

5.1.2 Click on the drop-down box to select the advertisement size (see Figure 6.25).

Figure 6.25 ▶

5.1.3 If you want a colour advertisement, click on the check box.

5.1.4 Choose the page where you want the advertisement placed (see Figure 6.26).

Figure 6.26 ▶

5.1.5 Use the spinner to adjust the number of weeks that you require. The price will be displayed automatically (see Figure 6.27).

Figure 6.27 ▶

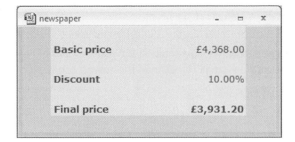

The final quotation screen will look the one in Figure 6.28.

Figure 6.28 ▶

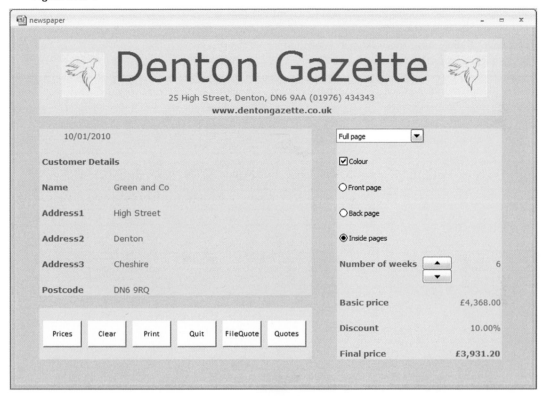

5.2.1 You have a variety of other options:

- clicking the **Prices** button allows you to see and edit prices
- clicking the **Clear** button deletes this customer's data
- clicking the **Print** button prints a quotation
- clicking the **Quit** button exits from the system
- clicking the **File the quote** stores the quotation on the QuoteFile worksheet.

This user guide would go on to describe:

- how to edit prices
- how to file quotations
- how to review quotations
- sorting quotations into order
- error messages
- adding a customer.

9: Technical documentation

You may also need to produce technical documentation for your solution. This is documentation for the people who will maintain the system, rather than those who use it.

Technical documentation should include:

- the original specification
- hardware, software and other resource requirements
- instructions for installing and opening the spreadsheet
- instructions for regular maintenance of the system – such as archiving records when a file is too big or adding additional customers to the system
- details of all calculations, formulas and functions used
- macro coding
- details of verification and validation procedures
- passwords and security information.

10: Evaluation

An evaluation report is an important part of a project at this level. You will need to ask yourself:

- What was I supposed to do?
- Have I done it?
- Have I done it well?
- What limitations are there that might affect the user?
- What improvements could I make to my system?

You must refer to the original user requirements.

Evaluation do's

- You must look at your original end-user requirements and report on whether you have achieved what you wanted – including successes, problems and possible solutions.
- No system is perfect – there will always be room for improvement. Outline any limitations and further possible developments.

Evaluation don'ts

- Don't moan about lack of time – time-management is your responsibility.
- Don't pretend it is all working when some parts are incomplete – do not be afraid to tell the truth.
- Don't report on how well you did but focus on how well your system achieved its aims.

Evaluation report

To evaluate my system I will look at the initial end-user requirements and also take on board comments made by the users when testing the system. There were originally 20 end-user requirements and I will refer to each one to see if I have met the requirement, giving evidence if appropriate.

1 I believe the system is user-friendly and easy to understand. Macros are used to help the user – for example in customising the screen and clearing the data.

2 The system does calculate the cost of an advertisement given the size, position, number of weeks and colour of the advertisement.

3 The user can select the different options with a mouse using the drop-down lists, the check box, the option buttons and the spinner.

4 The price is calculated automatically for the customer.

5 The new system saves the user time compared with the current manual method. The old system averaged nearly 30 seconds to complete a calculation, even using a calculator. The new system takes less than 5 seconds.

6 There is a file within the system in which quotations can be stored in sufficient detail so that they can be located easily and referred back to if necessary. This stops paperwork being misplaced and should help the company become more organised in their processing of quotations.

7 Filing the quotations is automated to make it quicker and easier for the user.

8   Users can clear quotations automatically with one mouse click. This will save time.

9   There is a quit icon to exit the system – but there is a double check in case the user quits accidentally.

10 A full printed quotation can be produced at the click of a button.

(The report would go on to consider the remaining 10 original user requirements.)

I believe that I have implemented the system well. The screens are easy to read, data input is via the mouse and so is quick and easy to do and my user testing threw up very few problems.

Limitations and possible enhancements

1   I might, in a future version of the system, remove the start-up screen by adjusting the Auto_open macro so that it is quicker for users to start work.

2   I could customise the user interface further by running the whole system from a UserForm.

3   It might be easier to handle if every quotation was issued with a quotation reference number and a date of issue to aid searching in the future.

4   Over a period of time this file will get very large and the user needs to establish procedures for clearing out quotations that are not needed. This could be done manually in Excel but I might try to automate this feature in the future.

5   Adding a customer is not easy at present and I would like to add a macro to do this.

6   My user was concerned about saving data and backups. I need to edit the FileQuote macro so that it saves the file whenever a quotation is filed. I can easily edit the VBA coding to do this. It is only one additional line: **ActiveWorkbook.Save**

7   I will need to discuss back-up options with my user and provide advice in the user guide.

8   I could extend the system to produce an invoice for customers who decide to place an advertisement and a receipt when they have paid.

Cell protection exercise

Cell protection can prevent cells being changed, either accidentally or mischievously, by the user. First you must set cells to locked or unlocked. Then you must protect the sheet.

To lock and unlock cells and to protect and unprotect the sheet, on the **Home** tab in the **Cells** group, click **Format > Lock Cell** or **Protect Sheet** or **Unprotect Sheet**.

In the spreadsheet **mileage.xlsx**, only cell A1 needs to change.

1 Set up the cell protection so that A1 can change but none of the other data/ formulas can be altered.
2 Test that it works for both protected and unprotected cells.

IF, check box and option button exercise

At the Hotel Manhattan, a single room costs £60 a night and a double room costs £90. An evening meal at the Delta Hotel costs £25. Set up a spreadsheet (Figure 7.2) to calculate the price of a stay.

Figure 7.2 ▶

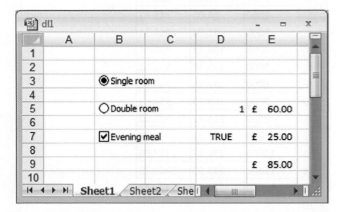

1 Set up two option buttons for the two different types of room. Make sure that the buttons are left aligned. Link the option buttons to cell D5.
2 Put a formula in cell E5 that will display the price of the selected room. Format this cell to currency.
3 Add a check box for an evening meal. Link the check box to cell D7.
4 Put a formula in cell E7 that will display the price of the evening meal if selected. Format this cell to currency.
5 Put a formula in cell E9 that will display the total price.

Nested IF exercise 1

Alan Richards lives in Birmingham and regularly travels to the following towns on business:

Bristol   87 miles away
Norwich   159 miles away
Wigan   91 miles away

■ 11: Getting your project ready to hand in

When your project is finished you should:

■ Produce a front cover – your name, centre and candidate number should be clear. Make it look good – you have spent a lot of time on this project, so don't hand in something that looks like you don't care.
■ Get your project in order – it should be in the order in which it will be marked. Page numbering and the use of headers and footers are to be encouraged.
■ Produce a contents page that clearly cross-references to each section in the project.
■ Bind your project securely. Coursework often has to be sent away for checking – it needs to be firmly held together, but ring binders are not encouraged.

7 Excel practice exercise

1: Data validation exercise

Data validation is important to ensure that only reasonable an entered into cells.

Look at the worksheet called **mileage.xlsx** shown in Figure 7.1

Figure 7.1 ▶

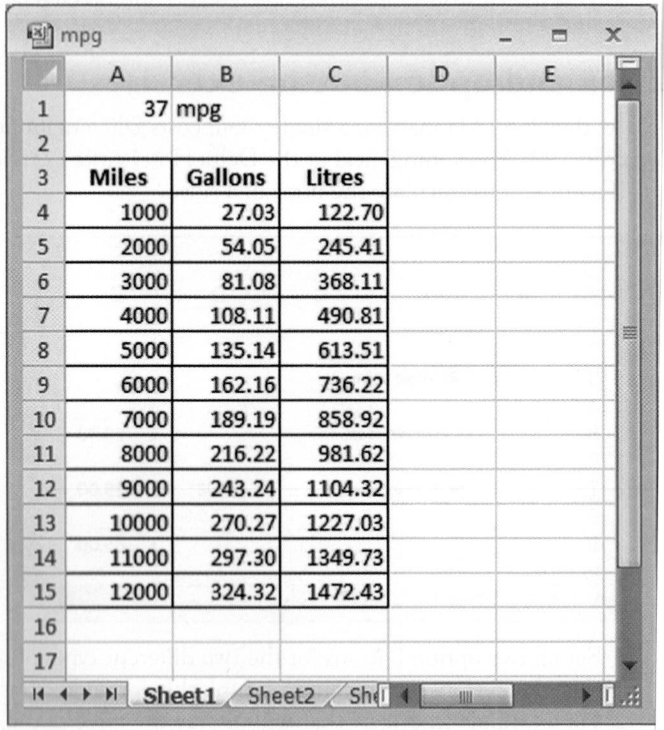

	A	B	C	D	E
1	37	mpg			
2					
3	**Miles**	**Gallons**	**Litres**		
4	1000	27.03	122.70		
5	2000	54.05	245.41		
6	3000	81.08	368.11		
7	4000	108.11	490.81		
8	5000	135.14	613.51		
9	6000	162.16	736.22		
10	7000	189.19	858.92		
11	8000	216.22	981.62		
12	9000	243.24	1104.32		
13	10000	270.27	1227.03		
14	11000	297.30	1349.73		
15	12000	324.32	1472.43		
16					
17					

1 Set up a suitable validation check for the miles per gallon i mpg should lie between 50 and 15 inclusive.

2 Test that it works – you will need to test it with data that i data that is invalid. In this example you would need to che
   a) numbers bigger than 50 are rejected – test it with 51
   b) numbers smaller than 15 are rejected – test it with 14
   c) 15 and 50 are accepted.

3 Save the file.

Because he uses his own car, his company pay him 38p a mile. If he gets back after seven o'clock, he can also claim a meal allowance of £12. Can you set up a spreadsheet to work out his mileage claim? Have a look at Figure 7.3.

Figure 7.3 ▶

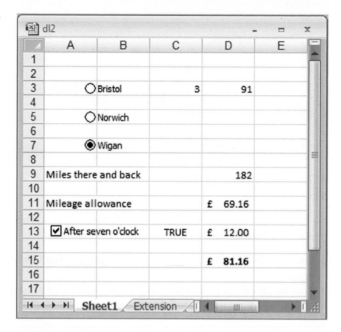

Extension

Extend the spreadsheet to include an additional town (Shrewsbury 47 miles away).

5: Nested IF exercise 2

1 Set up the spreadsheet shown in Figure 7.4.

Figure 7.4 ▶

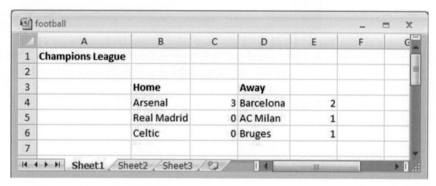

2 Save the file as **football.xlsx**.

3 Use the **IF** function to display in column F whether the result was a home win or an away win as shown in Figure 7.5.

Figure 7.5 ▶

	A	B	C	D	E	F	G
1	Champions League						
2							
3		Home		Away			
4		Arsenal	3	Barcelona	2	Home	
5		Real Madrid	0	AC Milan	1	Away	
6		Celtic	0	Bruges	1	Away	
7							

4 Test that it works by changing the scores.
5 Save your file.

So far it works for only two outcomes – a home win and an away win. Clearly in a football match there can be a draw.

6 Use a nested IF statement to say if a match is a home win, an away win or a draw.
7 Test by changing the score of the Celtic game to 1–1 as shown in Figure 7.6. Test it for the other matches too.

Figure 7.6 ▶

	A	B	C	D	E	F	G
1	Champions League						
2							
3		Home		Away			
4		Arsenal	3	Barcelona	2	Home	
5		Real Madrid	0	AC Milan	1	Away	
6		Celtic	1	Bruges	1	Draw	
7							

8 There are 3 points for a win, 0 for a loss and 1 for a draw. Extend your spreadsheet to include the number of points gained by the home team in column G.
9 Save your file.

6: LOOKUP exercise 1

1 In a new worksheet enter the information shown in Figure 7.7.

Figure 7.7 ▶

Productfile

	A	B	C	D
1	**Product number**	**Name**	**Price**	
2	C065	Mouse mat	£ 4.99	
3	C123	Poster	£ 2.50	
4	C157	Mug	£ 5.99	
5	C232	Six greetings cards	£ 4.50	
6	C306	Tea towel	£ 5.99	

Sheet1 Sheet2 Sheet3

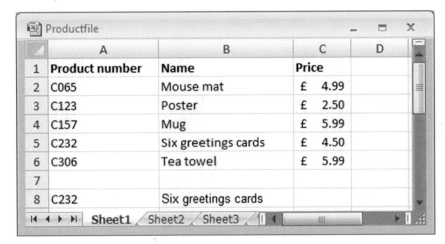

2 Define the area from A2 to C6 as **Items**. Highlight the cells. On the **Formulas** tab in the **Defined Names** group, click **Define Name** and set the name to **Items**.

3 In cell B8 enter **=VLOOKUP(A8,Items,2)**. It will say #N/A in B8.

4 Type a product number in A8, the product name will appear in B8 as shown in Figure 7.8.

Figure 7.8 ▶

Productfile

	A	B	C	D
1	**Product number**	**Name**	**Price**	
2	C065	Mouse mat	£ 4.99	
3	C123	Poster	£ 2.50	
4	C157	Mug	£ 5.99	
5	C232	Six greetings cards	£ 4.50	
6	C306	Tea towel	£ 5.99	
7				
8	C232	Six greetings cards		

Sheet1 Sheet2 Sheet3

5 Create another lookup so that the product's price (formatted to currency) appears in C8. Save the workbook as **productfile.xlsx**.

6 Check that the lookups work for all possible values. Investigate what happens if you type in a false product number in this workbook:

- try a value that is too big like C350
- try one that is too small like C050
- try one that doesn't exist like C150.

7: LOOKUP exercise 2

1 A gas company has a file on its customers, part of which is shown in Figure 7.9.

Figure 7.9 ▼

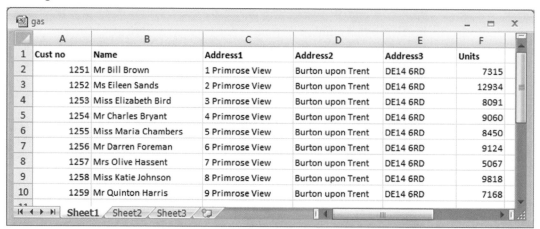

Gas costs 4.3p per KWh (unit). The bill also includes an 8p per day standing charge and 5 per cent VAT.

2 Open the file **gas.xlsx**.
3 Highlight the customer data and give the data a name.
4 On Sheet2 set up lookups so that if the customer number is typed in cell A2, the customer's name, address and units used appear as shown in Figure 7.10.

Figure 7.10 ▶

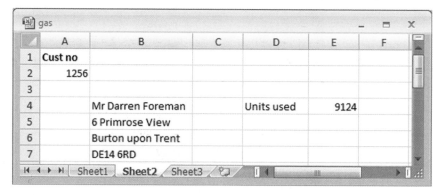

5 Check that it works for at least four different customer numbers.

6 Extend this sheet to calculate the whole bill as shown in Figure 7.11. To get the number of days use the formula: **=E2–E1**

Figure 7.11 ▶

	A	B	C	D	E	F
1	Cust no			Start of period	01/11/2011	
2	1256			End of period	01/02/2012	
3						
4		Mr Darren Foreman		Units used	9124	
5		6 Primrose View		Cost per unit	£ 0.043	
6		Burton upon Trent		Cost of gas	£ 392.33	
7		DE14 6RD				
8				No of days	92	
9				Standing charge per day	£ 0.08	
10				Standing charge	£ 7.36	
11						
12				Total	£ 399.69	
13						
14				VAT	£ 19.98	
15						
16				Total including VAT	£ 419.68	
17						

7 Test the workbook – as you enter different customer numbers, the bill will change.

8 Save the workbook.

Hint   Use the **Increase Decimal** button on E5 to format the cell to 3 decimal places.

8: LOOKUP exercise 3

In this exercise, you will practise taking data from a table and inserting it in a spreadsheet using Naming cells, LOOKUP functions and combo boxes

1 Open the file **postage.xlsx** that can be downloaded from the Internet. Data giving the cost of sending an airmail letter abroad is given in Sheet1 (Figure 7.12). The data defining which countries are in which zone for postage rates, is in Sheet2 (Figure 7.13).

Figure 7.12 ▶

	A	B	C	D	E	F
1	Airmail Letters					
2						
3		Weight in grams	Europe	World zone 1	World zone 2	
4	1	10	£0.48	£0.54	£0.54	
5	2	20	£0.48	£0.78	£0.78	
6	3	40	£0.69	£1.17	£1.24	
7	4	60	£0.90	£1.58	£1.74	
8	5	80	£1.10	£2.00	£2.24	
9	6	100	£1.31	£2.42	£2.74	
10	7	120	£1.52	£2.83	£3.23	
11	8	140	£1.73	£3.25	£3.72	
12	9	160	£1.94	£3.66	£4.22	
13	10	180	£2.15	£4.08	£4.71	
14	11	200	£2.35	£4.50	£5.20	
15	12	220	£2.54	£4.89	£5.67	
16	13	240	£2.74	£5.28	£6.13	
17						
18						

Figure 7.13 ▶

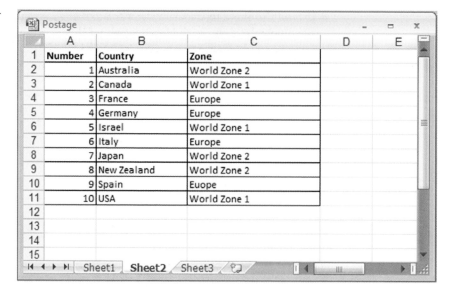

2 Go to Sheet1. Highlight the cells from A4 to E16. On the **Formulas** tab in the **Defined Names** group, click **Define Name.** Enter the name **Weight** and click **OK**.

3 Go to Sheet2. Highlight the cells from A2 to C11. On the **Formulas** tab in the **Defined Names** group, click **Define Name**. Enter the name **Zone** and click **OK**.

4 Click the Name Box drop-down arrow to see a list of all the named ranges – as in Figure 7.14.

Figure 7.14 ▶

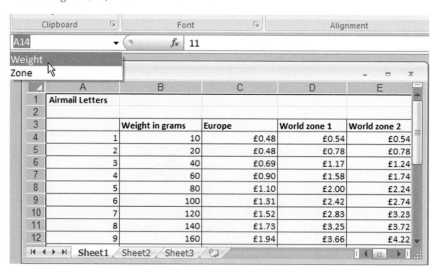

5 If Sheet2 is not already selected, switch to Sheet2. On the **Developer** tab in the **Controls** group, click **Insert > Combo Box (Form Control)** and drag out a box on the screen over cells E4 and F4 (see Figure 7.15).

Figure 7.15 ▶

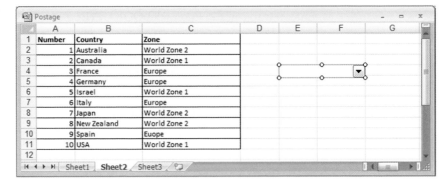

Note: If you hold the **ALT** key down, you will align the combo box with the cell gridlines. The smallest height for a combo box is slightly more than the default height for a cell.

6 Right click on the combo box and click **Format Control**. The Format Control dialogue box appears.

7 In the Input Range box enter **B2:B11**.

8 In the Cell link box enter **E2**.

9 Change the drop-down lines to **6**. Click **OK** and save your work.

If you click the arrow on your Combo box, you get six lines of different choices. If you choose the fourth item on the list (Germany) cell E2 changes to **4** (Figure 7.16).

Figure 7.16 ▶

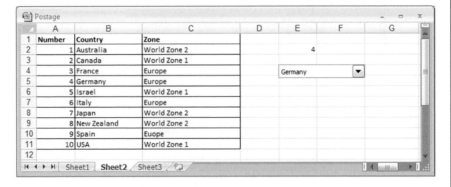

Remember: When you choose an item in a combo box list, the linked cell stores the number of that item, not the item itself. In this case E2 stores 4.

Linking the LOOKUP and combo boxes

A combo box and the LOOKUP function become very powerful when used together.

1 Enter **6** into cell **E2**. Enter **=VLOOKUP(E2,Zone,2)** into cell F2.

This looks in E2 and finds the value 6. Then it looks in the first column (column A) in the Zone table until it finds the row with 6 in it. It then finds the data in this row in column 2 of the table. It will return the value Italy as shown in Figure 7.17.

2 Check that it does return the value **Italy**.

Figure 7.17 ▶

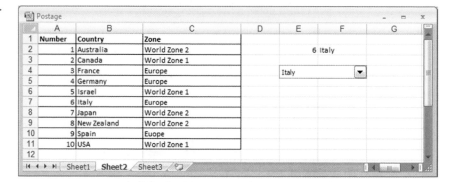

3 Change the value of E2 to **9**. Check that **Spain** appears in cell F2.
4 Using the combo box click **New Zealand**. Check that New Zealand appears in F2. The column may not be wide enough to fit in New Zealand so select cell F2. On the **Home** tab in the **Cells** group, click **Format > AutoFit Column Width**.
5 Enter **=VLOOKUP(E2,Zone,3)** into cell G2 and save your file.
6 Test that as you select a country using the combo box, the zone for that country appears in G2. You will need to make column G slightly wider as well. Figure 7.18 shows USA as the selected country.

Figure 7.18 ▶

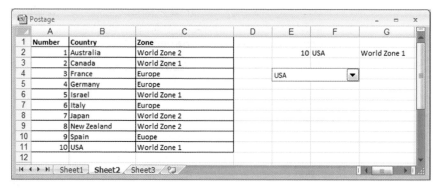

Looking up the prices for different zones

1 Switch to Sheet1. Set up a **combo box** over cell B18, as shown in Figure 7.19, linked to cell **B20**. The input range is **B4** to **B16**.
2 Set up the borders to cells **C20** to **E21** as shown in Figure 7.19. On the **Home** tab in the **Font** group, click the **Borders** drop-down box > **All Borders**.

3 Enter the headings in cells C20 to E20 as shown in Figure 7.19.

4 Use **VLOOKUP** in cells C21, D21 and E21 to find the price of postage to each zone (for the weight shown in the combo box).

Figure 7.19 ▶

Postage

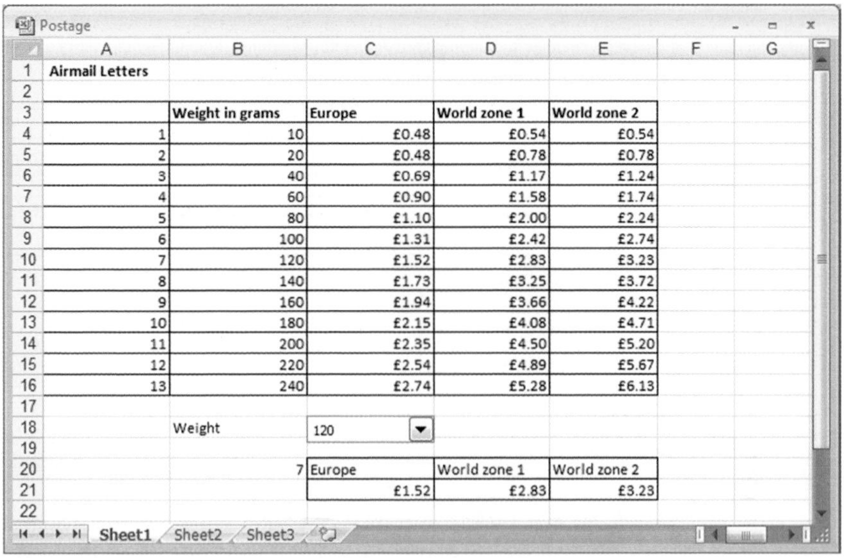

	A	B	C	D	E	F	G
1	**Airmail Letters**						
2							
3		**Weight in grams**	**Europe**	**World zone 1**	**World zone 2**		
4	1	10	£0.48	£0.54	£0.54		
5	2	20	£0.48	£0.78	£0.78		
6	3	40	£0.69	£1.17	£1.24		
7	4	60	£0.90	£1.58	£1.74		
8	5	80	£1.10	£2.00	£2.24		
9	6	100	£1.31	£2.42	£2.74		
10	7	120	£1.52	£2.83	£3.23		
11	8	140	£1.73	£3.25	£3.72		
12	9	160	£1.94	£3.66	£4.22		
13	10	180	£2.15	£4.08	£4.71		
14	11	200	£2.35	£4.50	£5.20		
15	12	220	£2.54	£4.89	£5.67		
16	13	240	£2.74	£5.28	£6.13		
17							
18		Weight	120				
19							
20		7	Europe	World zone 1	World zone 2		
21			£1.52	£2.83	£3.23		
22							

Sheet1 Sheet2 Sheet3

Hint The formula in cell C21 will be **=VLOOKUP(B20,Weight,3)**

5 Format cells C21, D21 and E21 to currency and test that as you select a weight in the combo box, the correct prices appear for each of the three zones.

Short cut: If you are in the middle of a lookup and you can't remember what name you used, press F3 and choose from the list of names in the Paste names dialogue box.

Using two combo boxes

You can use two combo boxes – one to select the weight (i.e. the row in the weight table) and the other to select the zone (i.e. the column of the weight table). The software will automatically calculate the cost of the letter.

1 Enter the data in cells **A23** to **B25** as shown in Figure 7.20.

Figure 7.20 ▶

Postage

	A	B	C
22			
23	1	Europe	
24	2	World zone 1	
25	3	World zone 2	
26			

Sheet1 Sheet2 Sheet3

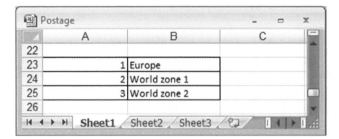

2 Enter the word **Zone** in cell D18.

3 Add another combo box over cell E18, linked to cell **B21**, getting its data from cells **B23** to **B25** as shown in Figure 7.21 and check that it works.

The link cell B21 will be used to find the correct column of the table.

4 Enter this formula in cell D24 =VLOOKUP(B20,Weight, B21+2).

Figure 7.21 ▼

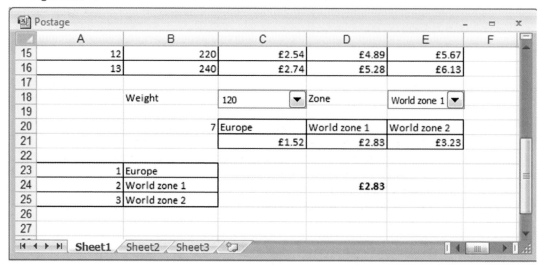

5 Format D24 to currency and bold. Fully test that the price in D24 is correct for all weights and zones. Then you can delete all the data in cells C20 to E21.

6 Format the data in cells B20, B21, A23, A24, A25, B23, B24 and B25 to font colour **white** and remove any borders (Figure 7.22).

Figure 7.22 ▼

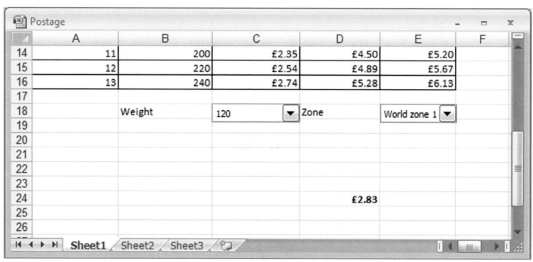

7 You may wish to add a title in cell C24.

Extension

Edit this spreadsheet so that it has a combo box for the weight and another combo box for the country.

9: Spinner exercise 1

When you format a spinner, you can set the incremental change to any whole number – but how can you set up a spinner so that it goes up and down by a half or a tenth?

Setting up a spinner to go up and down by 0.1

Suppose you want the spinner to have a minimum value of 0, a maximum of 10 and an incremental change of 0.1.

1 On a new spreadsheet, insert a spinner over cells **B2** and **B3**.
2 Right click on the spinner and choose **Format Control**.
3 Set the minimum value to **0**, the maximum value to **100**, the incremental change to **1** and set the cell link to **C3**.
4 In cell D3 enter the formula **=C3/10**.
5 Test that as you click the spinner, the number in D3 increases or decreases by 0.1 (Figure 7.23).

Figure 7.23 ▶

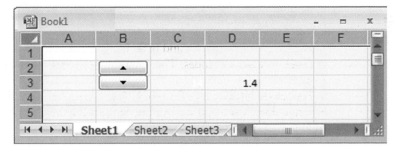

6 Hide the number in C3 by formatting the font colour to **white**.
7 Set up another spinner that makes a number go up and down by a half (0.5).

10: Spinner exercise 2

The following steps show you how to add a spinner to a spreadsheet used for storing details of share prices and profits made.

1 Enter the row, column headings and data as shown in Figure 7.24.

Figure 7.24 ▼

	A	B	C	D	E	F	G	H
		No of shares	Purchase	Current		Profit	Total	%
1	Company	held	price	price		per share	profit	profit
2	Standard Life	150	209	213				
3	BP	300	572	585				
4	Aviva	423	398	378				
5	ITV	79	45	53				
6	Prudential	700	497	639				
7								

2 In F2 enter the formula **=D2-C2**

3 Copy the formula into **F3, F4, F5** and **F6**.

4 In G2 enter the formula **=F2*B2** (number of shares multiplied by profit per share).

5 Copy the formula into **G3, G4, G5** and **G6**.

6 In H2 enter the formula **=F2/C2**. Remember, percentage profit is *profit/ purchase price*.

7 Copy the formula into **H3, H4, H5** and **H6**.

9 Format column **H** as percentage.

10 In G7 enter the formula **=SUM(G2:G6)**

We will use a spinner to edit the current price of the shares.

11 Add a spinner over cell E2 linked to cell **D2**.

12 Repeat this for rows **3, 4, 5** and **6** (Figure 7.25).

Figure 7.25 ▶

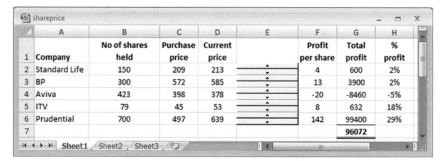

13 Save your file as **shareprice.xlsx**.

Note: Even when a cell has a spinner attached, you can still type a value into the cell.

11: Spinner exercise 3

Load the file **gas.xlsx** from Lookup exercise 2. Add a spinner to Sheet2 to increase and decrease the customer number by 1 so that you can cycle through all the records in the file.

12: Scroll bar exercise

A **scroll bar** enables you to increase or decrease the value in a cell by clicking the control or dragging the slide bar. As shown in Figure 7.26, a scroll bar can be either horizontal or vertical.

Figure 7.26 ▶

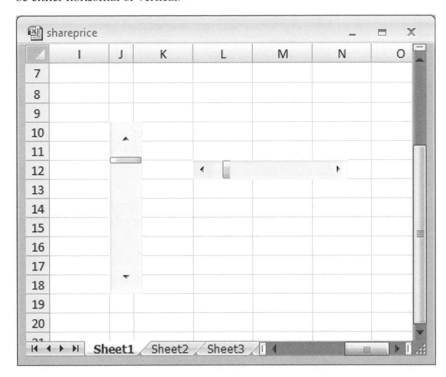

To insert a scrollbar, on the **Developer** tab, click **Insert > Scroll Bar (Form Control)** – the third button on the second row.

Figure 7.27 ▼

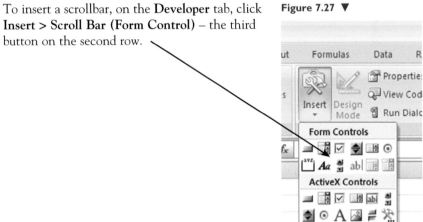

1 Load the file **shareprice.xlsx**.
2 Replace the spinners with scrollbars.
3 Set the maximum values to 1000 (Figure 7.28).

Figure 7.28 ▶

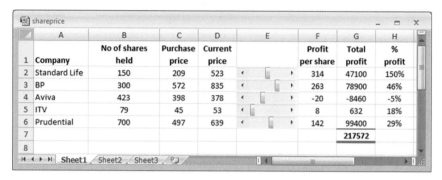

	A	B	C	D	E	F	G	H
		No of shares	Purchase	Current		Profit	Total	%
1	Company	held	price	price		per share	profit	profit
2	Standard Life	150	209	523	◄ ▌ ►	314	47100	150%
3	BP	300	572	835	◄ ▌ ►	263	78900	46%
4	Aviva	423	398	378	◄ ▌ ►	-20	-8460	-5%
5	ITV	79	45	53	◄ ▌ ►	8	632	18%
6	Prudential	700	497	639	◄ ▌ ►	142	99400	29%
7							217572	
8								

Sheet1 / Sheet2 / Sheet3

13: Macro exercise 1

Sometimes you need to remove the gridlines to customise an Excel spreadsheet. It is easy to do – on the **Page Layout** tab in the **Sheet Options** group, simply uncheck the **Gridlines View** box.

1 Record a macro called **GridOff** to remove the gridlines from the screen.
2 Record a second macro called **GridOn** to put the gridlines back.
3 Test both your new macros.

Extension – a toggle button

You can create a single macro that turns the grid off if it is on, and turns the grid on if it is off.

1 On the **Developer** tab in the **Code** group, click **Macros > GridOff > Edit** and type in the coding shown in Figure 7.29.

```
Sub GridToggle()
    mygrid = ActiveWindow.DisplayGridlines
    ActiveWindow.DisplayGridlines = Not mygrid
End Sub
```

Be careful – the wording has to be exactly right. This **GridToggle** macro toggles the gridlines, i.e. run it once to remove the gridlines; run it again to put them back. The second line reads the old value – are the gridlines on or off? The third line sets the new value to the opposite of the old value.

Figure 7.29 ▼

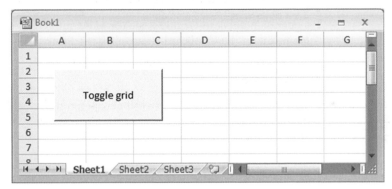

2 Close Visual Basic Editor and run the macro twice to test that it works.

3 Set up a button to run this macro (Figure 7.30).

Figure 7.30 ►

4 Set up a macro to turn the **sheet tabs** off – click **Office Button > Excel Options > Advanced** and uncheck the **Show sheet tabs** box.

5 Set up a second macro to turn the sheet tabs on.

6 Set up a third macro, called **TabsToggle**, to toggle the worksheet tabs on and off.

7 Remember to save your work as a macro-enabled file.

14: Macro exercise 2

You often need to update figures. A shop might store details of the number of items in stock and today's total sales (Figure 7.31).

Figure 7.31 ▶

Every time the shop sells a packet of Corn Flakes, the number in C2 has to be increased by one. You need set up a macro to automate this procedure.

1 Start recording the macro – call it **AddOne**.
2 Put a formula in cell D2 to add **1** to the number in **C2**.
3 Copy the number in D2 and paste the value into C2 – select C2 and on the **Home** tab in the **Clipboard** group, click the **Paste** drop-down list and click **Paste Values**.
4 Delete the number in **D2**.
5 Stop recording.
6 Test that the macro works. Each time you run it 1 should be added to the number in C2.
7 Save the file as **Update.xlsm** (macro-enabled).

15: Macro exercise 3

At the end of each day, the shopkeeper needs to update the stock levels – to see the new stock level and decide if any new stock needs to be ordered (Figure 7.32).

Figure 7.32 ▼

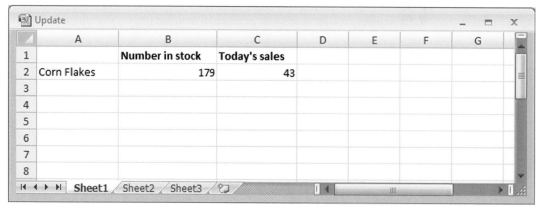

1 Record a macro called **Update** – this will calculate how many boxes of Corn Flakes are still in stock, update the number in stock and reset today's sales to zero.
2 Set up a button over cell **F2** to run the Update macro.
3 Test the macro thoroughly.
4 Save the file.

16: Macro exercise 4

Of course shops stock more than one product.

1 Enter at least four more products into Sheet1 as shown in Figure 7.33.

Figure 7.33 ▶

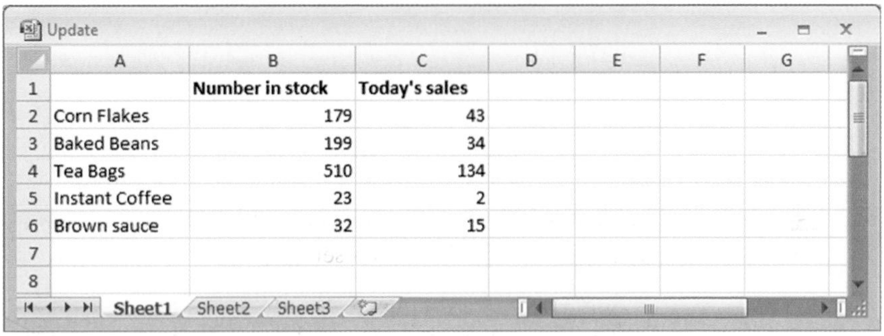

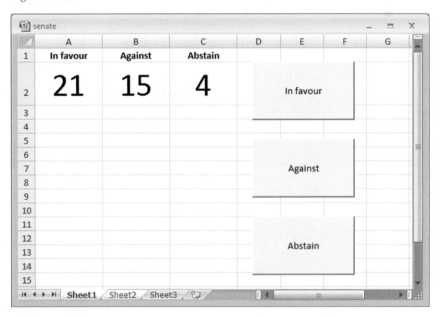

2 Record a macro called **Update2** to update all stock levels for all the products.

Extension

The US Senate is considering an electronic voting system for the 100 senators. When they vote, they will simply click a button on a screen as shown in Figure 7.34.

Figure 7.34 ▶

The computer automatically counts the votes.

Set up a system with three macros, so that each time a button is clicked the appropriate number increases by 1. Save the system as **senate.xlsm**.

17: Message box exercises

It is possible to customise message boxes in Microsoft Excel using a little Visual Basic coding.

The macro shown in Figure 7.35 will make a message box appear.

Figure 7.35 ▶

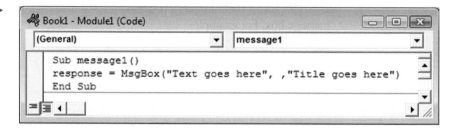

To set-up this macro:

1 On the **Developer** tab in the **Controls** group, click **View Code**.
2 Type in this code:

```
Sub message1()
response = MsgBox("Text goes here", ,"Title goes here")
End Sub
```

3 Save the file as a macro-enabled workbook.
4 Click **File > Close** and return to Excel.
5 On the **Developer** tab in the **Code** group, click **Macros > Sheet1.message1 > Run**. The message box shown in Figure 7.36 will appear.

Figure 7.36 ▼

We have seen that by adding **vbYesNo**, the message box can be changed so that it offers a choice of Yes and No as shown in Figure 7.37.

```
Sub Quit()
response = MsgBox("Are you sure you want to quit?", vbYesNo)
If response = vbYes Then Application.quit
End Sub
```

Figure 7.37 ▼

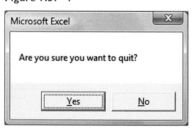

Other message box commands that you might want to experiment with include:

vbOKOnly	displays the OK button only
vbOKCancel	displays the OK and Cancel buttons.
vbAbortRetryIgnore	displays the Abort, Retry, and Ignore buttons.
vbYesNoCancel	displays the Yes, No, and Cancel buttons.
vbYesNo	displays the Yes and No buttons.

18: Message box icons

By adding an extra command, you can add one of four special icons to a message box. For example:

vbCritical displays the Critical Message icon. The macro would look like this:

```
Sub message2()
response = MsgBox("Created by Julian Mott © 2010", vbCritical, "Information")
End Sub
```

The message box looks like the one shown in Figure 7.38.

Figure 7.38 ▶

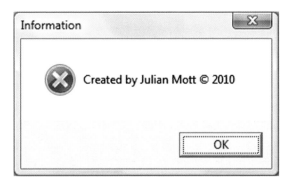

1 Experiment with the following visual basic commands:
   - **vbQuestion**
   - **vbExclamation**
   - **vbInformation**
2 You can combine a message box icon and a Yes/No answer by using **vbYesNo + vbCritical** – try it.
3 Can you combine the information icon and the Yes/No/Cancel buttons?

8 Tips and tricks

Here are fifty tricks and tips that have been found to be more than useful in implementing Excel projects. Many of them have been discovered by students themselves.

1   Getting more than one line of text in a cell
2   A quick way of displaying formulas
3   Putting a tick into a cell
4   Formatting non-adjacent areas
5   Using the fill handles
6   Using AutoFill to enter data quickly
7   What is a circular reference?
8   What is the difference between Paste and Paste Link?
9   Inserting multiple rows and columns
10 Quickly copying cell formats to other cells and cell ranges
11 Switching rows of cells to columns, or columns to rows
12 Displaying the date and time
13 Fixing problems with dates
14 Entering numbers as text
15 Calculating with dates
16 What day of the week is a date?
17 Hiding columns
18 Hiding the contents of a cell
19 Creating an automatic backup of your work
20 Adding Comments to your work
21 Automatically correcting common typing errors (AutoCorrect)
22 Stopping a header row disappearing off the screen (Freeze panes)
23 Combining the contents of two columns
24 LEFT, RIGHT and MID
25 A table stores names as 'John Smith'. How do you split this into 'John' and 'Smith'?
26 A quick way of entering the name of a range of cells (Paste name)
27 Using Go To Special
28 Highlighting changed cells
29 Splitting panes
30 Adding up a column of figures
31 Switching between relative and absolute references
32 Changing the status bar and caption text
33 Clicking a cell so it automatically changes 0 to 1 and 1 to 0
34 MsgBox Carriage Return
35 Running different macros depending on the value of a cell
36 A splashscreen in Excel
37 Synchronising one combo box with another

1: Getting more than one line of text in a cell

- Press **ALT** and **ENTER** to start a new line in the same cell.
- If your text is too long to fit in a cell, select the cell. On the **Home** tab in the **Alignment** group, click **Wrap Text**. The text will be displayed on multiple lines (Figure 8.1).

Figure 8.1 ▼

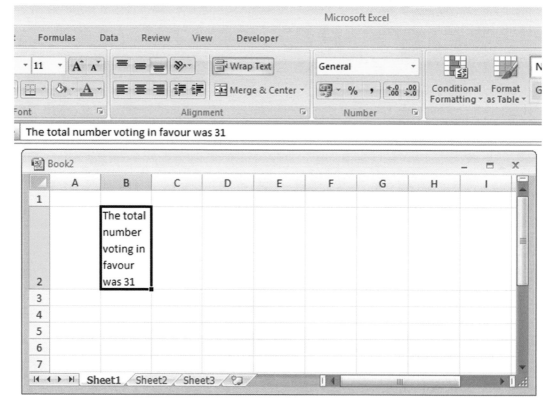

2: A quick way of displaying formulas

- Hold down the CTRL + the back tick key (next to 1 on the keyboard). This will switch to showing formulas (Figure 8.2).
- Press these keys again to return to normal mode.

Figure 8.2 ▶

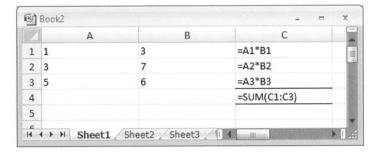

3: Putting a tick into a cell

- Type **=CHAR(252)** in the cell and then set the font to **Wingdings** font (Figure 8.3).

Figure 8.3 ▶

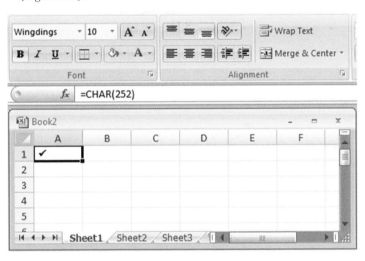

- You can now copy the tick to other cells.
- **=CHAR(251)** will give you a cross.

4: Formatting non-adjacent areas

If you want to format groups of cells on a worksheet that are not next to each other, you need to select them. Do this by:

- Dragging to select the first group of cells.
- Holding CTRL down and dragging across any other groups of cells.

Use this method if you want to draw a graph of data in non-adjacent cells.

5: Using the fill handles

When a cell is selected there is a small black square in the bottom right-hand corner – this is called the fill handle. If you move the cursor over this square, it changes from the usual white cross to a hairline black cross (Figure 8.4).

Figure 8.4 ▼

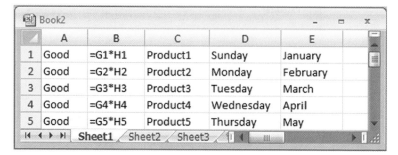

If you now drag this cross down to other cells it will copy the contents of first cell to all the others. It will also make an intelligent guess at a sequence.

Try the operation on a word, a formula, Product 1, a day of the week, a month in a cell (Figure 8.5).

Figure 8.5 ▶

	A	B	C	D	E
1	Good	=G1*H1	Product1	Sunday	January
2	Good	=G2*H2	Product2	Monday	February
3	Good	=G3*H3	Product3	Tuesday	March
4	Good	=G4*H4	Product4	Wednesday	April
5	Good	=G5*H5	Product5	Thursday	May

Book2 — Sheet1 / Sheet2 / Sheet3

If you enter the first two numbers of a number sequence or a date sequence, highlight both cells and drag down, and the sequence continues (Figure 8.6).

Figure 8.6 ▶

	A	B	C
1			
2	2	07 January 2011	
3	4	14 January 2011	
4	6	21 January 2011	
5	8	28 January 2011	
6	10	04 February 2011	
7	12	11 February 2011	

Book3 — Sheet1 / Sheet2

If the fill handles are not visible:

- Click **Office Button > Excel Options**.
- Click **Advanced**.
- Click the **Enable the fill handle and cell drag-and-drop** check box (Figure 8.7).

Figure 8.7 ▶

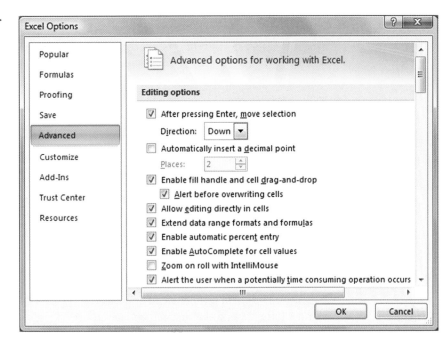

6: Using AutoFill to enter data quickly

Another way of performing the same operation is to:

- Enter the first piece of data in the series.
- Highlight the cells you want to fill.
- On the **Home** tab in the **Editing Group**, click **Fill > Series**.
- Click **AutoFill,** enter the **Step value**, and then click **OK** (Figure 8.8).

Figure 8.8 ▶

7: What is a circular reference?

Type **= A6 + A7** into A7. You will see this error message (Figure 8.9).

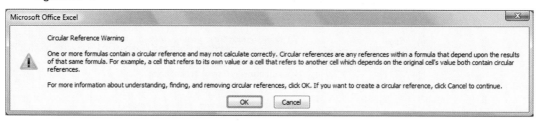

This is because the formula in A7 refers to A7. This error is called a circular reference.

8: What is the difference between Paste and Paste Link?

When you copy data from one cell and **Paste** it into another cell, if the first cell changes the second cell does not change.

Using **Paste Link** you can link the two cells, so that if the first cell is updated, so is the second.

- Click the source cell. On the **Home** tab in the **Clipboard** group, click **Copy**.
- Click the destination cell. On the **Home** tab in the **Clipboard** group, click the Paste arrow and click **Paste Link** (Figure 8.10).

Figure 8.10 ▼

9: Inserting multiple rows and columns

- If you need to insert one row, select a row by clicking the row number, right click and click **Insert**.
- To insert multiple rows (for example three) select three rows, right click and click **Insert**. Three rows will be inserted. This also works for columns.

10: Quickly copying cell formats to other cells and cell ranges

- Click the cell whose formatting you want to copy.
- On the **Home** tab in the **Clipboard** group, click the **Format Painter** button (a paintbrush picture).
- Click the cell or cell range you want to copy the formatting to.

Note: To format several different locations, double click the **Format Painter button** and click the button again when you have finished.

11: Switching rows of cells to columns, or columns to rows

How can we change Figure 8.11 …

Figure 8.11 ▶

… into Figure 8.12 without retyping or a lot of cut and paste?

Figure 8.12 ▶

- Select the cells that you want to switch.
- On the **Home** tab in the **Clipboard** group, click **Copy**.
- Click the top-left cell of the paste area. The paste area must be outside the copy area.
- On the **Home** tab in the **Clipboard** group, click the **Paste** arrow and click **Transpose**.

12: Displaying the date and time

To enter the date and time into an Excel worksheet:

■ Click the required cell.
■ Enter **=TODAY()** for today's date.

Figure 8.13 ▶

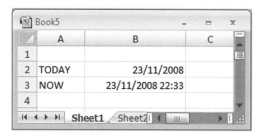

■ Enter **=NOW()** for today's date and the current time (Figure 8.13).

If the format is not exactly how you require the date, on the **Home** tab in the **Number** group, click the drop-down list and choose the required format.

Dates and times entered using =TODAY() or =NOW() will be updated when you next open the file.

Note: You can enter the current date or time quickly:
■ To enter the current date in a cell, press **CTRL** and **;** (semi-colon).
■ To enter the current time in a cell, press **CTRL** and **:** (colon).
Dates and times entered using this method will **not** be updated when you next open the file.

13: Fixing problems with dates

Sometimes the date appears as a number – like '36680'. This is because Excel stores dates as numbers in order starting on 1st January 1900 – which is stored as '1'.

For example, 3rd June 2000 is stored as '36680'. To change the number to a date, on the **Home** tab in the **Number** group click **Short Date** from the drop-down list.

14: Entering numbers as text

If you want to enter a number as a code (e.g. 000262), Excel will store it as a number and only display 262.

To enter 000262, type an apostrophe first **'000262**. The apostrophe formats the cell to text format. 000262 is displayed and not the apostrophe.

However, the apostrophe is displayed in the formula bar (Figure 8.14).

Figure 8.14 ▶

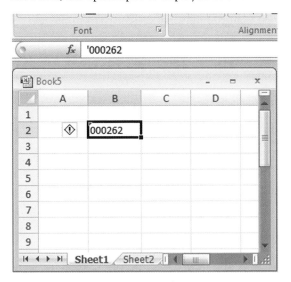

Similarly, you might have conducted a survey and typed 1-4, 5-8 and 9-12 into three cells. Excel changes them to 1 April, 5 August and 9 December respectively. This is because Excel has formatted the cells as dates. To prevent this, type an apostrophe at the start of the data, e.g. **'1-4**.

15: Calculating with dates

Use the DATEDIF function to calculate the number of days, months or years between dates – for example, to work out how old someone is or for how many days a book has been borrowed from a library.

- Put the first date in A1.
- Type **=NOW()** in A2.
- Type **=DATEDIF(A1,A2,"y")** in A3.

You will see the difference between the two dates in full years.

Use **"m"** for the number of full months in the period and **"d"** for the number of days.

16: What day of the week is a date?

- Type a date in A1.
- Type **=WEEKDAY(A1)** in A2.

1 means Sunday, 2 means Monday, and so on.

17: Hiding columns

Suppose you want to hide all of column C from the user.

- Select column C by clicking the **C** in the column heading at the top.
- Right click anywhere on the column.
- Click **Hide**.

To remove this feature:

- Highlight the two columns on either side of the hidden column (**B** and **D** in this case).
- Right click anywhere on one of these columns.
- Click **Unhide**.

18: Hiding the contents of a cell

- Select the cell(s) you want to hide.
- On the **Home** tab in the **Number** group, click the small arrow next to **Number** as shown in Figure 8.15.
- In the **Category** list click **Custom**.
- In the **Type** box select delete the existing codes and enter **;;;** (three semi-colons) as in Figure 8.16.
- Click **OK**.

Figure 8.15 ▼

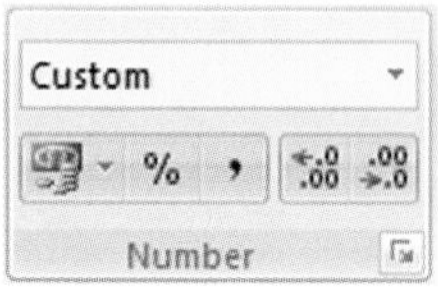

Figure 8.16 ▶

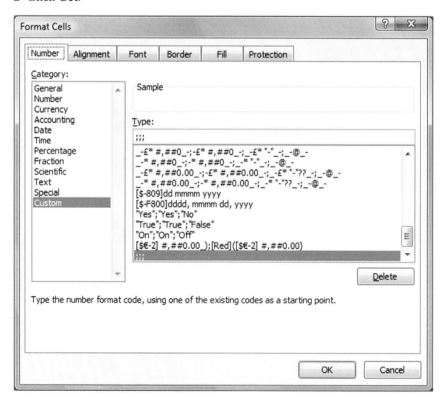

19: Creating an automatic backup of your work

Excel allows you to create an automatic backup of a file as you work, so that you cannot lose all your work if the system crashes.

- Click **Office Button > Excel Options** and click the **Save** tab.
- Set the **AutoRecover** settings to the appropriate time (Figure 8.17).

Figure 8.17 ▶

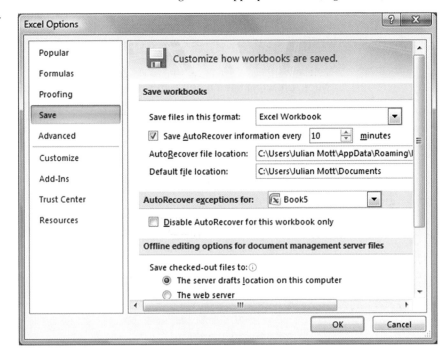

This feature is also available in Microsoft Word.

20: Adding Comments to your work

A comment is a small on-screen 'Post-it' note that you can attach to a cell to give the user some more information.

If a cell has a Comment attached, there is a red triangle in the top right-hand corner of the cell. As you move the cursor over the cell, the Comment appears (Figure 8.18).

Figure 8.18 ▶

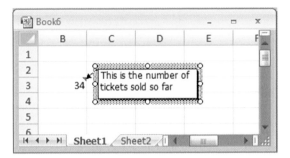

To enter a comment:

- Select the cell for the comment.
- On the **Review** tab in the **Comments** group, click **New Comment**.
- Enter the comment.

To delete a comment, right click the cell and click **Delete Comment**.

21: Automatically correcting common typing errors (AutoCorrect)

Microsoft Excel has a useful feature called AutoCorrect. Common spelling mistakes are automatically corrected as you type. For example *recieve* would automatically be corrected to *receive*. The word *I* is automatically capitalised.

You can customise it to add your own words using **Tools > AutoCorrect Options...**:

- Click the **Office Button** and choose **Excel Options**.
- Click **Proofing**.
- Click **AutoCorrect Options**.
- Click the **AutoCorrect** tab.
- Enter the incorrect word and the correct word into the boxes (Figure 8.19).
- Click **OK**.

Figure 8.19 ▶

There is another useful feature of AutoCorrect – if you accidentally leave the Caps Lock turned on and type in a name like *sMITH* it automatically changes the word to *Smith* and turns off Caps Lock.

The AutoCorrect feature is also available in Microsoft Word.

22: Stopping a header row disappearing off the screen (Freeze panes)

A company has details of customers stored in an Excel worksheet. As they scroll down the page the top line (the heading row) disappears (Figure 8.20).

Figure 8.20 ▼

You can keep the column headings on the screen by using **Freeze Panes**:

■ On the **View** tab in the **Window** group, click **Freeze Panes > Freeze Top Row** (Figure 8.21).

Figure 8.21 ►

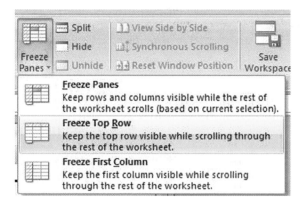

The top line is now locked – test it to see if it works (Figure 8.22).

Figure 8.22 ▼

■ To turn it off click **Freeze panes > Unfreeze Panes**.

23: Combining the contents of two columns

When storing details of customers' names, it is usual to store the data in three different fields – surname, first name and title (Figure 8.23).

Figure 8.23 ▶

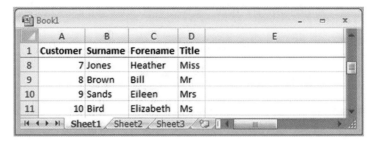

This means that you can sort into alphabetical order but can also send out personalised letters. The name on the invoice can be either Miss Heather Jones or Miss H. Jones.

Joining two or more words together into one word is called **concatenation**. To do this in Excel use the CONCATENATE function:

■ Enter the data shown in Figure 8.23.
■ In E8 enter the function **= D8&C8&B8**
■ Use the fill handles to replicate the formula in the cells below E8.

Figure 8.24 ▶

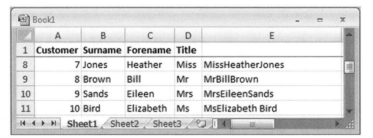

The function joins the text together (Figure 8.24). You then need to force spaces between the words.

■ In E8 change the function to **= D8&" "&C8&" "&B8** (there is a space between the quotation marks).
■ Copy and paste the function down the column (Figure 8.25).

Figure 8.25 ▶

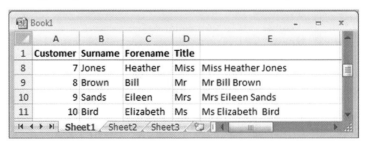

24: LEFT, RIGHT and MID

If we want the name Miss H. Jones to appear on the invoice, we need to use the LEFT function, which has the format =LEFT(C8,1**)**. This extracts the first letter of the word in C1.

Join the two functions together as follows:

- Enter **= D8&" "&LEFT(C8,1)&". "&B8** in E8.

Note: There are **RIGHT** and **MID** functions as well. For example:
- **RIGHT(D5,3)** will extract the 3 characters at the end of the word(s) in D5.
- **MID(E40, 5, 8)** will take 8 characters from the middle of the text in E40, starting at the fifth character.

25: A table stores names as 'John Smith'. How do you split this into 'John' and 'Smith'?

Suppose you have names in cells A1 to A3 as shown in Figure 8.26.

Figure 8.26 ▶

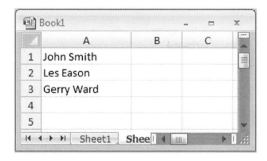

- Highlight the cells (in this case A1 to A3).
- On the **Data** tab in the **Data Tools** group, click **Text to Columns**.
- A wizard will start – click **Delimited** and then **Next**.
- Check the **Space** box as shown in Figure 8.27.
- Click **Finish** – Figure 8.28 shows the result.

Figure 8.27 ▶

Convert Text to Columns Wizard - Step 2 of 3

This screen lets you set the delimiters your data contains. You can see how your text is affected in the preview below.

Delimiters
- ☑ Tab
- ☐ Semicolon   ☑ Treat consecutive delimiters as one
- ☐ Comma
- ☑ Space   Text qualifier: "
- ☐ Other:

Data preview

John	Smith
Les	Eason
Gerry	Ward

Cancel   < Back   Next >   Finish

Figure 8.28 ▶

26: A quick way of entering the name of a range of cells (Paste name)

If you are using a named range of cells in a function, such as SUM or VLOOKUP, you do not need to type in the name. Just press **F3** to get a list of names available.

27: Using Go To Special

You can use this to highlight special cells on your workbook – for example cells with formulas, cells with validation, cells with comments or cells with conditional formatting.

■ Press **F5** to get the dialogue box shown in Figure 8.29.

Figure 8.29 ▶

■ Click the **Special** button.
■ Select the type of cell required.

28: Highlighting changed cells

■ On the **Review** tab in the **Changes** group, click **Track Changes > Highlight Changes**.

■ Check **Track changes while editing** (Figure 8.30).

Figure 8.30 ▶

Cells that are changed have a blue triangle in the top left-hand corner (Figure 8.31).

You can choose whether to accept or reject these changes by clicking **Track Changes > Accept/Reject Changes**.

Figure 8.31 ▼

	89

29: Splitting panes

■ On the **View** tab in the **Window** group, click **Split** to split your window into two sections. You can scroll on each section separately.

This is very useful if you want to work on two or more parts of the same worksheet that are not close to each other.

■ Click **Split** again to return to the conventional screen.

30: Adding up a column of figures

Suppose you want to add up amounts of money in a column. In this case (Figure 8.32) they are in cells C2 to C9. But if you add another row to the table, the data will be in C2 to C10 – in which case the formula will be different. How can you still add them up?

The simplest way to do this is to put the total in another column, say D6 and use the formula =SUM(C:C).

This will add up all the amounts in column C. It will works no matter how many records you have in column C.

Figure 8.32 ▶

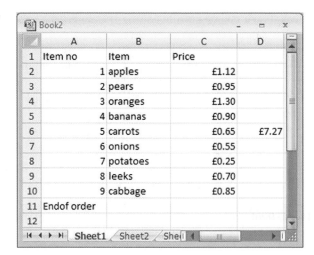

31: Switching between relative and absolute references

A relative reference looks like this **=SUM(C6:C10)**.

An absolute reference (which doesn't change when cells are copied) is indicated by $ signs and looks like this **=SUM($C$6:$C$9)**.

To switch between the two automatically, and so avoid having to enter the $ signs:

- Enter the formula with relative references.
- Highlight the formula in the formula bar.
- Press the **F4** key.

If you press **F4** again, only the rows are set as absolute references: **=SUM(C$6:C$9)**.

Press **F4** again for the columns to be set as absolute references: **=SUM($C6:$C9)**.

Press **F4** again to return to relative references.

32: Changing the status bar and caption text

Try this macro.

```
Sub display()
Application.Caption = "St Mary's School Play"
Application.DisplayStatusBar = True
Application.StatusBar = "Project by L.J.Smith ©2010"
End Sub
```

See Figure 8.33.

Figure 8.33 ▶

29	
30	
31	
32	

◄ ◄ ► ►◄ **Sheet1** / Sheet2 / Sheet3

Project by L.J.Smith ©2010

33: Clicking a cell so it automatically changes 0 to 1 and 1 to 0

You can run a macro so that when you click a cell containing a 0 its value changes to 1. If the cell contains a 1 it is changed to a 0. (This is useful for booking theatre seats – click a seat and it is booked; click again and it is unbooked.)

- Go into **Visual Basic Editor** (ALT and **F11**).
- Double click **Sheet1** in Project Explorer (top left of screen). A new module window will open. There are two drop-down boxes at the top of the window. Choose **Worksheet** and **SelectionChange** as shown in Figure 8.34.

Figure 8.34 ▶

Suppose that you want to change 0 to 1 when someone clicks a cell, and to change 1 to blank.

- In the blank middle line of the procedure in Figure 8.34, enter

```
If ActiveCell.Value = 0 Then ActiveCell.Value = 1 ElseActiveCell.Value = ""
```

as shown in Figure 8.35.

Figure 8.35 ▼

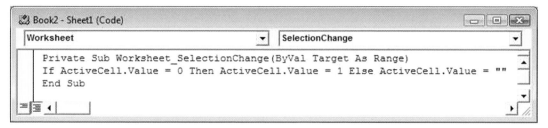

Go back to Excel (ALT and **F11**). Test it to see if works – it will only work for Sheet1.

34: MsgBox Carriage Return

Sometimes you may want to put a line of text on the second row of a message box. Try out this example.

- Press ALT and **F11** to open **Visual Basic Editor.**
- Click **Insert > Module** and enter this code:

```
Sub TwoLines()
MsgBox "Line 1" & vbCrLf & "Line 2"
End Sub
```

- Go back to Excel by pressing ALT and **F11** again.
- On the **Developer** tab in the **Code** group, click **Macros** > **TwoLines** (Figure 8.36).

Figure 8.36 ▼

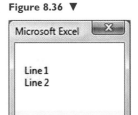

35: Running different macros depending on the value of a cell

Suppose that you want to run different macros depending on the value of a cell. For example, if the value of C4 is 1 then you want to run Macro1, if the value of C4 is 2 then you want to run Macro2, and if the value of C4 is 3 you want to run Macro3.

- Open **Visual Basic Editor** (ALT and **F11**).
- Type in this macro:

```
Sub Macrochoice()
If Range("C4").Value = 1 Then Macro1
If Range("C4").Value = 2 Then Macro2
If Range("C4").Value = 3 Then Macro3
End Sub
```

Another way of doing it is as follows:

```
Sub Macrochoice2()
Dim value
value = Range("C4").value
Select Case value
Case 1
Macro1
Case 2
Macro2
Case 3
Macro3
Case Else
Exit Sub
End Select
End Sub
```

36: A splashscreen in Excel

Sometimes it is a good idea to display a splashscreen – a message that appears on screen for only a few seconds when a file is loaded.

- Press ALT and **F11** to open **Visual Basic Editor**.
- Insert a UserForm with **Insert > UserForm**.
- If the **Control Toolbox** is not visible click **View > Toolbox**.
- Click the **Label** button in the Toolbox.
- Click the top left of the UserForm – **Label1** appears.

- Delete Label1 and replace it with **Welcome to Morgan's Jam,** or something appropriate. Choose the caption, fonts, font size and colour that you think are suitable (Figure 8.37).

Figure 8.37 ▶

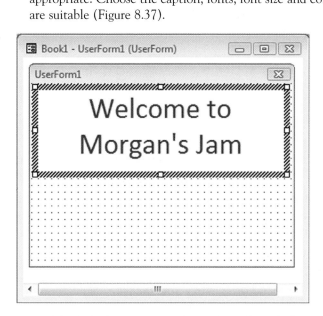

- Double click the **UserForm** (away from the Label).
- From the right hand drop-down box select **Initialize** (Figure 8.38).

Figure 8.38 ▶

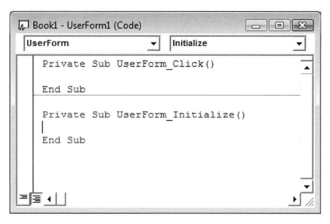

- Enter this code:

```
Application.OnTime Now + TimeValue("00:00:05"), "KillForm"
```

See Figure 8.39.

Figure 8.39 ▶

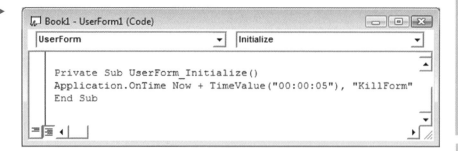

- Close this code window.
- Click **Insert > Module** and enter this code:

```
Sub KillForm()
   UserForm1.Hide
End Sub
Sub Auto_open()
   Load UserForm1
   UserForm1.Show
End Sub
```

- Close Visual Basic Editor. Save your Excel file (as a macro-enabled worksheet) and close it.
- Now re-open it – the UserForm should appear for just five seconds.

37: Synchronising one combo box with another

The data in one combo box is often linked to another. For example, a company may sell two makes of cars, Ford and Honda. The models sold are as shown in Figure 8.40.

Figure 8.40 ▶

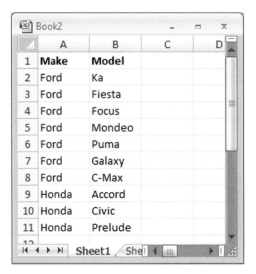

How can you set up a combo box for the make so that if Ford is chosen, only Ford models appear in a second combo box and so on?

- Open a new file in Excel.
- Enter the data as shown in Figure 8.40. Save your file as combo exercise. Again it must be a macro-enabled worksheet.
- Type **Ford** in cell D2 and **Honda** in cell D3.
- On the **Developer** tab in the **Controls** group, click **Insert** and set up a combo box over cells D5 and E5.
- Right click the combo box and format it so that the input range is **D2:D3** and the linked cell is **F5**.
- Set up a second combo box over cells D8 and E8. Do not format it.
- Hold down the ALT key and press **F11** to open **Visual Basic Editor**.
- Click **Insert > Module**. In the window that opens enter this code exactly as shown:

```
Sub Dropdown1_Change()
Dim Make As Integer
Make = Range("F5").Value
Select Case Make
Case 1
ActiveSheet.Shapes("Drop-down 2").Select
With Selection
.ListFillRange = "B2:B7"
.LinkedCell = "F8"
.DropDownLines = 6
.Display3DShading = False
End With
Case 2
ActiveSheet.Shapes("Drop-down 2").Select
With Selection
.ListFillRange = "B8:B10"
.LinkedCell = "F8"
.DropDownLines = 3
.Display3DShading = False
End With
Case Else
End Select
Range("A1").Select
End Sub
```

- Go back to Excel by clicking the **View Microsoft Excel** button.
- Right click the first combo box and choose **Assign Macro**. Choose the macro **Dropdown1_Change()**.

It should now work. Save the file and test it – you should get results like those shown in Figure 8.41.

Figure 8.41 ▶

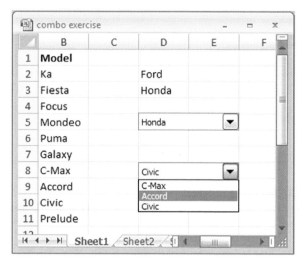

If you want to have more makes of car, it is easy enough to edit the macro to include Case 3, Case 4 etc.

38: A real-time clock in Excel

You can set up a real-time clock (Figure 8.42) in an Excel UserForm that ticks by second by second, as follows:

Figure 8.42 ▶

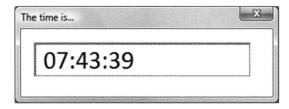

- Open a new Excel workbook or open the workbook in which you want to put the clock.
- Open **Visual Basic Editor** by pressing ALT and **F11**.
- Click **Insert > Module**.
- In the new window that opens type in this code:

```
Dim flag As Boolean

Sub auto_open()
flag = False
Load UserForm1
UserForm1.Show
clock
End Sub

Sub clock()
If flag = True Then Exit Sub
Range("a1").Value = Format(Now, "hh:mm:ss")
Application.OnTime (Now + TimeSerial(0, 0, 1)), "clock"
End Sub

Sub stopclock()
UserForm1.Hide
flag = True
End Sub
```

What the code does
- The first line sets *flag* as a global variable – a variable that is available in all the macros.
- The first macro loads the UserForm.
- The second macro puts the time in cell A1 and updates it every second.
- The third macro stops the clock and removes the UserForm.

- Still in Visual Basic Editor set up a UserForm with **Insert > UserForm**.
- In the Properties window set the caption to **The time is**...
- Still in the Properties window, set the **ShowModal** property to **False** – this is critical.
- Add a **List box** to your UserForm.
- Select the List box and in the Properties window set the **RowSource** to **A1**.

- Resize the UserForm and the List box as appropriate and choose appropriate colours, borders and fonts (Figure 8.43).

Figure 8.43 ▶

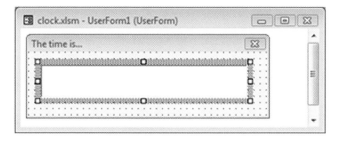

- Close Visual Basic Editor.
- Set the font colour of cell A1 to white.
- Add a button to run the Stopclock macro. Make the text on the button **Stop the clock**.

If you want to, you can add a button to run the Auto_open macro too.

- Save your file and test that it works.

Note: You can't exit from this program while the macro is still running but you can do other work on your Excel file.

39: Using Select Case for different responses to different message box buttons

Select Case allows you to set up more options than IfThenElse where you are limited to two alternatives. Try this macro:

```
Sub message()
Select Case MsgBox("Are you sure you want to do this?",
vbYesNoCancel)
Case vbYes
MsgBox "You chose Yes"
Case vbNo
MsgBox "You chose No"
Case vbCancel
MsgBox "You chose Cancel"
End Select
End Sub
```

40: Importing data from the Internet into Excel

For this to work and for the information to be continually updated you need:

- an always-on connection to the internet

■ a website with regularly updated data such as the foreign exchange site www.x-rates.com/ (Figure 8.44).

Figure 8.44 ▼

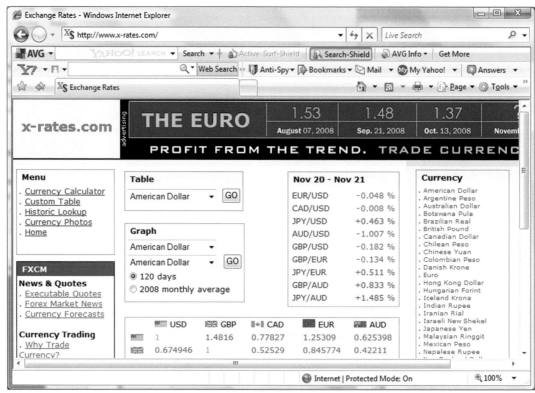

Suppose you want to get updated currency information – you would use the table at the bottom of this webpage that gives rates for the US dollar, British pound, Canadian dollar, the Euro and the Australian dollar.

■ Open a new worksheet in Excel.
■ Click cell **B2**.
■ On the **Data** tab in the **Get External Data** group, click **From Web**

■ The **New Web Query**.dialogue box opens. Type the address e.g.
www.x-rates.com/ in the address box and click **Go** (Figure 8.45).

Figure 8.45 ▼

■ Scroll down and across to the required table (Figure 8.46).

Figure 8.46 ▼

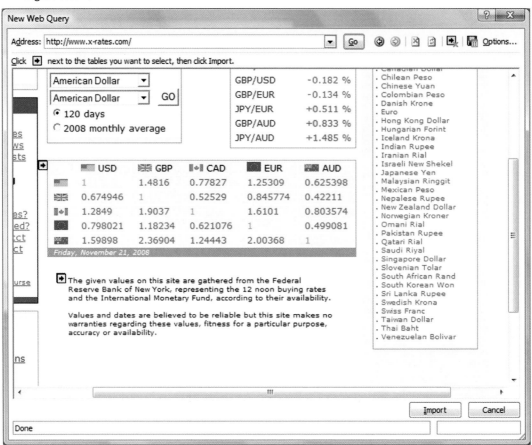

■ Click the little black and yellow arrow to the top left of the table. The arrow goes green and the table is highlighted (Figure 8.47).

Figure 8.47 ▶

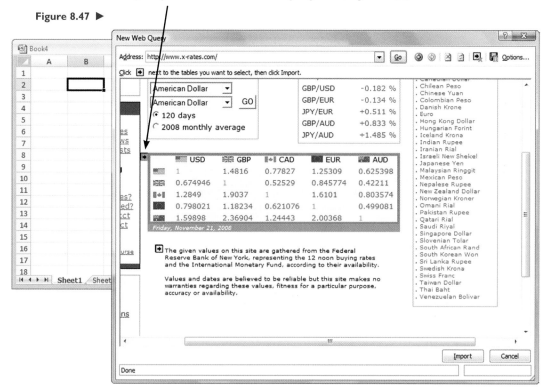

■ Click **Import > OK**.The data will appear on your worksheet as shown in Figure 8.48.

Figure 8.48 ▶

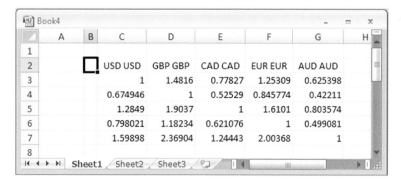

- You can format it as required (Figure 8.49).

Figure 8.49 ▶

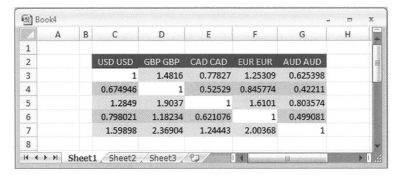

- Save the file.
- To update the data, highlight cells C3 to G7. On the **Data** tab in the **Connections** group, click **Refresh All** (Figure 8.50).

Figure 8.50 ▶

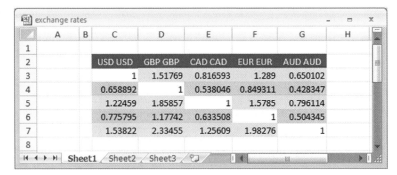

You can use macros to transfer data to cells on a different sheet and enter the date. It is possible to create graphs tracking the exchange rates.

41: Are you sure?

When you exit from Excel, would it be reassuring to be asked this question (Figure 8.51)?

Figure 8.51 ▶

You need it set up so that if **Yes** is selected the user leaves Excel, otherwise nothing happens.

- Open **Visual Basic Editor** (ALT and **F11**).
- Click **Insert > Module**.
- Enter this code:

```
Sub message()
Answer = MsgBox (Prompt:= "Are you sure?", Buttons: = 4)
End Sub
```

- Click the **Run** button to test the macro. It displays just the message box.
- Add an additional line as shown in Figure 8.52.

Figure 8.52 ▶

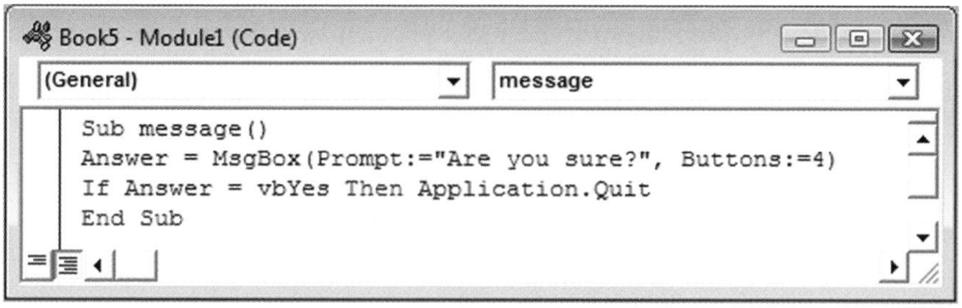

- Don't forget to save your work before testing it.

42: Sending an email from Excel

How can you send an email from Excel with the spreadsheet file attached?

- Press ALT and **F11** to open **Visual Basic Editor**.
- Click **Insert > Module** and enter this code:

```
Sub EmailFile()
  ActiveWorkbook.SendMail _
  Recipients:="put the email address here", _
  Subject:="Here is the file you wanted " & Format(Date, "dd/mm/yy")
End Sub
```

- Save your file.
- Go back to Excel by pressing ALT and **F11** again.
- Click **Tools > Macro > Macros > EmailFile** to test it.

43: Incrementing an invoice number

Invoices are normally numbered. How can you increase the invoice number by 1 when you clear the old data ready for a new customer?

Suppose that you have already recorded a macro called **Clear** to clear the old data and that the invoice number is stored in cell B7.

- Press ALT and **F11** to open **Visual Basic Editor**.
- Click **Insert > Module** and enter this code:

```
Sub Newinvoice
Range("B7").Value = Range("B7").Value + 1
Clear
End Sub
```

- Save your file.
- Go back to Excel by pressing ALT and **F11** again
- Click **Tools > Macro > Macros > Newinvoice** to test it.

44: Automatic updating of stock levels

Suppose you have the number of widgets in stock stored in cell B5. Some more widgets are delivered and this is stored in cell D5. How can you update the stock levels to take account of the delivery?

- Press ALT and **F11** to open **Visual Basic Editor**.
- Click **Insert > Module** and enter this code:

```
Sub Update
Range("B5").Value = Range("B5").Value + Range("D5").Value
Range("D5").Value = 0
End Sub
```

- Save your file.
- Go back to Excel by pressing ALT and **F11** again
- Click **Tools > Macro > Macros > Update** to test it.

45: Automatic updating of stock levels (2)

Your spreadsheet stores the stock levels and deliveries of 20 items. The numbers in stock are in column B; the numbers delivered are stored in column D. Can you update all the stock levels at once?

Suppose that the first item is stored in cell B5. Open a macro and enter the following code:

```
Sub Update2()
Range("B5").Select
For Count = 1 To 20
ActiveCell.Value = ActiveCell.Value + ActiveCell.Offset(0,
2).Range("A1").Value
ActiveCell.Offset(0, 2).Range("A1").Value = 0
ActiveCell.Offset(1, 0).Range("A1").Select 'go down a line
Next Count
End Sub
```

46: Using the Calendar control to enter dates

- Open **Visual Basic Editor** (ALT and **F11**).
- Insert a UserForm by clicking **Insert > UserForm**.
- Right click the Toolbox and choose **Additional Controls**.
- Scroll down until you see **Calendar Control 12.0** – the number is different for different versions of Excel (Figure 8.53).

Figure 8.53 ▶

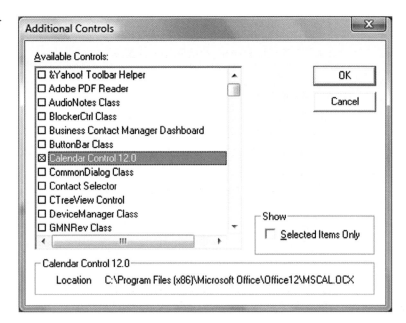

- Check the box next to Calendar Control and click **OK**.
- A new button appears in the toolbox (Figure 8.54).

Figure 8.54 ▼

- Click this button and drag out a rectangle over the whole of the UserForm. A calendar appears (Figure 8.55).

Figure 8.55 ▶

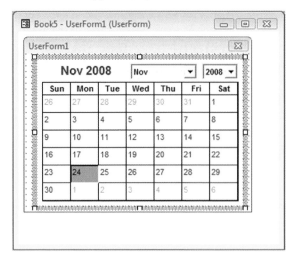

You now need to set up the UserForm so that when you click a date, that date is entered into a cell, say cell A2.

■ Double click the calendar – this VB code appears (Figure 8.56):

Figure 8.56 ▶

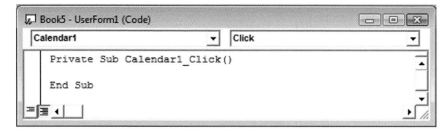

■ Edit the code so that it reads as shown in Figure 8.57.

Figure 8.57 ▶

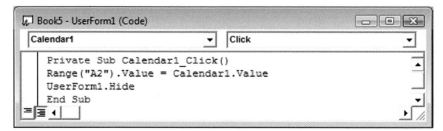

■ Insert a module by clicking **Insert > Module**.
■ Enter the macro shown in Figure 8.58.

Figure 8.58 ▶

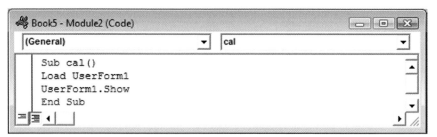

■ Close Visual Basic Editor.
■ Make column A slightly wider and run the macro. On the **Developer** tab in the **Code** group, click **Macros**. Select the **Cal** macro and click **Run**. The UserForm with the calendar should load with today's date highlighted.
■ Click a date in the calendar. You can use the drop-down boxes to select a different month and year. The chosen date will appear in cell A2 (Figure 8.59).

Figure 8.59 ▶

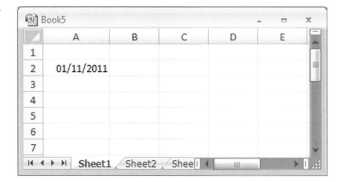

47: Adding data at the bottom of a table

Suppose you have the data shown in Figure 8.60. You want to add lettuce, £0.72, at the bottom – how can you do this?

Figure 8.60 ▶

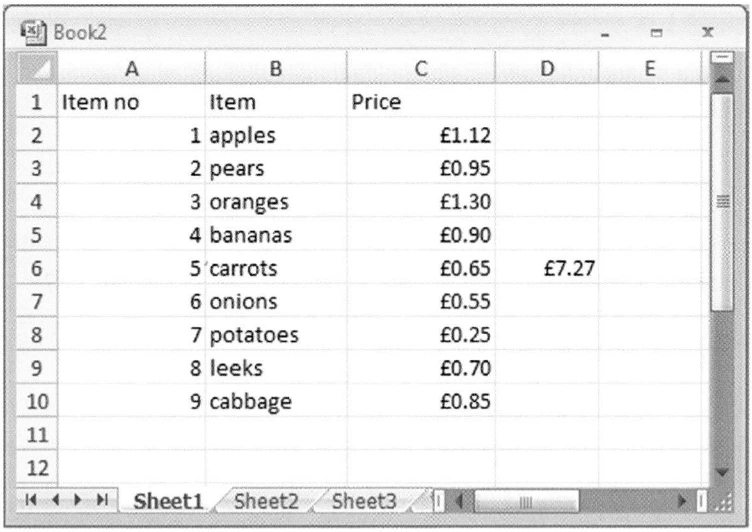

	A	B	C	D	E
1	Item no	Item	Price		
2		1 apples	£1.12		
3		2 pears	£0.95		
4		3 oranges	£1.30		
5		4 bananas	£0.90		
6		5 carrots	£0.65	£7.27	
7		6 onions	£0.55		
8		7 potatoes	£0.25		
9		8 leeks	£0.70		
10		9 cabbage	£0.85		
11					
12					

Book2

Sheet1 Sheet2 Sheet3

- Click anywhere on the table.
- Click the **Form button** in the **Quick Access** toolbar. This button should still be there from Unit 15 – if not then go back to Unit 15 and follow the instructions.
- Click **New**.
- Enter the data.
- Click **Close** (Figure 8.61).

Figure 8.61 ▶

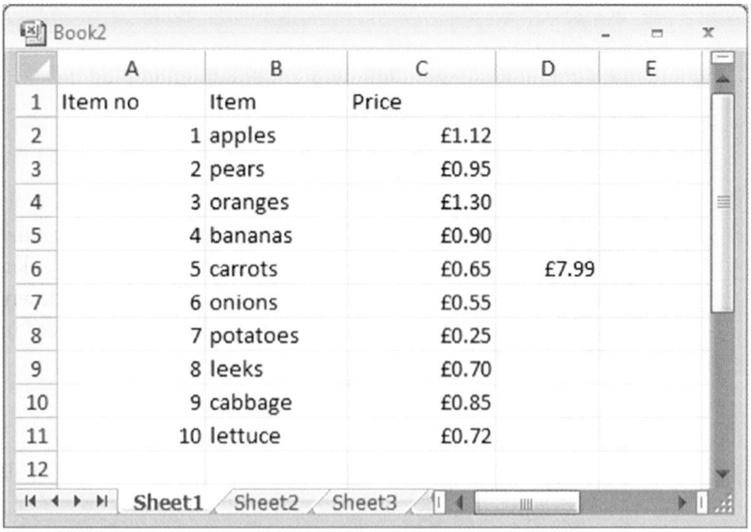

	A	B	C	D	E
1	Item no	Item	Price		
2		1 apples	£1.12		
3		2 pears	£0.95		
4		3 oranges	£1.30		
5		4 bananas	£0.90		
6		5 carrots	£0.65	£7.99	
7		6 onions	£0.55		
8		7 potatoes	£0.25		
9		8 leeks	£0.70		
10		9 cabbage	£0.85		
11		10 lettuce	£0.72		
12					

Book2

Sheet1 Sheet2 Sheet3

48: Password-protecting your files

Sometimes it is a good idea to protect your files with a password.

■ Click **Office Button > Prepare > Encrypt Document**.

Figure 8.62 ▶

■ In the **Encrypt Document** dialogue box, you will need to type a password, and then click **OK**. You won't see the password on the screen – just dots as shown in Figure 8.62
■ In the **Confirm Password** dialogue box, in the **Re-enter password** box, type the password again and then click **OK**.
■ Save the file.

You will be asked to type the password when loading the document (Figure 8.63).

Figure 8.63 ▶

But be careful – if you forget your password you will not be able to access your file, which could be months of work. It is best **not** to use a password.

Remember that passwords are case sensitive so check that **Caps Lock** is turned off.

49: Changing the colour of the gridlines

■ Click **Office Button > Excel Options**.
■ Click **Advanced**.
■ Scroll down through the options until you see the **Display Options for this Worksheet** section.

Figure 8.64 ▼

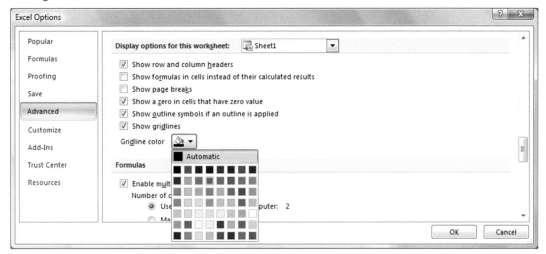

- Make sure that the **Show Gridlines** check box is selected.
- Use the **Gridline Colour** drop-down box to choose the colour you want (Figure 8.64).
- Click **OK**.

50: Zooming in and out with the mouse wheel

If you have a computer mouse with a wheel as well as the two buttons, you can use it to zoom in and out.

- Click **Office Button > Excel Options**.
- Click **Advanced**.
- In the **Editing Options** section, click **Zoom on roll with IntelliMouse**.
- Click **OK**.

Now when you turn the mouse wheel away from you, it zooms in. Turn it back to zoom out.

Index